DEADLY DOZEN

TRAINING MANUAL & RULEBOOK

ISBN: 9798870388472

Published by **www.strengthandconditioningcourse.com**

Copyright © 2023 Strength and Conditioning Course Limited

The moral right of this author has been asserted.

www.strengthandconditioningcourse.com

www.deadlydozen.co.uk

Facebook & Instagram: **@strengthandconditioningcourse**
Facebook: **@deadlydozen** Instagram: **@deadly.dozen**
YouTube: **@DeadlyDozen** / **@CoachJCurtis**

Cover Image Copyright: Strength and Conditioning Course

Image Copyright: Strength and Conditioning Course

Contents

Table of Contents

Introduction

The Deadly Dozen (DD) has been designed to be one of the hardest yet most accessible fitness races in the world.

The race involves 12x 400m runs, which we refer to as "Journeys," and 12x exercise stations, which we refer to as "Labours." The Labours only use bodyweight (BW), kettlebell (KB), dumbbell (DB) and weight plate (WP) exercises. Therefore, race training is incredibly accessible in any setting, whether in a gym, at home or outdoors. Ultimately, an individual could effectively train for the event with just a pair of KBs.

Another benefit of only using KBs, DBs and WPs is that they are easy to store and transport and extremely unlikely to break or get damaged.

Official Deadly Dozen races are held on athletics tracks (both outdoor and indoor) and involve running a 400m lap (2x 200m laps indoors) before crossing over into the centre and completing a Labour and repeating the process until the athlete has completed all 12 Labours – 6 of the Labours move between a 30m lane (Distance Labours – D Labours) and 6 are stationary (Rep Labours – R Labours).

Of course, Deadly Dozen races can hosted on an open area with a 200-400m loop.

The Deadly Dozen Labours (exercises) have been selected so that they develop a well-rounded training program that develops the Half Dozen Fundamental Movements: Hinge, Squat, Lunge, Push, Pull and Carry, all of which require some level of bracing and/or rotational movement.

The Deadly Dozen is NOT just a fitness race; it is an entire training methodology.

In short, the Deadly Dozen Method (DDM) splits training down into three major disciplines: Collectively, these are called the Deadly Dozen Triad (DDT).

The Deadly Dozen Triad:

1. **Strength Training:** Resistance training sessions (usually gym-based) that concentrate on low and mid-volume sets (lower reps) with higher training intensities (heavier).

2. **Labour Fitness:** Circuit training sessions that include some or all of the Labours performed at higher volumes (for high reps or time). These sessions can include or not include Journeys (runs and other forms of cardio).

3. **Journey Fitness:** Running training sessions that are usually split between long-duration work at lower intensities or interval work at higher intensities. However, Journey fitness does not have to be a run; it can be a row, ski, cycle or swim, etc.

Note: Alongside the main running-based event, variations such as Deadly Dozen Row, Deadly Dozen Ski and Deadly Dozen Cycle can also be practised: DD Row and Ski use the same Journey distance (1:1 Run to Row/Ski Ratio: 400m on all), whereas DD Cycle doubles the Journey distance (1:2 Run to Cycle Ratio: Cycle 800m).

Other potential Deadly Dozen variations include DD Swim (4:1 Run to Swim Ratio: 100m swim) or DD Climb, where a rock wall or obstacle/obstacle course is completed as a Journey.

My Story

Hi, my name is Jason Curtis, and I am the founder and race director of the Deadly Dozen.

From a young age, I started training and competing in combat sports. I was never going to be a world champion, but this background got me into hard physical training, and I was always fascinated by how physical fitness is developed.

After school, I joined the British Army with the aim of becoming a Physical Training Instructor (PTI) in the Infantry. Unfortunately, you can't join the army as a PTI, but the recruitment sergeant ensured that if my fitness stood out, I would be a PTI within a year or two, and fortunately, that was the case. I served six years as a PTI, with the last two being at Catterick training infantry recruits. It was in these last two years that my own training took a real shift.

As a young lad, I was small for my age (I used to compete at 57kg/125lbs), and when I eventually shot up to over 6ft, I was as thin as humanly possible. Fundamentally, this was a good thing for my boxing/Thai boxing and sports like cross-country running, which I did A LOT of. However, throughout my army career, I began to develop my expertise as a strength and conditioning coach and started to lean into the strength training side of things, which meant I wanted to be stronger and, of course, I wanted to look stronger – who wants a skinny strength coach?

This drive to gain muscle mass resulted in me getting into Powerlifting and Weightlifting. Because marching and running was essentially my job, heavy lifting became my primary training focus – when I joined the army, I was 64kg/140lbs, and when I left the army, I was 90kg/200lbs.

After leaving the army, I set up a strength and conditioning gym and also an educational academy that qualifies new personal trainers and S&C coaches. In the gym, the bulk of what I was coaching athletes and teaching to students was strength training, and although the gym has always run conditioning classes, my personal focus remained under the BB, and around the year 2022, my weight peaked at 109kg/240lbs – after leaving the army, I wasn't doing a great deal of my own conditioning (running or other forms).

At 109kg, I felt strong, but I also felt a little unhealthy. At this point, I had also started to prioritize my work over training. In between sets, I would answer emails or edit a paragraph from a book I was writing, and although I will always love the BB, I released I was getting no real buzz from the training. Something was missing.

Side Note: I have young children, so when I considered for the first time in my life that I was clearly less healthy than I could be (always bulking for muscle), it was a real wakeup call: As a young lad, I would choose performance over health, as a father, I choose health above all else – I want to give myself the best shot at being around for my kids for as long as I can be (you get dealt a hand by the genetic lottery and the key is to play it the best way you can – you can win a round of Poker with a starting hand of 2-7 offsuit).

It was around 2022 when more gym members were getting into fitness races, and one of my members asked if I would do an event with him. I reluctantly said yes, as it would give me a kick to do more hard conditioning. And what can I say? After a couple of weeks of training, I realised what I had been missing over the last few years. I was missing getting my heart rate up through the roof and feeling like I was going to die. I missed pushing my body that hard that afterward, the endorphins were flowing so fast that I felt on top of the world, regardless of how my day had been thus far: I often say, don't judge how you feel until you have got your heart rate up: If you have had a bad day, get your heart rate above 80% (of your max heart rate) and see if you still care about whatever it was you were stressed about.

Alongside realising what I was missing, I realised what style of fitness I really loved. It is what I refer to as "Conventional" Fitness Racing (CFT). Now I can't knock CrossFit, they are some of the most impressive athletes in the world, and people love the sport. However, I was never into combining Olympic Weightlifting and gymnastic-type movements (handstand walking, etc) into my conditioning style work; it just isn't for me (simply my preference). I call CrossFit "Specialist" fitness racing, which is the term I also use for sports like Obstacle Course Racing. For me, these races have high technical demands, whereas conventional fitness racing places far more emphasis on core performance qualities like endurance, speed and strength.

Of course, having good running or rowing technique is going to benefit you greatly, but fundamentally, when it comes to a race that involves running, rowing, loaded carries, burpees, etc. It is more about fitness than skill.

Note: When I use the word "conventional," I don't mean it to imply that this style is the "primary standard" or in any way superior to others. It just seemed to be the best word to describe fitness races whose only barrier to entry is "are you fit enough." You could be the fittest man or woman on earth, but if you haven't been practicing ring muscle ups, then a race with a lot of ring muscle ups is probably going to write you off.

After a good 6-months of fitness race training and loving the different races that I tried, I wanted to make a race of my own, and I wanted it to be what I consider to be the most complete race in the world while also being extremely accessible. Although I love rowing and pushing heavy sleds, etc. I wanted to design a race that could be truly trained for in every gym in the world, at any outdoor bootcamp or home gym, even a garage or living room with a single set of weights.

I wanted the race to act as a complete training system, an entire methodology that goes beyond just a training program and into a training ethos.

I feel I have achieved that, and I hope you think so too. I hope this manual acts as a bridge for more people to get into this style of training (and thinking) and improve themselves in ways they never thought possible.

Coach Jason Curtis

Founder & Race Director

P.S. I used to put a lot of pressure on myself about competitions against others. However, when it comes to fitness racing, I just see it as me vs the race: The aim is to **Beat the Race** and do the best I can – this thought process has definitely helped me to enjoy the sport even more!

Fitness Racing

At this point, we have already taken a good leap into the Deadly Dozen and who I am as the founder and race director. However, I feel now is a good time, before we take a deep dive into the Deadly Dozen, to take a step back and explain exactly what fitness racing is in a little more depth.

Fitness Racing is a sport where athletes race through a series of physical activities as an individual or team. These activities can include running, rowing and other modes of cardio, bodyweight exercises, lifting and carrying weights, and maneuvering over obstacles.

As touched upon briefly in the previous section, I consider there to be two main categories of fitness racing:

1. **Conventional Fitness Racing:** Races with low technicality.

2. **Specialist Fitness Racing:** Races with higher technical demands.

For me, there are **Six Key Components of Fitness Racing:**

1. **Cardio:** This refers to the cardiovascular activities within a race. For example, running, rowing, skiing, cycling.

2. **Muscular Endurance:** This refers to the bodyweight and sub-maximal resistance exercises that are performed for longer durations (high reps, etc).

3. **Strength:** This refers to the heavy (near-max) resistance exercises.

4. **Speed:** This refers to how much emphasis is placed on speed.

5. **Technicality:** This refers to how technical the activities are within the race.

6. **Novelty:** This refers to additional aspects of the race that are designed to be fun, scary, arduous, etc. For example, slides into water or inflatable obstacle courses.

Conventional Fitness Racing has a high emphasis on Cardio, Muscular Endurance and Speed, while having a lower emphasis on Strength and a very low emphasis on Technicality. The Novelty aspect of conventional fitness races can be varied.

Of course, strength is a vital attribute for conventional fitness racers as it will greatly improve an athlete's performance (the weights will feel lighter) and reduce their risk of injuries. However, when I say, "lower emphasis on strength," I mean the race doesn't include weights that are likely to be near maximal loads for the athletes. For example, the KB Goblet Squat weight in the Deadly Dozen may only be 10-25% of an athlete's 1RM Back Squat with a BB (BB).

All races will have biases towards different components. For example, a race may have a Cardio Bias and involve a lot of running. A Strength Bias and consists of a lot of heavy lifting. Or a Novelty Bias with the main aim being fun and enjoyment.

I truly believe Fitness Racing to be the ultimate "Lifelong Sport." Everyone should aspire to include both cardiovascular and resistance training throughout their entire life and fitness racing allows people to do this with a sport that is, in essence, the most adaptable sport in the world: Sport provides goals – goals encourage consistency – consistency leads to success!

The Concept & Inspiration for The Deadly Dozen

When it comes to running, there are certain distances that are particularly horrific, and that is because they are not short enough to be over quickly (there's plenty of time to suffer), yet they are not long enough to warrant slowing down and pacing yourself.

On the athletics track, the 400m and 800m are exactly that, and when it comes to road running, the ability to run a fast 5km has always been noteworthy to me. Whenever an athlete I worked with had a fast 5km time (relative to their gender, bodyweight, and age, etc), they ALWAYS stood out in both their physical and mental capacities, especially when that individual was also strong in the gym – when someone has good physical strength, and can also smash out a good 5km time, they are not just a Hybrid Athlete, they are an absolute beast!

One of the best ways to train for a fast 5km time is with the infamous interval session, 12x 400m runs, usually with around 45-120 seconds recovery (slow jog: 200-300m), and it was this training session that was the initial inspiration for the race.

Fitness racing, by nature, is leg-heavy, and that's good because running on tired legs separates the men from the boys and the women from the girls. However, I wanted to create a race that also involved a lot of upper body movements and rather than going from cardio to cardio, transitioned from cardio (the run) to a resistance exercise, or at least a bodyweight movement that requires a lot of muscular energy to perform.

I wanted these exercises to develop the key fundamental movements such as Hinge, Squat, Lunge, Push, Pull and Carry. I wanted them to be accessible to all, hence only using basic equipment. And most of all, I wanted them to feel "laboursome." I wanted each exercise station to feel like a real "Labour" between each run, and this, of course, got me thinking about the 12 Labours of Hercules and how he would "Journey" to each – unfortunately, I don't have Namean Lion's or Hydra's for people to slay.

I was worried about linking Greek mythology to the Deadly Dozen at the risk of being cliché. However, on second thought, Greek mythology is extremely cool (I get that referring to something as "extremely cool" is NOT very cool), and I have always been a massive advocate of Stoicism (a school of philosophy from ancient Greece and Rome). People confuse Stoicism with having a stiff upper lip and bottling things up, but in actuality, it is the exact opposite. Stoicism is about having a deeper understanding of how you react to the challenges life throws at you and handling these things with emotional intelligence, fortitude, and self-discipline. It is about understanding what you can and can't control and the beneficial regulation of emotions.

I feel many Stoic principles go hand in hand with hard physical training and will ultimately help you to become a better athlete. Therefore, I have sprinkled this manual with lots of Stoic wisdom, along with some of the wisdom or insight that I have picked up over the years. I also think that making things fun is vital because enjoyment promotes consistency. Therefore, I have aimed to use gamification where possible by utilising Greek mythology with fun ranking systems, etc – I hope you find value in the ways I have tried to make the Deadly Dozen an exceptionally challenging yet fun training system.

Fitness Racing and Stoicism have helped me to become a fitter, healthier, happier and an all-round better human being (husband, father, friend, colleague, boss, athlete) – the mind develops the body, and the body develops the mind.

"Difficulties strengthen the mind as labour does the body." – **Seneca**

"The trials you encounter will introduce you to your strengths." – **Epictetus**

The Race

The Deadly Dozen Fitness Race works off a Dozenal (duodecimal) system. Therefore, all distances and reps are based around the number 12 (a superior highly composite number) and can be increased or decreased by 25, 50 or 75% while maintaining round numbers – this is a key element of the training methodology.

Race Structure

- 400m Run

- **1. KB Farmers Carry:** 240m

- 400m Run

- **2. KB Deadlift:** 60 Reps

- 400m Run

- **3. DB Lunge:** 60m

- 400m Run

- **4. DB Snatch:** 60 Reps (Alternate)

- 400m Run

- **5. Burpee Broad Jump:** 60m

- 400m Run

- **6. KB Goblet Squat:** 60 Reps

- 400m Run

- **7. WP Front Carry:** 240m

- 400m Run

- **8. DB Push Press:** 60 Reps

- 400m Run

- **9. Bear Crawl:** 120m

- 400m Run

- **10. WP Clean & Press:** 60 Reps

- 400m Run

- **11. WP Overhead Carry:** 180m

- 400m Run

- **12. DB Devil Press:** 20 Reps

Total Journey Distance: 4800m / **Total Distance Labours:** 900m / **Total Rep Labours:** 320 Reps

Here is an illustration of how the event is set up on a 400m athletics track:

Note: This can be replicated on a sports field. You can even perform the Labours within an open gym space and then go outside and run 200m from the gym and 200m back (accessibility!)

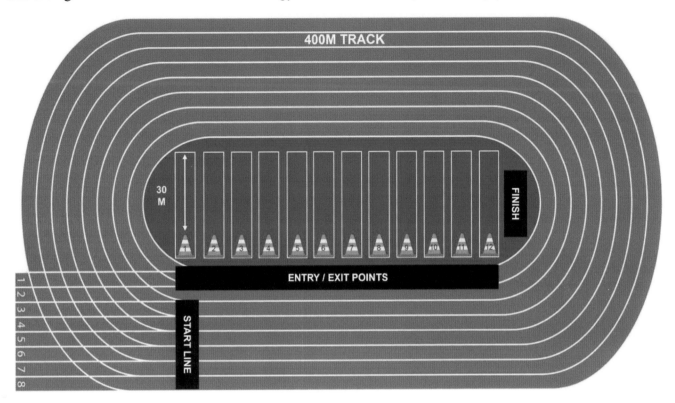

Here are the weights that are used by male and female athletes:

Labours	Male Weight	Female Weight
KB Farmers Carry	2x 24kg KB	2x 16kg KB
KB Deadlift	1x 32kg KB	1x 24kg KB
DB Lunge	2x 12.5kg DB	2x 7.5kg DB
DB Snatch	1x 15kg DB	1x 9kg DB
Burpee Broad Jump	Bodyweight (BW)	Bodyweight (BW)
KB Goblet Squat	1x 16kg KB	1x 12kg KB
WP Front Carry	1x 25kg WP	1x 20kg WP
DB Push Press	2x 12.5kg DB	2x 6kg DB
Bear Crawl	Bodyweight (BW)	Bodyweight (BW)
WP Clean & Press	1x 15kg WP	1x 10kg WP
WP Overhead Carry	1x 15kg WP	1x 10kg WP
DB Devil Press	2x 10kg DB	2x 5kg DB

Race Variations

Solo Race

The Solo Race involves running the entire event as an individual.

There is no time limit on the race. However, each Labour (exercise) must be completed in the right order, and athletes cannot move on until the Labour is completed – athletes are seeded with our Seeding Labour prior to the event and are set off in waves (two men and two women at a time).

If an athlete is unable to complete a Labour to the set standard (modified technique or range of motion, etc), their final race time will be followed by "(s)" which denotes that they have "scaled" the race.

Pairs Race

The Pairs Race involves running the event in teams of two.

Both athletes run every 400m Journey together and are involved in completing each Labour. However, they can split each Labour between them in any way they see fit: One athlete can complete an entire Labour independently, or the athletes can alternate how they see fit.

Athletes can be same-sex or mixed - mixed teams use the male weights (female-only teams use the female weights). Athletes can be any age combination (above 18).

If either athlete needs to scale a Labour, the final time will be followed by (s).

Equipment must be placed down on the floor before the other athlete takes over – the equipment can NOT be passed to your partner. Athletes must move together on the Distance Labours (one walking/jogging).

Only one athlete wears the timing chip.

Relay Race

The Relay Race involves running the event in teams of four.

Each athlete runs 1x Journey and 1x Labour before the next team member goes. Therefore, each athlete completes 3x Journeys and 3x Labours to complete the race – athletes must stick to their order, i.e., Athlete A does Labour 1, 5 & 9. Athlete B does Labour 2, 6 & 10. Athlete C does Labour 3, 7 & 11. Athlete D does Labour 4, 8 & 12.

Athletes can be same-sex or mixed (2x male + 2x female) - mixed teams use the male weights (female-only teams use the female weights). Athletes can be any age combination (above 18).

If any athlete needs to scale a Labour, the final time will be followed by (s).

Equipment must be placed down on the floor before the next athlete goes.

Only 1 athlete at a time wears the timing chip (the one doing the work): The non-chipped team members stand on the outer lanes of the track in line with the Labour station the chipped team member is on. The next team member to go crosses into the centre of the track (once the working athlete has finished their 400m and gets to the Labour station), ready to take the timing chip once the Labour station is completed. The newly chipped athlete then crosses the timing mat onto the track and completes their Journey and Labour.

Equipment

When I decided that I wanted to create a fitness race that combined resistance exercises with running, and I wanted that race to be one of the most accessible fitness races and training methodologies in the world, I knew the race had to include only Bodyweight (BW), Kettlebell (KB) Dumbbell (DB), and Weight Plate (WP) exercises.

Of course, you can use any KBs, DBs and WPs that are available to you. However, Official Deadly Dozen Races use a set style of equipment – this equipment is available from equipment providers worldwide.

- The KB Labours use both Competition and Cast Iron KBs: The KB Deadlift and Farmers Carry use Competition KBs and the Goblet Squat uses a Cast Iron KB

- The DB Labours use Hex Dumbbells (metal handles with rubber hexagonal bells)

- The WP Labours use Thick Rubber Bumper Plates (Diameter: 45cm)

WP Thickness (give or take 1cm): 25kg: 10cm / 20kg: 8cm / 15kg: 6cm / 10kg: 4cm

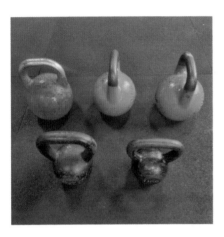  

The following tables include everything you need to run a race simulation at the official race weights – of course, you can use the same weight(s) for multiple Labours (this is noted in bold brackets)

Male Weights:

KBs	Dumbbells	Weight Plates
1x 32kg	1x 15kg	1x 25kg
2x 24kg	4x 12.5kg **(2x)**	2x 15kg **(1x)**
1x 20kg	2x 10kg	

Female Weights:

KBs	Dumbbells	Weight Plates
1x 24kg	1x 9kg	1x 20kg
2x 16kg	2x 7.5kg	2x 10kg **(1x)**
1x 12kg	2x 6kg	
	2x 5kg	

Equipment needed to run 2x Male + 2x Female per wave:

Official Deadly Dozen Races send 2x male and 2x female solo racers every 12 minutes for a total of 20 solo racers per hour.

Pairs teams share the equipment, so 20 pairs teams (40 people in total) get through the event per hour.

Relay teams share the equipment, so 20 relay teams (80 people in total) get through the event per hour.

Official races have an extra 1-2 pieces of equipment per Labour Lane to minimize the risk of bottle necks during the event (people catching up to each other).

Male Weights		
KBs	**Dumbbells**	**Weight Plates**
2x 32kg	2x 15kg	2x 25kg
4x 24kg	8x 12.5kg	4x 15kg
2x 20kg	4x 10kg	
Female Weights		
2x 24kg	2x 9kg	2x 20kg
4x 16kg	4x 7.5kg	4x 10kg
2x 12kg	4x 6kg	
	4x 5kg	
Total		
2x 32kg	2x 15kg	2x 25kg
6x 24kg	8x 12.5kg	2x 20kg
2x 20kg	4x 10kg	4x 15kg
4x 16kg	2x 9kg	4x 10kg
2x 12kg	4x 7.5kg	
	4x 6kg	
	4x 5kg	

If you are interested in running Official Deadly Dozen Fitness Races, drop me an email at **info@deadlydozen.co.uk**

"External things are not the problem. It's your assessment of them. Which you can erase right now." – **Marcus Aurelius**

The Rulebook

The Deadly Dozen Fitness Race involves athletes competing against each other to complete 12x 400m runs (Journeys) and 12x exercise stations (Labours). Therefore, specifically when it comes to the Labours, it is essential that movement standards are strictly standardized for everyone to ensure a fair race.

In this section, we look at the overall rules of the race and an in-depth look at each of the Labours, detailing the key rules.

Registration

- Deadly Dozen Fitness Race Registration can only be done via the official Deadly Dozen Website: **www.deadlydozen.co.uk**

- Athletes must select their gender category (Male or Female), input their age and select the race category they are entering (Solo, Pairs, Relay)

- The athlete must be at least 18 years old on the day of the Deadly Dozen race

- The athlete must agree to the terms and conditions set upon registration

- Race spots are non-refundable. If an athlete wants to defer their entry to a future race or transfer their entry to another athlete, they must contact us at **info@deadlydozen.co.uk**

- For ticket transfers, both parties need to email **info@deadlydozen.co.uk** – Deadly Dozen is NOT responsible for any transfer of funds external to the Deadly Dozen website.

Age Groups

Age groups are determined by their age on the race date – if the athlete turns 50 the following day, they are still in the 40-49 category.

- 18-29
- 30-39
- 40-49
- 50-59
- 60-69
- 70-79
- 80-89
- 90-99+

Pairs and Relay age groups are created by dividing the age difference between the youngest and oldest athletes by 2 and then adding it to the youngest athletes' age to generate the age group. For example, if Athlete A is 22 and Athlete B is 56: (56-22 = 34) (34 / 2 = 17) (22 + 17 = 39). So, they fall into the 30-39 age category.

Equipment

The following equipment **can** be used/carried during the race:

- Appropriate clothing: Shorts/joggers/t-shirt/vest – athletes can go topless

- Appropriate trainers: Trainers can have carbon plates

- Watch/heart rate monitor

- Sweatbands – headbands and wristbands

- Knee sleeves or joint supports

- Athletes can choose to carry a hydration pack (worn on their back) and can carry snacks/energy gels, etc. However, these must be carried by the athlete and all rubbish must be kept on the athlete

The following equipment **can NOT** be used/carried during the race:

- Trainers with spikes

- Phones

- Headphones

- Rings or jewellery that could cause injury if it were to get caught

- Gloves

- Belts

- Lifting straps

- Peaked caps

- Chalk – powdered or liquid (no tacky)

- No water bottles

Hydration and Nutrition

Athletes can NOT receive any hydration or nutritional products from a spectator. Water is available on the final bend of the track prior to entering the Labour stations.

It is advised that athletes hydrate fully and eat around 2-3 hours before their race wave.

We recommend you trial the appropriate nutrition protocol for the race day weeks/months prior: Program some form of race simulation/hard training session and trial your morning routine.

Race Day Protocol

- Athletes must turn up 1 hour before their wave time

- Upon arrival, athletes head to the registration area (clubhouse) with a copy of their race confirmation (printed) and a form of government issued ID (Passport or Driving License)

- Once registered, the athlete will receive a numbered timing chip that is worn on their ankle – this number becomes their race number (bib number)

- Athletes can wear their bib number on their tops or shorts or have it written on their left forearm

- One person from the pairs team wears the timing chip

- Relay teams change the timing chip over after the completion of the Labour

- Timing chips MUST be given back – a Deadly Dozen official will take the chip back after the last Labour before the athlete leaves the centre of the track (this is also where you get your medal)

- Toilets are available at the athletics track

- Athletes are responsible for their training equipment and valuables on the day

- Athletes can use the areas surrounding the track for warm-ups

- Athletes must be on the track (starting box) 12 minutes before their wave starts (waves are every 12 minutes) – they can use the designated area within the track to warm up during this time

Scaling

All activities involved in the Deadly Dozen Fitness Race can be "Scaled" (s) to accommodate for the needs of the athlete. Athletes with specific needs should contact the race director prior via email (info@deadlydozen.co.uk) to ensure we can accommodate for the athlete to the best of our ability – we stand by our aim to be the most accessible fitness race in the world.

Race Declaration

The athlete agrees to race in a fair and honourable manner, and to show good sportsmanship throughout the race. The athlete agrees to show the utmost of respect to Deadly Dozen officials and volunteers, other athletes, and spectators. If these standards are not met, the athlete will be disqualified from the race and potentially banned from future races. No refunds will be given to athletes that are disqualified or banned.

In consideration of being permitted by Deadly Dozen to participate in its activities and to use its equipment and facilities, now and in the future, I hereby agree to release, indemnify and forever discharge Deadly Dozen, its agents, owners, members, shareholders, directors, partners, employees, volunteers, manufacturers, participants, lessors, affiliates, its subsidiaries, related and affiliated entities, successors and assigns (the "RELEASED PARTIES"), on behalf of myself, my spouse, my children, my parents, my heirs, assigns, personal representative and estate as follows:

I acknowledge that my participation in Deadly Dozen activities and use of Deadly Dozen facilities entails known and unknown risks that could result in physical or emotional injury, paralysis, death, or damage to myself, to property or to third parties. I understand that such risks simply cannot be eliminated without jeopardising the essential qualities of the activity.

The 12 Rules

These are the overarching rules of the race.

1. The first rule of Deadly Dozen: You must tell as many people as possible about the Deadly Dozen.

2. All athletes must complete the Seeding Labour and post their time to **info@deadlydozen.co.uk** at least 2-weeks prior to the race: Wave times are released 1-week prior to the race (those that don't post a seeding time will be placed in later waves).

3. All athletes must arrive and register for the race at least 1 hour before their wave time.

4. All athletes must wear appropriate sportswear and trainers for the race – carbon trainers are allowed, but spikes are NOT allowed.

5. All athletes must abide by all Deadly Dozen rules and regulations and treat other athletes with respect.

6. All athletes must stay within the lanes of the athletic track when completing Journeys. Athletes should NOT run in the first lane (closest to the Labour entry point) while on the initial 100m stretch – athletes should be aware of incoming runners when leaving the Labour Lanes.

7. Athletes must NOT purposefully block other athletes while on the track.

8. All athletes must aim to perform the Labours to the correct standard (unless scaled) and must ensure they cover the correct distance/perform the correct number of reps. If an athlete cannot complete a Labour to the correct standard or cannot complete the programmed distance or reps, they get an "(s)" (scaled) by their final time. Athletes can be given "No Reps" by judges if a rep is not to standard or told to adjust their form.

9. During Labours, rests can be taken at any time, but the equipment must be placed down under control and the rest is taken on that exact spot. Upon completion of the Labour, the equipment is placed down ready for the next athlete.

10. All athletes must respect the judge's decisions – if a judge doesn't count a rep, your form was off.

11. Waves (2x male + 2x female) are set off every 12 minutes on the dot: 09:00 – 09:12 – 09:24 – 09:36 – 09:48 – 10:00.

12. If an athlete gets to a Labour and there is no available equipment, they are credited the missed time back – with seeding, 12-minute waves and spare equipment, this shouldn't happen.

Journey Rules

- The race starts with a 400m Journey around the track. This starts in line with the first Labour station on the outside lanes

- Athletes can move into the second lane as soon as they want and into the first (inside) lane once they have passed the final Labour station (approach the first curve of the track)

- Athletes must NOT purposefully block or hinder other athletes – athletes take over on the outside

- Athletes can get a drink of water that is available on the outer lanes of the final curve of the track before approaching the Labours – cups/bottles must be thrown into the bins provided

- Upon reaching the first 100m stretch (the Labour entry and exit points) the athlete can run down the inside lane and once they reach the first Labour, the athlete steps onto the inside area of the track (across the timing mat) and begins the Labour

- Upon completing the first Labour, the athlete steps across the timing mat and back onto the track (the athlete must give way to running athletes) and moves into the second lane (to avoid other athletes) until they reach the first curve of the track

- The athlete completes another 400m run and crosses onto the inside of the track in line with the second Labour

- This process is repeated until all 12 Labours are complete

- Pairs teams complete all 12 Journeys together

- Relay teams only complete 3 Journeys each – timing chips are exchanged in the centre of the track by the Labour station that has just been completed

Labour Rules

The following pages describe the rules of each of the 12 Labours:

1. KB Farmers Carry
2. KB Deadlift
3. DB Lunge
4. DB Snatch
5. Burpee Broad Jump
6. KB Goblet Squat
7. Plate Front Carry
8. DB Push Press
9. Bear Crawl
10. Plate Clean & Press
11. Plate Overhead Carry
12. DB Devil Press

1. KB Farmers Carry

The KB Farmers Carry involves carrying a KB in each hand and walking or running a distance of 240m over a 30m lane (8x 30m lengths / 4x there and back).

Distance: 240m

Male weight: 2x 24kg (KB)

Female Weight: 2x 16kg (KB)

Key Rules:

- No chalk is allowed

- Any style of grip can be used

- The athlete can walk or run

- The KBs can be placed down at any time. The athlete must place them down where they are stood and remain in that position until they pick them up again

- At each end of the 30m lane, the athlete must cross over the line with their entire body (both feet)

- Upon completion of the full distance, the KBs must be placed down so that they are ready for the next athlete

2. KB Deadlift

The KB Deadlift involves picking up a KB from the floor with straight arms and fully extending the knees and hips so that the shoulders come behind the KB at the top. The KB is then returned to the floor and must touch the floor (not dropped) before subsequent reps are completed.

Reps: 60

Male weight: 1x 32kg (KB)

Female Weight: 1x 24kg (KB)

Key Rules:

- No chalk is allowed

- Any style of grip can be used

- The feet can be slightly wider than shoulder-width, but NOT a wide sumo stance

- The hands do NOT have to leave the handle of the KB between each rep, but the athlete can take their hands off at any time to rest

- Rests must be taken in a stationary position – the athlete can NOT walk around

- The KB must touch the floor between each rep, otherwise the lift is a no rep

- Both the knees and hips must fully extend at the top and the shoulders must finish behind the KB

- On the last rep, the KB must be placed down so that it is ready for the next athlete

3. DB Lunge

The DB Lunge involves holding a DB in each hand in a farmer's carry position (straight arms at your sides) and performing walking lunges for 60m (2x 30m lengths – 1x there and back).

Distance: 60m

Male weight: 2x 12.5kg (DB)

Female Weight: 2x 7.5kg (DB)

Key Rules:

- No chalk is allowed

- Any style of grip can be used

- The athlete can put the DBs down at any time and rest. However, they must place the DBs down under control and rest in a stationary position where they stopped

- The rear knee must touch the floor during each lunge, and the knee that touches the floor must alternate (the athlete can NOT lunge forward with the same leg twice)

- The knees and hips must fully extend at the top of each lunge

- If the knee does not touch the floor or the hips and knees do not fully extend at the top, the athlete gets 1 warning before being told to stop and take one step back

- The athlete can stride through with the rear leg into the next lunge without setting their foot down, or they can place the foot down before proceeding into the next lunge

- The athlete can NOT take any steps forward in between lunges. If they do, they will be told to stop and take a step back

- At each end of the 30m lane, the athlete must cross over the line with their entire body (both feet)

- On the last rep, the DBs must be placed down so that they are ready for the next athlete

4. DB Snatch

The DB Snatch involves taking a single DB from the floor to overhead in one movement. This is done in an alternating fashion from one arm to the next – the athlete can NOT perform multiple successive reps on the same side.

Reps: 60 (30 Each Side)

Male weight: 1x 15kg (DB)

Female Weight: 1x 9kg (DB)

Key Rules:

- No chalk is allowed

- Any style of grip can be used

- At the bottom of the movement, the DB is on the floor and the athlete grips it with one hand. Their other hand can be supported on their leg

- The DB is pulled upward and taken overhead, and the elbow must extend fully – if the elbow does not extend fully, it is a no rep

- If an athlete is unable to extend their elbows fully due to anatomical reasons, they must let the judge know prior to starting by showing the range of motion they have (extend arms overhead)

- The athlete can change hands on the way down (the working arm must extend before the DB is changed to the other hand) or while the DB is on the floor

- Only one of the bells (the end of the DB) has to touch the floor – if it doesn't touch the floor, it is a no rep

- Rests must be taken in a stationary position – the athlete can NOT walk around

- On the last rep, the DB must be placed down so that it is ready for the next athlete

5. Burpee Broad Jump

The Burpee Broad Jump involves performing a burpee (going from a standing position to lying chest down on the floor) before standing up and jumping forward with both feet and landing with both feet (broad jump, aka horizontal jump). This is done for 60m (2x 30m lengths – 1x there and back).

Distance: 60m

Male weight: Bodyweight (BW)

Female Weight: Bodyweight (BW)

Key Rules:

- The athlete must start behind the line and perform a burpee with their chest and thighs touching the floor – the athlete can step or jump down into the bottom position, but the hands can't crawl forward

- The athlete can step up or jump up from the bottom position (the body does NOT have to fully extend before jumping

- If jumping up, where the feet land is where the broad jump is performed from – athletes can NOT step forward after jumping up. If stepping up, after the initial step, the rear foot steps up in line with the front foot and the broad jump is performed from there – no additional steps can be taken

- The athlete must perform the jump with both feet and land with both feet

- Upon landing the jump, no additional steps can be taken and if the athlete stumbles forward or steps forward by accident, they must stop and take a step back

- Upon landing the jump, the athlete can place their hands down anywhere in front of their feet and perform the next burpee by jumping or stepping back with their legs (NOT crawling forward with their hands) – the athlete can NOT dive or leap forward with their body into the bottom of the burpee

- The athlete can rest at any time in any position (on their knees, etc). However, they must remain where they stopped – they can NOT crawl forward

- At each end of the 30m lane, the athlete must cross over the line with their entire body, i.e., jump over the line

6. KB Goblet Squat

The KB Goblet Squat involves holding a KB to the front (above the waist) and performing squats to parallel or below (thighs in relation to the floor). Therefore, the thighs must be at least parallel to the floor.

Reps: 60

Male weight: 1x 16kg (KB)

Female Weight: 1x 12kg (KB)

Key Rules:

- No chalk is allowed

- Any style of grip can be used – the athlete can hold the KB how they like

- The KB must be held above the athlete's waist – if the KB drops below the waistline, it is a no rep

- The stance can be slightly wider than shoulder width, but a sumo squat position can NOT be used (athletes would struggle to achieve the appropriate depth if the squat stance is too wide)

- The athlete must squat to at least a parallel position, where their thighs are parallel to the floor, i.e., the hips are at the same height at the knees

- The forearms can NOT push on the legs at the bottom of the squat

- Both the knees and hips must fully extend at the top of the movement

- Rests must be taken in a stationary position – the athlete can NOT walk around

- On the last rep, the KB must be placed down so that it is ready for the next athlete

7. WP Front Carry

The WP Front Carry involves carrying a WP to your front (with both arms) and walking or running a distance of 240m over a 30m lane (8x 30 lengths / 4x there and back).

Distance: 240m

Male weight: 1x 25kg (WP)

Female Weight: 1x 20kg (WP)

Key Rules:

- No chalk is allowed

- Any style of grip can be used – the athlete can hold the WP how they like as long as it is held with both hands/arms at the front of their body (NOT on their shoulder or head)

- The athlete can walk or run

- The WP can be put down at any time, but the athlete must remain where they are

- At each end of the 30m lane, the athlete must cross over the line with their entire body (both feet)

- On the last rep, the WP must be placed down so that it is ready for the next athlete

8. DB Push Press

The DB Push Press involves pressing a pair of DBs from the shoulders to overhead. A leg drive can be used (a bend and extension of the knees to propel the DBs upwards). The elbows must extend fully overhead.

Reps: 60

Male weight: 2x 12.5kg (DB)

Female Weight: 2x 6kg (DB)

Key Rules:

- No chalk is allowed

- Any style of grip can be used

- At the bottom of the movement, the DBs should be either touching the shoulders or be just above the athlete's shoulders (no higher than the athlete's ears)

- The athlete can press the DBs overhead using a strict press (upper body only). However, a bend of the knees followed by an explosive extension of the knees can be used to propel the DBs overhead (Push Press)

- The elbows must fully extend overhead, otherwise it is a no rep.

- If an athlete is unable to extend their elbows fully due to anatomical reasons, they must let the judge know prior to starting by showing the range of motion they have (extend their arms overhead)

- Rests must be taken in a stationary position – the athlete can NOT walk around

- On the last rep, the DBs must be placed down so that they are ready for the next athlete

9. Bear Crawl

The Bear Crawl involves crawling on all fours (hands and feet – NOT knees) over a distance of 120m (4x 30m lengths – 2x there and back).

Distance: 120m

Male weight: Bodyweight (BW)

Female Weight: Bodyweight (BW)

Key Rules:

- The athlete must start behind the line and get onto their hands and feet and start crawling
- The knees are not allowed on the floor while crawling
- There should always be at least one hand and one foot on the floor at all times.
- The athlete can NOT use a "galloping" action where both hands and/or feet are off the floor at the same time
- The athlete can rest at any time in any position (on their knees, standing, etc). However, they must remain where they stopped – they can NOT crawl forward while on their knees
- At each end of the 30m lane, the athlete must cross over the line with their entire body (both hands and feet). They can NOT stand up and step across the line, or crawl on their knees across the line

10. WP Clean & Press

The WP Clean & Press involves taking a WP from the floor to overhead. The WP must touch the floor between each rep and the elbows must fully extend overhead.

Reps: 60

Male weight: 1x 15kg (WP)

Female Weight: 1x 10kg (WP)

Key Rules:

- No chalk is allowed
- Any style of grip can be used
- At the bottom of the movement, any part of the WP can touch the floor (usually the top edge as pictured) – if the WP doesn't touch the floor, it is a no rep
- The centre of the WP must be taken directly overhead, and the elbows must fully extend – if the elbows do not fully extend overhead, it is a no rep
- If an athlete is unable to extend their elbows fully due to anatomical reasons, they must let the judge know prior to starting by showing the range of motion they have (extend their arms overhead)
- On the last rep, the WP must be placed down so that it is ready for the next athlete

11. WP Overhead Carry

The WP Front Carry involves carrying a WP overhead (with both arms) and walking or running a distance of 180m over a 30m lane (6x 30 lengths / 3x there and back).

Distance: 180m

Male weight: 1x 15kg (WP)

Female Weight: 1x 10kg (WP)

Key Rules:

- No chalk is allowed

- Any style of grip can be used – the athlete can hold the WP how they like as long as the centre of the WP is directly over their head

- The athlete's elbows can be straight or bent, but the plate can NOT touch the head – if the WP touches the athlete's head, they will be asked to stop and given a caution (after 3 warnings the athlete is scaled)

- The athlete can walk or run

- The WP can be put down at any time, but the athlete must remain where they are – the athlete can NOT rest the WP on their head (even while stationary)

- At each end of the 30m lane, the athlete must cross over the line with their entire body (both feet)

- On the last rep, the WP must be placed down so that it is ready for the next athlete

12. DB Devil Press

The DB Devil Press involves holding a DB in each hand, performing a burpee with the chest and thighs touching the floor before jumping or stepping up, lifting the DBs and taking them overhead.

Reps: 20

Male weight: 2x 10kg (DB)

Female Weight: 2x 5kg (DB)

Key Rules:

- No chalk is allowed

- Any style of grip can be used

- With a DB in each hand, the athlete performs a burpee and touches their thighs and chest to the floor. The athlete can jump or step down

- The athlete then jumps or steps up and stands up with the DBs and takes them overhead – this movement can be performed as a strict DB clean and press, or a swinging motion can be used

- The athlete's elbows must fully extend overhead – if the elbows do not fully extend overhead, it is a no rep

- If an athlete is unable to extend their elbows fully due to anatomical reasons, they must let the judge know prior to starting by showing the range of motion they have (extend their arms overhead)

- On the last rep, the DBs must be placed down so that they are ready for the next athlete

Labour Technique

1. KB Farmers Carry: Technique Variations & Tips

To start, when you get to the KBs, make sure to brace your body if you need to. Creating tension in the body can make the initial lift easier and reduce the risk of straining your back or your hamstrings, etc.

You can simply walk with the KBs. However, moving fast means the station gets completed quicker as a whole, so you will be less likely to have to put the KBs down.

The faster you can move, the less time the KBs will be in your hands. However, breaking into a full run will create vertical movement (up and down), which will put more stress on your grip. Therefore, it is best to use a shuffling technique where there is less leg lift (the knees are kept lower), but the feet are moving quickly.

I recommend using a full grip (fingers and thumb wrapped around the horn/handle of the KB). However, you can use a false/hook grip where the thumb is not wrapped around the horn/handle of the KB. Athletes may start with the full grip but transition to the false/hook grip as their grip starts to go (at this point, it may be worth speeding up).

Full Grip	**Hook Grip**

When performing loaded carries, it is generally best to use quick, forceful breaths – I exaggerate the exhale (blow the air out like you are blowing out candles on a birthday cake).

2. KB Deadlift: Technique Variations & Tips

To start, stand directly over the KB. You don't want to be too far behind the KB, as it will make it a harder lift. You can take a wide shoulder-width stance, but it cannot be a sumo stance.

Athletes will often prefer to take a full grip on the KB (fingers and thumb wrapped around). However, I tend to use a false/hook grip. I know I have the finger/grip strength to do this, and using this grip essentially lengthens my arms by a couple of inches and shortens the range of motion.

There are two ways in which you can perform the deadlift:

1. **Quad Heavy Lift:** Sit more into the deadlift (increase your knee bend and lower your hips) to maximize the work from the quadriceps (thighs).

2. **Posterior Chain Heavy Lift:** The posterior chain refers to the muscles that run up the rear of the body. Therefore, this lift involves less knee bend and a higher hip position, meaning more of the load is focused on the hamstrings, glutes, and back muscles.

Athletes can lean into one style or be anywhere on the spectrum between the two. They can also vary the style over the 60 reps.

Your knees and hips have to fully extend at the top, and your shoulders have to fall behind the KB. Therefore, you should think about pushing your chest out at the top.

Quadriceps Heavy Lift   **Posterior Chain Heavy Lift**

3. DB Lunge: Technique Variations & Tips

To start, hold the DBs in each hand and stand in a hip-width stance. From there, stride into the first lunge with a comfortably long stride – too short, and you won't cover much ground, and it will limit your ability to touch your knee to the floor / too long, and it will require too much force to extend the legs from such a stretched-out position, and therefore, create a harder movement.

There are 2 ways in which the lunge can be performed:

1. Striding right through with the rear leg without setting it down.

2. Placing the rear foot down for a second before striding forward with it into the next lunge.

Striding through with the rear leg without placing it down results in a faster lunge. However, it is more tiring on the legs. Also, it can encourage people to not fully extend the supporting leg at the top before proceeding into the next lunge, so ensure you come up tall and fully extend the knee and hip of the stance leg; otherwise, it will be counted as a no rep, and you will be asked to take one step back.

Placing the rear leg down for a second before going into the next lunge is a little slower, but it provides some respite and helps to ensure you fully extend at the top.

Note: When you place the foot down before striding into the next lunge, it only needs to be a quick tap with the ball of the foot to deload a lot of the stress from the supporting leg.

During a lunge, the front leg generally does around 75% of the work, while the back leg does arounds 25% of the work. However, while striding out from the bottom of the lunge, it is beneficial to make a conscious effort to push up and forward hard with the back foot as well as pushing hard with the front foot. The back foot can work harder when using a shorter lunge stride.

If you struggle with balance when lunging, straddle your stance slightly so that your legs are wider apart (when looking from the front). However, going too wide will place more stress on your groin muscle.

| **Back Leg Swings Through** | **Back Leg Steps Down** |

4. DB Snatch: Technique Variations & Tips

To start, stand directly over the DB with a wide shoulder-width stance.

A pronated (palm facing the athlete) or neutral grip (palm facing out to the side) can be used.

I use a neutral grip as only one bell (rubber block at the end of the metal bar) has to touch the floor. Therefore, the bell furthest away from me is tilted to touch the floor.

It is key during the snatch to use the legs to propel the DB upwards. Once the force is transferred from the legs and the elbow is pulled up high, you should be able to comfortably "turn the arm over" (the elbow goes from being higher than the wrist to coming underneath it) and extend the DB overhead.

The arm that is performing the snatch must fully extend before the DB is transitioned into the other hand, but from that point onwards, it can be transitioned. The transition can happen directly after the arm extends, on the way down, or on the floor – I like to transition the DB as soon as I start to bring the DB down (I throw it down into my other hand, which is at chest height).

It is fine to have the hand without the DB in on your thigh, and this can help during the pull phase off the floor and can ease the load on the back on the way back down.

Bottom Position

High Pull

Receive Overhead

Hand Transition

5. Burpee Broad Jump: Technique Variations & Tips

You can step or jump down and up during burpee broad jumps. Many people prefer to jump down but step up to conserve energy (the jump up prior to the broad jump is very taxing). You can also alternate the legs that you use to step up with.

Jumping up from the bottom position is faster than stepping up, but it can be far more taxing on the legs and the cardiorespiratory system. Jumping up from the bottom position gives the benefit of loading the legs up, ready to jump (as soon as the feet touch down, you can spring forward).

When jumping up from the bottom position, you want the flexibility to get your feet as close to your hands as possible; otherwise, you are losing distance – if you are jumping up to 1ft behind your hands, you are losing 1ft on your jump. Your feet can jump up between your hands, just behind your hands, or on the outside of your hands.

During the broad jump, the greater the distance you jump, the fewer jumps you are going to have to perform in total. However, performing repeated maximal jumps is going to be very taxing. Therefore, you want to aim to perform a good jump, but not a maximal jump – stay relaxed.

To maximize the length of the jump, you need some height. However, it is key that you concentrate on jumping horizontally and not waste energy on gaining too much height.

After stepping or jumping up from the burpee, I like to stay low and transition into the jump. I then stay low upon landing to place my hands straight down to go into the next burpee.

| **Step Up** | **Narrow Jump Up** | **Wide Jump Up** |

6. KB Goblet Squat: Technique Variations & Tips

Any grip can be used on the KB as shown below, as long as the KB has to be above waist height – the position can be changed at any time during the 60 reps.

If your stance is too wide or too narrow, you will struggle to reach the depth requirement (parallel or below). Therefore, it is key to find the stance and foot placement that suits you – most people will find a shoulder-width or slightly wider stance with their toes angled outward slightly optimal.

When squatting, it is key to drive your weight through your heels, big toes, and little toes to stay balanced.

Both the hips and knees need to fully extend at the top, so be sure not to rush the extension of the legs.

Parallel Squat **Deep Squat**

Although parallel is the standard, athletes do not have to limit depth and may benefit from utilizing the stretch reflex and "springing" out of a slightly deeper squat.

7. WP Front Carry: Technique Variations & Tips

You can carry the WP however you like, as long as the WP is held to the front of your body (NOT on your shoulders or overhead).

Here are a few variations:

My personal favourite is carrying the WP with straight arms with the WP pressed into my lower abdomen/groin area. Yes, this can be a little uncomfortable in that area. However, I have found it to be by far the most efficient position to carry the WP. I find this technique allows for a little respite after the first half of the Deadly Dozen Fitness Race, especially after working the legs hard on the Goblet Squat. However, if I pick up the pace (shuffle) with the WP in this position, I bend my arms slightly to keep the WP stable.

I lean back slightly and shuffle – I find this technique to be quite heavy on the hamstrings, which isn't necessarily a bad thing after Goblet Squats have hit my quads hard.

When performing loaded carries, it is generally best to use quick, forceful breaths – I exaggerate the exhale (blow the air out like you are blowing out candles on a birthday cake).

8. DB Push Press: Technique Variations & Tips

You can have your palms facing away or towards each other (neutral grip) while performing the DB push press. I personally prefer to use a neutral grip.

To maximize the work from the legs, you bend your knees (dip with the knee), not sit back with your hips as if you are squatting. The knees should bend to a point where you drop about 10% of your height (around 7 inches for a 6ft guy), and then they should extend explosively to propel the DBs from the shoulders.

Due to the fact the DBs are not a near max load, a full knee dip is not always necessary to propel the DBs off the shoulders. Just a slight dip of the knees to cushion the DBs as they drop down from the top of the movement, followed by an explosive plantarflexion of the ankles (come up onto your heels – almost a small jump), can be a fast way to perform high rep DB Push Press.

I will often create mind-body connection (think about the body part) with my elbows as they extend overhead to ensure I get the full extension (this is similar to mind-muscle connection, where you consciously think about the muscle you are working to maximize its engagement).

As the DBs lower back down to the starting position (the downward phase is called the eccentric phase), you can use the downward momentum to go straight into the next knee dip (bend), or you can catch the weights at your shoulder before proceeding with the next knee dip.

Starting Position	The Dip and Drive	Full Extension

9. Bear Crawl: Technique Variations & Tips

During the bear crawl, as long as your hands and feet are on the floor, you can have your hips as high or as low as you want, so choose a position that suits you.

Some find bear crawls quite hard on their wrists. In this case, they can come up onto the pads of their thumbs and fingers as pictured (this is quite hard on your fingers, but you can build up resilience with progressive training).

I often use a technique where my fingers are forward facing, and I drive the base of my palm into the floor as I aim to sprint with the legs, and move my hands as quickly as possible.

Rests can be taken in a kneeling or standing position. Although you can't move around the lane when resting, sometimes standing can be beneficial as you can shake your legs off.

Woodchop

Woodchops can be performed with DBs, resistance bands (as shown on the previous page), or a cable machine, and you can hold the resistance in one or both hands) – you can also whack a sledgehammer onto a truck tyre to create an awesome rotational exercise.

Performing the exercise with DBs maximizes the need to decelerate the movement towards the end of the lift, while bands create accommodating resistance as you progress through the movement (it gets harder as band tension increases).

The woodchop is performed by rotating the resistance from one side of the body to the other and can be practiced from a variety of starting and finishing positions:

- Swinging side to side at chest height – this is great for mobilizing the thoracic spine

- From above your shoulder to shin or thigh height and vice versa – diagonally across the body

- From overhead to between your legs

During any of the woodchop variations, you can produce even power as you go both up and down or left to right, or you can emphasize the power in one direction, i.e., the downward action. You can also isolate the movement to your thoracic spine with no movement from your lower body, or you can increase the range of motion by pivoting on your feet and rotating with both your hips and thoracic spine.

1. Grab a dumbbell with one or two hands or grab the end of a band that is attached to a solid structure.
2. Rotate into the starting position.
3. Explosively rotate back and forth in the direction of your choosing – play with difference starting and finishing positions.
4. Complete successive reps.

Coach Curtis Core Routine

The **Coach Curtis Core (CCC) Routine** is a 360 Core Workout that develops flexion, rotation, lateral flexion, lateral extension and extension of the spine. This is an **ADVANCED** Core Routine. Yes, a healthy spine can and should perform all the above movements. However, some may not yet have the strength and conditioning in their structures to accommodate the stress or previous injuries may currently prevent them from performing movements of this kind with maximal range of motion.

The Core Routine consists of 4 key exercises, all performed on the GHD back-to-back. However, you can break up the movements however you like (supersets are great).

1. **GHD Sit-Up:** Maximal Extension into Maximal Flexion (4-12 Reps)

2. **GHD Rotation:** Maximal Rotation (2-12 Reps on Each Side)

3. **GHD Side Bend:** Maximal Lateral Flexion to either side (4-12 Reps on Each Side)

4. **GHD Back Extension:** Maximal Flexion into Maximal Extension (8-25 Reps)

Complete 3-4 sets with 30-60 seconds rest between sets.

12. DB Devil Press: Technique Variations & Tips

You can step or jump up from the bottom position. Jumping up is more taxing, but I tend to find with it being the last Labour and it being 20 reps, I prefer to power through and jump up.

There are 2 ways in which you can jump up:

1. Jump up so your feet are directly behind or in between the DBs (narrow stance).

2. Jump up into a wide stance so your feet are on the outside of the DBs.

I personally like to use the wide stance method as I find it more efficient.

Once you are in a standing position and holding the DBs on the floor, there are two ways in which you can proceed to take the DBs overhead:

1. Swing the DBs back into your groin before taking them overhead – this requires less brute force and, therefore, saves energy. However, it is a little slower.

2. Lift the DBs directly upward in a vertical path – this is quicker but is more energy-intensive.

I often start with the more energy-intensive method but transition to the swinging method if I need to.

When I go to place the DBs down for the next burpee, I ensure I don't place them too far forward as this would require me to jump further forward when getting back up – I like to perform the push-up of the burpee with the DBs at my lower chest.

Swinging the DBs	**No DB Swing**

Awards

Meet *Mori*, our SkullBell Logo and the official mascot of the Deadly Dozen.

Note: The Mori Medal has exactly 12 teeth – that's attention to detail right there!

We recommend you get a Stoic Quote of your choice engraved on the back (or any quote you like) – find a quote within this book that resonates with you: Memento Mori / Amor Fati / or my acronym G.Y.H.R.U.

Upon successful completion of the Deadly Dozen Fitness Race (even if Labours have been Scaled), every participant receives a Mori Medal, i.e., Our SkullBell Pendant – this is NOT a "participation medal" because you do NOT get a medal for just participating, you have to complete one of the hardest fitness races in the world to earn your Mori Medal! Scaled (s) attempts do get a medal because although we are tough, we are not monsters. The Mori Medal also makes a cool keyring.

The Deadly Dozen is split into two gender categories (male and female) and there are three race variations: Solo, Pairs and Relay. The latter two have both same-sex and mixed categories. Therefore, there are 8 race divisions in total.

- **Solo Race:** Male / Female
- **Pairs Race:** Male / Female / Mixed
- **Relay Race:** Male / Female / Mixed

The top three fastest times (non-scaled) from each division win 1st, 2nd and 3rd place, and we also account for age group winners and runners-up – age groups are 18-29 and 10-year increments after that (we have a calculation to work out the age category when there are age differences within Pairs and Relay teams).

We do NOT have award ceremonies on the race day, as we feel it drags the day out. Instead, we send Race Certificates to all athletes with a full breakdown of their times for each Journey and each Labour – it is you vs the race – **BEAT THE RACE!**

The overall winners and runners-up (not age groups) also get awarded discounts on future Deadly Dozen Race entries (this can be stacked on top of any other discount).

- **1st Place: Solo:** 100% Off / **Pairs:** 50% Off / **Relay:** 25% Off
- **2nd Place: Solo:** 50% Off / **Pairs:** 25% Off / **Relay:** 15% Off
- **3rd Place: Solo:** 25% Off / **Pairs:** 15% Off / **Relay:** 10% Off

Note: Only one discount code is given to Pairs or Relay teams to use on future registrations.

The Top 12 Athletes: The Deadly Dozen

Alongside the podium (top 3), the solo race also has an additional award system – **The Deadly Dozen**.

- Top 6 Male Athletes
- Top 6 Female Athletes

If an athlete makes it into the top 12, they are sent an Official Deadly Dozen Patch that is only available to those who make it into the top 12.

Have you got what it takes to become one of the Deadly Dozen or the Deadliest of the Dozen?

The Hercules and Atalanta Patches

There are two patches that are awarded to just two athletes from the race. However, both patches can be awarded to the same athlete on the day.

- **The Hercules Patch:** Awarded to the athlete (male or female) that showed the most heart during the Labours
- **The Atalanta Patch:** Awarded to the athlete (male or female) who showed the most heart during the Journeys

The athletes are chosen by the Deadly Dozen officials who have overseen the event, along with recommendations from the judges.

You may be asking, "What do you mean by the most heart?" Well, it could be the slowest person that was seen to be struggling the most but still got through it. Or it could be the fastest person pushing themselves well beyond their limit, what we call RPE 12 – "Isn't 10 the highest?" you ask. Yeah, well, our RPE Scale jumps to 12!

Note: RPE means Rating of Perceived Exertion and is explained in the section on Quantifying Training Loads – Page-71.

Mori Collecting: Stoic Patches

Every time you complete an Official Deadly Dozen Fitness Race, you are awarded a Mori Medal (SkullBell Pendant). When you collect a specific number of Mori Medals, we will send you the relevant Stoic Patch + a race discount + more!

- Collect **3** Mori's: **Zeno Patch** + 50% off your next race
- Collect **6** Mori's: **Seneca Patch** + 50% off your next race + a Deadly Dozen T-Shirt
- Collect **9** Mori's: **Epictetus Patch** + 75% off your next race + a Deadly Dozen Cap or Beanie Hat (your choice)
- Collect **12** Mori's: **Aurelius Patch** + 100% off your next race + a Signed Hardcover Copy of the Deadly Dozen Training Manual

An Introduction to Physical Training

The aim of this section is to give you an overview of what physical training is and the theory behind how we go about improving it. From there, we will perform a Needs Analysis for the Deadly Dozen and its athletes and then dive headfirst into the Deadly Dozen Method (DDM).

What is Physical Training?

The definition of physical training is the systematic use of exercise to promote bodily fitness and strength.

Not a bad definition if you ask me, but it brings us to the next question:

What is Fitness?

The definition of fitness is the condition of being physically fit and healthy.

Again, not a bad definition, but let's take a look at what fitness really means. To be a well-rounded athlete is not just about physical fitness. It is also about what is commonly referred to as Total Fitness.

- **Physical Fitness:** The well-being of the body's systems, including the heart, lungs, muscles, bones, and joints. It covers health-related and skill-related components

- **Mental and Emotional Fitness:** The well-being of the mind; a positive mental state and harmony between the mind and emotions. It includes a person's ability to manage stress – I see Stoicism as a form of training for mental and emotional fitness

- **Medical Fitness:** Being free from injury, chronic disease, and illness

- **Nutritional Fitness:** Having access to healthy food; eating a healthy diet with a balanced nutritional intake for fuel, growth and repair

- **Social Fitness:** Having healthy interactions and relationships with others. Having quality social interactions is more important than you think – many experts consider loneliness to be as damaging, if not more damaging, to an individual's overall health than severe stress

Of course, in this manual, the primary focus is Physical Fitness, so let's take a look at the components of that.

"Only the educated are free." – **Epictetus**

48

Components of Physical Fitness: Performance Qualities

Generally, there are considered to be eleven components of physical fitness, with five being health-related qualities and six being skill-related qualities. However, I include an additional health-related component, which is Mechanical Strength, something I will talk in-depth about in the section on injury prevention.

With the additional performance quality, it makes 12 components – that number keeps cropping up! Even the race's long tagline is 12 words: "One of the hardest yet most accessible fitness races in the world!" – Our short tagline is Beat the Race!

Note: We refer to the components of fitness as Performance Qualities.

Health-Related Qualities	Skill-Related Qualities
Muscular Strength The ability of a muscle or group of muscles to exert maximal force	**Agility** The ability to move, change direction and body position quickly and efficiently while maintaining control – often in reaction to a stimulus
Muscular Endurance The ability of a muscle or group of muscles to sustain repeated contractions	**Balance (Static & Dynamic)** Static balance is the ability to maintain equilibrium when stationary. Dynamic balance is the ability to maintain equilibrium when moving. (Equilibrium – a state in which opposing forces are balanced)
Cardio-Respiratory Endurance The ability of the heart, lungs, and blood vessels to deliver oxygen to the tissues	**Coordination** The ability to move two or more body parts under control, smoothly and efficiently
Mobility / Flexibility Flexibility is the passive length a muscle can achieve. Mobility is the range of motion a joint can achieve (includes flexibility)	**Speed** The ability to move quickly across the ground or move limbs rapidly
Body Composition The percentage of muscle, fat, bone, and water in the human body	**Power** The ability to exert high force in minimal time
Mechanical Strength The ability of your tissues to withstand the stress of physical forces: Tension / Compression / Bending / Shear / Torsion	**Reaction Time / Quickness** The ability to respond quickly to a stimulus

As you can see, there is far more to fitness than just being aerobically fit. This being said, there is usually a bias towards specific performance qualities depending on the activity that is being practised – we will cover this in much greater detail when we get to the next section, The Needs Analysis.

Movement Qualities

On top of the **12 Performance Qualities**, we have **12 Movement Qualities**.

Note: I have always taught my 11 Movement Qualities. However, I have added Crawl to fit all movements that are carried out in the Deadly Dozen.

Unfortunately, there are no throws in the Deadly Dozen. Although having Olympic throwing events like the Javelin and Discus would suit the Greek sub-branding, the risk of other racers being impaled by a Javelin or knocked out by a flying disc was a deciding factor – Greco-Roman wrestling would also have been a nice way to finish after the Devil Press, but I actually want people to sign up for the race.

1. **Brace:** The ability to create tension and maintain a position. Bracing is vital in maintaining posture, both statically (standing still) and dynamically (moving).

2. **Hinge:** Bending at the hips while keeping the knees straight and maintaining a neutral spine (neutral spine simply means unbent and untwisted).

3. **Squat:** Bending at the hips, knees, and ankles.

4. **Lunge:** Single-leg exercises that work the legs independently from one another (unilateral).

5. **Push:** Pushing with the upper body.

6. **Pull:** Pulling with the upper body. The deadlift exercise is often classified as a "Pull" exercise (pulling from the floor). However, the deadlift can be better classified as a hinge exercise as the emphasis is on hip extension.

7. **Rotate:** Rotation is primarily performed at the hips and shoulders (ball and socket joints) and at the spine through a series of facet joints. These structures can work in isolation or together to produce a greater range of motion.

8. **Gait:** Walking, running, and carries.

9. **Change of Direction (COD):** The ability to change direction at speed while maintaining balance and coordination – Multidirectional Speed (MDS) is the ability to accelerate, decelerate, change direction, and maintain speed in multiple directions and movements.

10. **Crawl:** Moving across the floor using both your feet and hands.

11. **Jump:** Throwing your entire body off the floor either vertically or horizontally. Jump = taking off with two feet and landing with one or both feet / Bound = Taking off with one foot and landing on the opposite foot / Hop = taking off with one foot and landing on the same foot.

12. **Throw:** Throwing an object into the air with one or both hands in any direction.

"As long as you live, keep learning how to live." – **Seneca**

Biceps Curl

The biceps are responsible for elbow flexion and forearm supination, and the long head of the biceps attaches to the shoulder blade and plays a small role in shoulder flexion. Therefore, to fully work the biceps, you should start with the DBs at your sides in a neutral grip (palms facing your thighs).

You can work all three movements with DBs: As you flex your elbows, you supinate your forearms (turn your palms up), and as you come towards the top, your elbows come forward slightly to create a small degree of shoulder flexion to maximize the peak contraction at the top.

Of course, DB curls can be varied in several ways. For example, instead of starting in a neutral grip, you can keep your forearms supinated. Although this removes the need to supinate during the lift, it maximizes the stretch through the biceps brachii as you work through the eccentric phase (keep more tension on the muscles).

DB curls can be performed bilaterally (working both arms simultaneously) and unilaterally (working one arm at a time).

A unilateral curl's benefit is that it increases the weight that can be lifted as all the effort can be driven into that one arm performing the curl. However, on the flip side, the benefit of performing bilateral curls is that you can achieve more reps in a shorter amount of time with both arms working in a continuous fashion rather than one resting while the other is working.

To maximize time under tension during unilateral curls, you can hold the non-working arm at the halfway point or at the top while the working arm performs a set number of reps.

One of my favourite ways to perform a DB biceps curl is the Zottman Curl (named after George Zottman, an 1800s Strongman). The Zottman curl involves using the full DB curl on the way up, rotating your forearms at the top so your palms face forward before lowering the DB down in a reverse curl position. All this makes the Zottman curls arguably the most complete curl variation there is.

Alongside DB curls, you can also perform BB curls or use a variety of specialist bars, such as EZ bars. You can also use KBs or WPs – cable machines are also effective tools for working the arms.

1. Stand up tall with good posture.
2. Hold the DBs at your side in a neutral grip – starting in a neutral grip allows you to supinate your forearms as you perform the curl, helping to increase biceps engagement.
3. Contract your biceps, bringing the DBs upwards, as this happens, begin to supinate your forearms – this should all be done in a fluid motion.
4. As your elbows pass 90 degrees of flexion, bring your elbows forward slightly to increase the engagement of your biceps as you reach the top of the lift.
5. As you get to the top of the lift, supinate your palms as hard as you can to increase the engagement of the biceps – push your little fingers in towards your chest.
6. A shift grip can be used to increase the work required to supinate your forearms (hand placed off centre on the DB, towards the bell on the outer side at the top of the movement)
7. Lower the DB down under control to the starting position.
8. Don't swing the DB backward.
9. Continue with successive reps.

Triceps Extension

Triceps extensions can be performed while standing or seated with an upright torso and are a great way to build triceps strength and elbow resilience – triceps strength is absolutely key for pushing movements.

A DB, WP, various bars, or a KB can be used to perform the movement:

- When performing the exercise with a DB, you cup the DBs top bell in your hands and take it overhead. Or, if performing a single-arm triceps extension, grab the bar of the DB with one hand

- While performing the exercise with a WP, you grab each side of the WP and take it overhead

- When using a straight BB or EZ bar, you can perform the action with a pronated or supinated grip

- When using a KB, you need to ensure you grip the horn/handle of the KB tightly – raising the bell up at the top encourages peak contraction of the triceps at the top of the movement

Regardless of what equipment is used, you should aim to keep your elbows as forward-facing as you can (during bilateral triceps extensions). You should also ensure you do not pull the weight overhead to the front using your latissimus dorsi, and instead, concentrate on extending your elbows, taking the weight upward, not forward.

Triceps extensions can also be performed with one arm, holding a DB behind your head and extending it from behind your head in a lateral motion to overhead. During a lateral (single arm) triceps extension, rather than facing forwards, your elbows face away from your body (to the side).

Another great way to build the triceps and build resilience around the elbows is with triceps pushdowns on a cable machine or resistance band.

1. Stand upright with good posture or sit on a bench with good posture – having a proud chest with your shoulders back and thoracic/upper spine extended allows for better overhead mobility.
2. If using a DB, pick it up, grabbing the underside of one bell and extend it overhead.
3. If using a WP, grab each side of the plate and extend it overhead.
4. While keeping your elbows as forward facing as possible, bend your elbows and allow the DB/WP to lower behind your head.
5. Once your elbows are fully bent, extend them and return the DB/WP back to the starting position – a common fault is bringing the weight too far forward in front of the head – cue to "push the weight up towards the ceiling" / "extend the weight upward not forward".
6. Continue with successive reps.

Delayed Onset Muscle Soreness (DOMS)

To finish this section on physical training, it is important to briefly explain DOMS, or Delayed Onset Muscle Soreness, because it is a phenomenon that anyone who trains will experience at some point.

DOMS refers to the pain/discomfort and stiffness felt in the muscles several hours or days after exercise - the soreness is felt most strongly 24-72 hours after exercise. Contrary to popular belief, DOMS is not caused by lactic acid buildup. Lactic acid typically dissipates within an hour or two after exercise. Instead, DOMS is a byproduct of muscle trauma that leads to inflammation of the tissues.

Key points:

- Eccentric contractions (muscles lengthening under tension) are known to cause greater DOMS as they result in more micro-trauma to the tissues (which leads to inflammation) in comparison to concentric contractions (muscles shortening under tension)

- The key to preventing DOMS is progressive training and good training frequency – DOMS increase when there is a spike in volume/intensity or a sudden change in the type of stressors included in the session

- DOMS should not be chased – muscle soreness is NOT an accurate indicator of a "good session." Instead, DOMS is usually a good indicator of a lack of training frequency and irregular exposure to specific stressors

Coming from a prolonged rest period to even moderate training is essentially a spike in stress, and it is not uncommon for an athlete to suffer from notable DOMS even after a short period of inactivity (we take this into account early on in the program). DOMS can have a negative impact on the training plan and, therefore, should be limited – it is key to build resilience progressively.

This all being said, although we should aim to minimize DOMS, it is quite normal to get some level of DOMS when exposed to new stressors (especially early in a program), and ultimately, we shouldn't shy away from a bit of discomfort when our aim is to get to a high level of physical performance.

There are countless remedies for DOMS that people promote, but many are more placebo than anything else (placebos have their place). However, if something aids relaxation or increases circulation to an area, then it is not a bad thing – my suggestion is to go for a walk or do low-intensity cardio to increase circulation.

Note: The placebo effect is a psychological and physiological phenomenon in which a person experiences real or perceived improvements in their condition or symptoms after receiving a treatment that has no active therapeutic effect. In other words, the placebo effect occurs when a person's belief in the effectiveness of a treatment leads to actual improvements in their health despite the treatment having no intrinsic therapeutic properties.

Conversely, the nocebo effect occurs when a person experiences negative outcomes due to their belief in the harm or ineffectiveness of a treatment. This belief can lead to the worsening of symptoms or the occurrence of side effects.

The Needs Analysis

To design an optimal plan, we first need to understand the sport and the athlete, which is done with a **needs analysis**, a 2-stage process where we first analyse the sport, then the individual athlete.

Sports Categories

Here are some examples of the different types of sports (some categories merge). We also have youth and veteran age categories and special populations such as Paralympians.

- **Strength Sports**: Powerlifting, Strongman, Weightlifting

- **Strength and Speed Sports (Athletics)**: Track and Field (Throwing, Jumping and Sprinting)

- **Team Sports (Invasion Ball Games)**: Football, Soccer, Rugby, Hockey

- **Team Sports (Fielding/Striking Games)**: Cricket, Rounders, Baseball, Softball

- **Net/Wall/Racket Games**: Tennis, Squash, Badminton, Table Tennis

- **Endurance Sports (Cyclic Sports)**: Long Distance Running, Cycling

- **Combined Sports**: Biathlon, Triathlon, Decathlon

- **Combat Sports (Martial Arts)**: MMA, Boxing, Karate, Judo

- **Gymnastics**: Floor Work, Parallel Bars, Vaulting

- **Complex Coordination Sports (Dance)**: Artistic Skating, Synchronized Swimming

- **Aquatic Sports**: Swimming, Surfing, Sailing

- **Outdoor Pursuits**: Mountaineering, Rock Climbing, Orienteering

- **Target Sports**: Archery, Rifle, Pistol, Shotgun

- **Extreme sports**: Skateboarding, Mountain Biking, Base Jumping

- **Motorized sports**: Formula Racing, Motorcycling

- **Fitness Racing Sports**: Conventional fitness racing sports like the Deadly Dozen, Hyrox and Deka. Specialist fitness racing sports like CrossFit and Obstacle Course Racing (OCR)

Most sports can be classified into one of the four categories below, with some sports having events in each. For example, there are individual duel (singles) and duel (doubles) events in tennis.

- **Individual**: Competing as an individual against the event

- **Individual Duel**: Competing as an individual against another individual

- **Duel**: Competing as a pair against another pair

- **Team**: Competing with 3 or more individuals against another team

Sports Analysis

- **Sports Overview:** What is the typical sporting season and the main events throughout the year?

- **Movement Analysis**: What movement patterns are common in the sport and, therefore, need to be trained? Kinetics is the study of the forces that create motion, and kinematics is the study of motion

- **Physiological Analysis**: What are the strength, power, hypertrophy, muscular endurance, metabolic, speed, agility, and mobility requirements of the sport?

- **Injury Analysis**: What are the common sites for injury, and how is the risk of injury effectively minimized?

- **Position-Specific Analysis**: What are the different needs of each position? For example, the demands placed on a prop are different from those placed on a winger in rugby

Much of the information above can be gained by watching the sport, attending competitions, and speaking to coaches, athletes, and other spectators. Even just watching the sport on television or searching for videos online will provide you with invaluable insight once you approach being a spectator with a coach's eye.

On top of all this, there is a plethora of information online in regard to the analysis of different sports. You will find articles discussing the physical demands of a sport, injury surveillance studies that provide you with information on the prevalence of injuries, and incredibly well-edited videos that demonstrate the movement requirements of specific positions – do your research!

The analysis of sport is much easier with the accessibility of various technologies such as video software, GPS (Global Positioning System) and heart rate monitors, etc.

An example of using these technologies is time-motion analysis. For example, video and GPS can be used to assess how much a mid-fielder in soccer moves during 15 minutes of play. Add a heart rate monitor, and you will gain data on the average heart rate during a game and how often specific positions go into what is often referred to as a "red zone" heart rate (above 90% of maximum heart rate).

The Deadly Dozen is an easy event to analyse as there are fewer variables. It is an individual sport where the athlete is competing as an individual against the event (or as a pair or team against the event), i.e., No other athlete is directly impacting their performance. On top of this, every aspect of the event is planned out. We know exactly how long the athlete is running for and what movements/exercises they are required to complete.

"If you desire philosophy, prepare yourself from the beginning to be ridiculed, to expect many will sneer at you. Remember, that if you abide in the same principles, these men that first ridiculed will afterward admire you." – **Epictetus**

Sports Seasons

Most sports follow an annual plan that works towards the main season where the major events occur. For example, rugby players will be well aware of intense pre-season training prior to the main season. However, some sports, such as combat sports (MMA), may not follow an exact season each year, with athletes potentially accepting big fights at different times of the year.

Four parts of the conventional sporting season:

- **Pre-Season**: A time when athletes prepare physically for the season and when teams often play exhibition/warm-up games

- **Regular Season**: The time that most of the games are played (league competitions, etc)

- **Post-Season**: The time after the season. Teams often have a tournament to win a championship (playoffs)

- **Off-Season**: The time before the season starts that teams use to rest, recover and prepare for the next preseason/season

The Deadly Dozen Season

Although the Deadly Dozen can host races year-round, the primary season is in the summer. Therefore, the winter is seen as the Off-Season (although it is a great time for an indoor track season), where an aerobic base is usually established. The spring acts as a Pre-Season where training ramps up and places more emphasis on race-specific movements and qualities, and the Summer is the main/regular Season – late summer is where major championships take place.

Athlete Analysis

- Analyse the age, gender, and anthropometrics of the athlete (height, weight, limb lengths, etc) – what are the pros and cons of each for their sport?

- Look at their training and injury status

- Conduct tests to evaluate the athlete

- Evaluate the results compared to your research and their peers' testing results (considering positional demands) – use normative data

- Based on the results and comparisons, decide what the training priorities should be for this athlete in consultation with them

An analysis of the athlete should always start with a simple conversation (for a personal trainer, this would be the initial consultation). To truly understand the needs of an athlete, you must get to know them and build rapport. Having good rapport will result in the athlete giving honest feedback, which is essential, as honest feedback about how the athlete feels and responds to the training will best inform your programming.

From there, testing will provide you with relevant data, and normative data informs this.

Normative Data

Normative data is data from a reference population that establishes norms that can be compared against. However, there are a few things we must consider.

If using "norms" or "rating tables" to interpret your test results, you must consider whether the tests were carried out using the same protocol – many tests have a number of variations but are still given the same name.

- Is the equipment different in any way?

- Are the distances the same: Metric or imperial system – is the test laid out in meters or yards?

- Was the same starting stance used?

- Was the same starting command given? i.e., 3-2-1 Go!

- Were the weather conditions the same?

It is also important to consider what population group the normative data was derived from. For example, the age group or ability level – many studies have been carried out with college/university students/athletes.

Published norms are generally based on the range of scores around the mean. However, this doesn't necessarily mean the above-average score is good. For example, the test group may have achieved poor results across the board, and therefore, an above-average score is still fairly poor.

Smallest Worthwhile Change

Fitness testing is generally conducted several times a year to evaluate changes in an athlete's performance and identify where programming adaptations may need to be made.

Unfortunately, there are countless factors that can influence test scores on a given day. For example, an athlete's arousal level, caffeine consumption, sleep quality the night before and overall fatigue and stress levels. Therefore, changes in test scores cannot always be put down to increases or decreases in overall performance. There is also going to be a certain amount of variety between test scores no matter how perfect the conditions are, and this is more problematic when there is less wiggle room in the test, i.e., A test that lasts less than 10 seconds.

This being said, it is important that we determine what is a worthwhile or meaningful change in an athlete's test results and this is obviously going to depend on the test. Ultimately, when deciding on the SWC of a test, it comes down to the coach's experience and knowledge of the test and normative data.

Fortunately, when it comes to the Deadly Dozen Testing Battery (DDTB), which we will look at in the next section, all of the tests allow for much greater room for improvement than those that only last a few seconds, for example, a short agility test.

"I judge you unfortunate because you have never lived through misfortune. You have passed through life without an opponent—no one can ever know what you are capable of, not even you." – **Seneca**

Deadly Dozen Normative Data

The following data has been collected from my Strength and Conditioning gym in Macclesfield in the UK – these are subject to change as I gather more data from races.

If you want the most current data, feel free to email me at **info@deadlydozen.co.uk**

Note: Unlike regular normative tables that use terms like "Average" and "Good" over five or six data points, we use a 12-level system due to the fact that it fits well with our ranking systems and provides people with much more data – 1 is the lowest level and 12 is the highest.

The Full Deadly Dozen Race (Labours + Journeys): Normative Data

Note: G = Gender / M = Male / F = Female

G	L1	L2	L3	L4	L5	L6	L7	L8	L9	L10	L11	L12
M	<100m	<85m	<70m	<60m	<58m	<56m	<54m	<52m	<50m	<48m	<46m	<44m
F	<105m	<90m	<75m	<65m	<62m	<60m	<58m	<56m	<54m	<52m	<50m	<48m

Labour Only Deadly Dozen (Back-to-Back Stations): Normative Data

Note: G = Gender / M = Male / F = Female

G	L1	L2	L3	L4	L5	L6	L7	L8	L9	L10	L11	L12
M	<50m	<45m	<35m	<31m	<30m	<29m	<28m	<27m	<26m	<25m	<24m	<23m
F	<58m	<48m	<38m	<33m	<32m	<31m	<30m	<29m	<28m	<27m	<26m	<25m

1x 400m (Journey) Best Effort: Normative Data

Note: G = Gender / M = Male / F = Female

G	L1	L2	L3	L4	L5	L6	L7	L8	L9	L10	L11	L12
M	<110s	<95s	<85s	<80s	<75s	<70s	<65s	<62s	<60s	<58s	<56s	<54s
F	<120s	<105s	<95s	<90s	<85s	<80s	<75s	<70s	<65s	<62s	<60s	<58s

"What would have become of Hercules, do you think, if there had been no lion, hydra, stag or boar – and no savage criminals to rid the word of? What would he have done in the absence of such challenges?" – **Epictetus**

12 Labours: Average Times

These times are a rough average across male and female times (performed fresh – no prior fatigue).

1. **KB Farmers Carry:** 2 mins – 2 mins 30 secs (120-150 secs)

2. **KB Deadlift:** 1 min 30 secs – 2 mins (90-120 secs)

3. **DB Lunge:** 2 mins – 3 mins (120-180 mins)

4. **DB Snatch:** 2 mins 15 secs – 3 mins 15 secs (135-195 secs)

5. **Burpee Broad Jump:** 2 mins 15 secs – 3 mins 15 secs (135-195 secs)

6. **KB Goblet Squat:** 2 mins 15 secs – 3 mins 15 secs (135-195 secs)

7. **Plate Front Carry:** 2 mins – 2 mins 30 secs (120-150 secs)

8. **DB Push Press:** 1 min 45 secs – 2 mins 15 secs (105-135 secs)

9. **Bear Crawl:** 2 mins 30 secs – 3 mins 30 secs (150-210 secs)

10. **Plate Clean & Press:** 2 mins 15 secs – 3 mins (135-180 secs)

11. **Plate Overhead Carry:** 1 min 30 secs – 2 mins (90-120 secs)

12. **DB Devil Press:** 2 mins 15 secs – 3 mins 15 secs (135-195 secs)

During the full race, these times will vary due to progressive fatigue. They will also vary due to an individual's strengths and weaknesses. For example, some athletes may be strong on upper body movements but not great at lower body movements or might excel at all of the weighted movements but struggle with the bear crawl or burpee broad jumps.

I recommend setting a "fresh" (not fatigued) time for each Labour at what you would consider to be a steady but good pace (7 out of 10). From there, see how you compare during a full race simulation.

Tip: Set your watch off at the start of the first 400m run, and then LAP your watch each time you come to a Labour or go off for your next 400m. That way, you will see your split times for each 400m and each of the Labours – you get all of this information on a Race Certificate when you complete the Official Deadly Dozen Fitness Race.

Deadly Dozen Analysis

So far, we have established a few things about the needs of the DD Race:

- The race involves the athlete competing against the event, i.e., other competitors are not directly impacting on their performance

- The race involves 12x 400m runs, which is a total of 4800m. Other than the first run, these are performed in a fatigued state, and the legs are often worked heavily prior

- Key movements include loaded carries, deadlifting, squatting, lunging, pressing overhead, crawling, and going down into a prone position before getting up and jumping horizontally

- For the average athlete, the weights would be considered fairly low in a strength training setting (performing sub-10 rep sets), but for the high rep ranges (60 reps / 100+ meters), the weights are reasonably high. In a fatigued state, most athletes will have to break the exercise stations down into multiple sets, i.e., sets of 10-20 reps

- The race is going to last between 40 and 120 minutes depending on the ability level of the athlete

Looking at the bullet points above, the athlete will need a good aerobic base (aerobic capacity – work for long periods) and great aerobic power.

Aerobic power is the ability to work at higher intensities while still primarily using the aerobic system. If an athlete ventures too far past their anaerobic threshold (aka lactate threshold), they won't recover and will burn out – you can find more info on the energy systems on page-67.

Good anaerobic fitness and the ability to tolerate the discomfort of the anaerobic system working hard is also key.

Muscular endurance is key to ensure the muscles can keep working after bouts of intense exercise.

The athlete needs good running speed to cover the 400m as quickly as possible and high levels of muscular strength, so the weighted Labour stations do not take too much out of them. If an athlete is not as strong, then the weights used during the deadlift, squat, and push press, etc will cause huge fatigue.

With hybrid events like the Deadly Dozen, it is a balancing act of having enough muscle mass and strength to move the weights with greater ease, yet not being too heavy that it negatively impacts the athlete's running ability – a leaner athlete may have the advantage when it comes to running, but a more muscular athlete may have the advantage when it comes to the KB, DB and WP Labours.

Good lower body power is required to jump, and good lower and upper body power is required to take the weights overhead.

The athlete needs good balance, coordination, and agility to transition between the different stations and execute the proper form and technique. They need to be able to change direction quickly during Distance Labours like the Farmers Carry.

Good mobility and flexibility are required to ensure the athlete can perform exercises like the KB Goblet Squat to the proper depth.

"How does it help, to make troubles heavier by bemoaning them?" – **Seneca**

Performance Triangle

A great way to illustrate the physical requirements of a sport and where an athlete's strengths lie is to place dots within the performance triangle.

The performance triangle denotes Force (F) on the bottom left, Velocity (V) on the bottom right and Endurance (E) at the top.

Note: Force = Strength / Velocity = Speed.

Strength x Speed = Power

Endurance is placed at the top because we have max force and velocity at the base. From there, as we climb up each axis, we develop the ability to repeat these actions over and over again – power endurance, speed endurance and muscular endurance, etc.

We can assess where the sport lies across the F-E, V-E and F-V axis, and from there, decide what performance qualities need to be prioritised.

I have placed Mori where I feel the Deadly Dozen lies on this Performance Triangle.

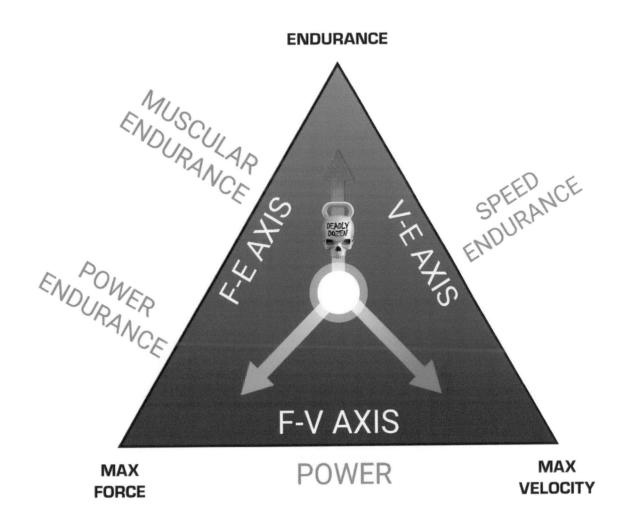

The Deadly Dozen Testing Battery (DDTB)

Once a Needs Analysis has been carried out on the sport and the athlete. The next step is to establish a battery of tests that are going to provide us with relevant data.

We want this data to:

- Inform us of the athletes' current abilities (set a baseline)

- Allow us to create a profile of the athlete: We don't just want data on one performance quality. We want to measure the different qualities that the athlete requires – establish their strengths and weaknesses

- Inform our programming: The program should be influenced by the test results – once we have analysed the test results, we set SMART Goals

Below is the Official Deadly Dozen Testing Battery: 3x Journey Fitness Tests (the 10km is optional) and 1x Labour Fitness Test – I like to carry out these tests every 12-weeks (best effort 400m runs are carried out throughout the interval training program, so we are gathering data on this regularly).

Journey Fitness Tests: Running Fitness

- 400m Dash

- 1-Mile (1600m) MAS Test (Maximum Aerobic Speed) Test (more info on the following page)

- 30-Minute Lactate Threshold Heart Rate (LTHR) Test (see page-76)

- Alternative (or additional) to LTHR Test = 5km Time Trial

Note: A 5km best effort may equate to around the 30-minute mark for many, but if an athlete has a sub-20-minute 5km or faster, the longer 30-minute run will provide more accurate data.

Labour Fitness Tests: Muscular Endurance

- The Deadly Dozen Seeding Labour

Seeding Labour: All exercises performed at race weights

3 Rounds for Time: Max effort

- **KB Deadlift:** 20 Reps
- **DB Snatch:** 20 Reps (Alternate: 10 Each Side)
- **KB Goblet Squat:** 20 Reps
- **DB Push Press:** 20 Reps
- **WP Clean & Press:** 20 Reps
- **DB Devil Press:** 10 Reps

Additional/Optional BB Strength Tests:

For those who want to gain data on their muscular strength, they can perform 1RM, 3RM, or 5RM on the following lifts.

- **BB Squat** (Back or Front Squat)

- **BB Deadlift**

- **BB Strict Press / BB Push Press**

- **BB Bench Press**

Note: Add 10% to 3RMs or 15% to 5RMs to estimate your 1RM.

Maximum Aerobic Speed (MAS) Test

In short, Maximum Aerobic Speed is the slowest speed at which you reach your V02 Max (maximum oxygen uptake). Therefore, it shows us how fast we can move while primarily using the aerobic system.

Note: VO2 max is defined as the maximum volume of oxygen (VO2) that a person can consume per minute during intense, maximal exercise. It is usually expressed in milliliters of oxygen per kilogram of body weight per minute (ml/kg/min).

The MAS test involves performing a 1-Mile (1.6km) best-effort run – it can be performed as a row (or even as a swim, etc). However, due to the fact that the Deadly Dozen is a running-based event, it makes sense to perform the MAS test as a run (my second choice would be a row).

Note: 1 Mile (1600m) is 4 laps of an athletics track. However, the run can be performed on any route that is relatively flat.

Your Maximum Aerobic Speed (MAS) is expressed in meters per second (m/s). Therefore, to work out your MAS score, take the distance in meters (1600) and divide it by the time it took you in seconds – let's say you covered the distance in 6 minutes (6 minutes = 360 seconds).

MAS Score: 1600 / 360 = 4.4m/s

Note: The higher the MAS score, the better.

If you want a FREE Excel MAS Calculator, email: **info@deadlydozen.co.uk**

MAS Test: Normative Data

This data has been established by testing a broad range of individuals (abilities and ages) from my gym.

G	L1	L2	L3	L4	L5	L6	L7	L8	L9	L10	L11	L12
M	2.6	2.8	3.0	3.2	3.4	3.6	3.8	4.0	4.4	4.6	4.8	5.0
F	2.2	2.4	2.6	2.8	3.0	3.2	3.4	3.6	3.8	4.0	4.4	4.6

Test Analysis: Profiling the Athlete

Once we have completed the fitness testing, it is time to analyze the results.

A **GAP Analysis** looks at the difference between where you are and where you want to be.

If you know where you are and know where you want to be, you can program backward from where you want to be and set realistic benchmarks at key stages within the plan.

Programming backward like this will show you whether your goals are realistic and will help you to organize training loads and retesting, etc.

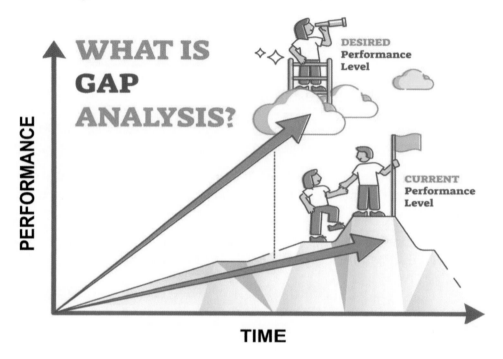

When it comes to profiling the athlete, we are not only assessing each performance quality that we have tested as an individual element that needs improving, but we are also comparing them against each other. This is why it is key not just to perform tests that focus on one performance quality like strength or aerobic fitness. We want to see whether an athlete is strong but not very fast, aerobically fit but not very strong, etc (this is what we call profiling the athlete).

Profiling the athlete like this will inform both our goal setting and the way in which we program.

We, of course, want to work on the athlete's weaknesses, but we also want to lean into the athlete's strengths. Leaning into strengths is something that is not often emphasized, but if someone is good at something (maybe has talent in that area), we want to capitalize on that, and more often than not, if they are good at it, they will probably enjoy it more.

This being said, as a strength and conditioning coach, if I see an athlete with clear weak links, I am going to put a bias towards that, especially if it is an area that has been undertrained historically. If it is undertrained, the chances are you will see novice/newbie gains, which refers to the rapid improvements you tend to see from an individual in the first few weeks and months of performing a novel activity. For example, someone who has put little effort into running over three to four years will likely see HUGE improvements while performing a six-week running program compared to the developments you would expect in a seasoned runner – a weakness is an awesome opportunity to see BIG improvements in a short space of time.

Goal Setting

Once testing and analysis of the results (GAP analysis, etc) has been done, it is time to set goals – These goals need to be SMART.

Three Types of Goals:

- **Outcome Goal(s):** The main goal(s) you are working towards and looking to achieve after a set period of time

- **Performance Goals:** These are benchmarks you are looking to achieve on your way to the main outcome goal(s)

- **Process Goals:** These are the processes we will take to achieve our outcome goal(s), i.e., I will train 3x a week

Goals are classed as **Short-Term** (0-1 Month), **Medium-Term** (1-6 Months) and **Long-Term** (6+ Months). However, you can adapt these timeframes to suit your programming.

SMART Goals

Acronym	Description
Specific	The goal must be well-defined and clear.
Measurable	The goal must be defined in measurable terms – quantifiable/comparable.
Achievable	The goal must be realistic and manageable.
Relevant	The goal must relate specifically to what you are trying to achieve.
Timed	The goal must be time-bound.

Alongside SMART goals, you may also see SMART**ER** goals, and the final "ER" usually refers to evaluated or exciting/enjoyable and Rewarded or Reviewed. I often tell people they can make the "ER" whatever they want to be – what fits for you?

"No person has the power to have everything they want, but it is in their power not to want what they don't have, and to cheerfully put to good use what they do have." – **Seneca**

Quantifying Training Loads

After we have set goals, it is time to develop the plan. However, before we look at how we design an optimal plan, we need to look at how we quantify training loads as these methods will be mentioned throughout the following sections on Periodization and Programming.

When it comes to training, you could just train as hard as possible during every training session. However, that's a surefire way of causing burnout and, more often than not, injuries. Anyone can write a program that, on paper, looks like it will result in huge improvements in performance, but is the program realistically sustainable? Does it provide enough frequency, volume, and intensity while not so much that it results in overuse injuries, or negatively impacts on other areas of the athlete's training and lifestyle?

The key to training is to take an educated approach where we consider how an individual session may impact the rest of the training week and beyond – what good is an incredibly intense session if the athlete is then unable to perform well for the rest of the week?

The best way to ensure that a training program is as optimal as it can be is to quantify the work that is being done, and this can be done subjectively and objectively. Subjective refers to a personal viewpoint (how hard the athlete thought the activity was), whereas objective refers to factual data (the athlete's heart rate during the activity).

Remember, Optimal is an ever-changing state for an athlete and requires constant evaluation and modification of the program. What is optimal one week may not be the next. However, this doesn't usually mean drastic changes need to be made; the coach just needs to be a little more dynamic with their sessions: We need to be Proactive with Programming and Reactive in the Real world (on the ground/gym floor). One of the most important soft skills for a coach is being able to read how an athlete is feeling – you can usually get a feel for an athlete's training readiness in the first 5-10 minutes of a session (although never fully judge someone until they are warmed up – you might feel terrible, but then have a great session once warmed up).

Note: Soft skills refer to the non-technical skills that describe how you work and interact with others, such as communication and having empathy and understanding. Hard skills, on the other hand, are specific capabilities and skills that an individual can possess and demonstrate in a measured way, like reading and writing, computer literacy, or being able to practically demonstrate a movement/skill.

In this section, we will look at how we quantify training loads for both strength training and conditioning (Labour and Journey Fitness). However, before we dive in, it is best to define a few terms first.

Strength and Conditioning, or S&C for short, refers to the physical development of competitive athletes at all levels, including elite-level sport, grassroots players or even hobbyists who want to succeed in sporting or fitness events.

Although, the S in S&C is quite self-explanatory, as it refers to the strengthening of the muscles and other soft tissues like our tendons. The term **Conditioning** can be a little more ambiguous. We can argue that all physical activities "condition" the body. For example, strength training conditions the muscles, plyometrics (jump training) conditions the tendons, and long-duration running conditions the aerobic system.

This being said, for the most part, when we say conditioning, we mean metabolic conditioning, which relates to the development of the energy systems that fuel the training we do. Of course, lifting weights works the energy systems. However, we can draw the line by defining training modes by their primary aim. For example, is the aim to build muscular strength or develop the energy systems that fuel the strength?

Energy Systems

We have 3 energy systems: All 3 work to produce ATP (Adenosine Triphosphate) which is a molecule that provides all livings things with fuel/energy (we eat food and plants use photosynthesis to produce it).

- **ATP-CP System** – this is anaerobic and doesn't utilize oxygen

- **Lactate System** – this is anaerobic and doesn't utilize oxygen

- **Aerobic System** – this does utilize oxygen

Note: All three of the energy systems have countless names, so don't get confused if you hear someone refer to the ATP-CP system as the Creatine Phosphate system or Phosphocreatine system. In a training setting, we tend to refer to activities as either anaerobic or aerobic.

The term "energy system" (bioenergetic systems) refers to metabolic processes (chemical processes) that create energy (ATP) in the body. These energy systems produce energy at different speeds (**power**) for varying durations (**capacity**), and therefore, training can be tailored to specifically target each system.

Although we can target specific systems, the three energy systems will develop holistically. For example, when multiple sprints are performed (working within the anaerobic energy systems), aerobic fitness will improve because the aerobic system is working throughout the entire training session to replenish what has been used – do not see it as one system doing all the work, see it as one taking the lead.

Some sports place emphasis on the energy system that provides energy the fastest, such as track and field events like the shot put, while others require all three in varying amounts, such as boxing or football. Sports will often have a bias towards one energy system, like a marathon runner, or that bias may change depending on the sporting situation.

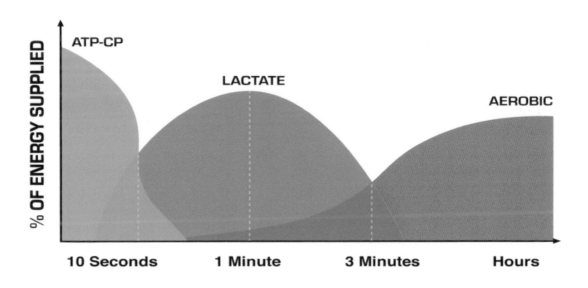

The ATP-CP system has the highest power (produces energy the fastest) but the lowest capacity (can't produce energy for very long). In contrast, the aerobic system has the lowest power (produces energy the slowest) but the highest capacity (can produce energy for a long time). The lactate system is in the middle of the two: The lactate system produces energy fast, and for much longer than the ATP-CP system, but it has nowhere near the capacity that the aerobic system has.

The Lactate threshold (often referred to as the anaerobic threshold), so named due to blood lactate levels being used to measure it, is the intensity at which the body transitions from primarily using the aerobic system to using the anaerobic lactate system, and therefore, waste products build up and performance diminishes – depending on genetics and an individual's fitness levels, the LT is generally around 75-90% of max heart rate, but most commonly described as 85% of max heart rate (it can be as low as 50-60% of max heart rate in untrained individuals).

We identify two lactate thresholds:

First Lactate Threshold (LT1): LT1 represents the exercise intensity at which lactate production starts to increase, but it is still being effectively cleared by the body. At this point, the body predominantly relies on aerobic energy production (using oxygen) to meet the energy demands of the exercise. This is often referred to as the point where you transition from light to moderate exercise and can be referred to as the **Aerobic Threshold**.

Second Lactate Threshold (LT2) or Onset of Blood Lactate Accumulation (OBLA): LT2 is the exercise intensity beyond which lactate production exceeds the body's ability to clear it and is considered to be the **Anaerobic Threshold**. This is considered a marker of the transition from aerobic metabolism to anaerobic metabolism. At LT2, there's a noticeable increase in blood lactate levels, and this is accompanied by a significant increase in perceived exertion and a decrease in the ability to sustain the exercise intensity for an extended period.

In fitness racing, we spend a lot of time at LT2 (working at threshold pace): We need **Aerobic Power** to sustain high-intensity exercise over longer durations through oxygen-dependent processes. However, a lot of activities (lifting weights) will throw us over LT2, and it is common to finish races with a fare few heart rate spikes and a surprisingly high average heart rate.

Once we venture over LT2, our ability to sustain the activity levels starts to diminish rapidly and if we venture too far across, we may burn out completely and be unable to recover – we have all been there, starting off too fast and regretting it BIG TIME. This is why **Aerobic Power** is a key attribute for many athletes.

Aerobic power refers to the quality of being able to produce energy quickly and hence maintain high intensities of work while remaining primarily within the aerobic system. In short, during a fitness race, if an athlete is able to work faster than you while remaining below LT2, then they are going to be able to maintain it and will be incredibly hard to beat.

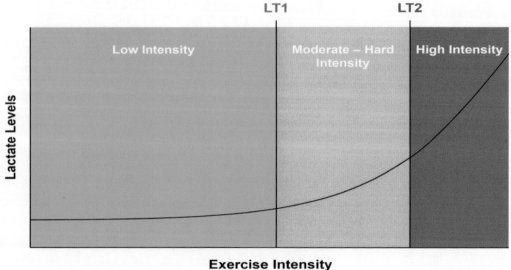

Remember, although the anaerobic system is still kicking in, especially during times when the intensity ramps up (going up a hill or performing a Labour station), it is ultimately the aerobic system that allows us to recover from the additional fatigue caused – the aerobic system is the backbone of energy production.

Aerobic Power can often be described as "Speed at VO2 Max" (maximal oxygen uptake: the "V" is for Volume and the "O2" is for Oxygen), which refers to how fast someone can go at their VO2 Max.

VO2 Max is a physiological measure that reflects the maximum amount of oxygen your body can utilize during intense aerobic exercise. It's often considered a gold standard indicator of cardiovascular fitness and aerobic endurance. VO2 max provides valuable information about your body's ability to transport oxygen to your muscles and use it efficiently to produce energy during prolonged physical activity.

This all being said, athletes need to be well-trained to race at high percentages of their VO2 Max. An untrained individual might only be at 50-60% of their VO2 Max when they hit LT2. Well-trained individuals will be around 80% while elite athletes will likely be around the 90% mark.

There are several ways an athlete can develop their ability to hit high percentages of their VO2 Max before crossing LT2:

- Developing an aerobic base through a large volume of low-intensity training below LT1 (often 60-120 minutes) – in a lot of endurance training programs, this takes up as much as 80% of the training

- Specific threshold training (tempo work: holding a faster pace for a set time) to bring LT2 closer to your VO2 Max. The tempo runs usually involve 20-40 minutes of work at or just below LT2, or multiple bouts of 10-minute efforts (longer intervals) at or just below LT2 (note: typically "tempo" runs are slower than this and classed as continuous "moderately hard" runs)

- Intervals and High-Intensity Interval Training (HIIT) to improve the ability to work within the upper limits of the energy systems – see below for a brief explanation of interval training

- Strength training to develop efficiency, strength, power and fatigue resistance – this helps to improve **Energy Utilization**

Interval training is a broad term that encapsulates work involving bouts of moderate to high-intensity exercise followed by active or passive recovery/rest. Active recovery refers to engaging in low-intensity activity during the rest period rather than resting in a static position without deliberate activity (passive recovery).

HIIT is a specific form of interval training characterized by short bouts of high-intensity exercise followed by short periods of rest. SMIT (Supramaximal Interval Training, aka, Speed Endurance Interval Training or just speed/sprint interval training) involves very short bouts of maximal intensity work followed by much longer rest periods.

Note: We often describe low-intensity training (building an aerobic base) as PUSHING up the lactate threshold and higher-intensity training as PULLING up the lactate threshold – alongside "Push + Pull" Conditioning, we also have "Push + Pull" Strength Training: Pushing with the lower and upper body and pushing and pulling with the upper body.

VO2 max is expressed as a numerical value (which can be found on many smart watches) that represents the maximum amount of oxygen an individual can consume per kilogram of body weight per minute (ml/kg/min) during intense aerobic exercise. Let's break down what each component of this expression means:

- **ml (milliliters):** This is a unit of measurement used to quantify the volume of a substance. In this case, it represents the volume of oxygen consumed

- **kg (kilograms):** This is a unit of measurement for mass or weight. In the context of VO2 max, it refers to the individual's body weight

- **min (minute):** This is a unit of time, indicating that the measurement is taken over the course of one minute

Put together:

- **ml/kg/min (milliliters of oxygen consumed per kilogram of body weight per minute):** This unit expresses the amount of oxygen a person's body consumes while exercising, standardized by their body weight and measured over one minute of intense aerobic activity

For example, if an individual's VO2 max is measured as 45 ml/kg/min, it means that they are able to consume 45 milliliters of oxygen for every kilogram of their body weight per minute of intense exercise. Therefore, it is clear to see how an individual's VO2 max score is a key indicator of cardiovascular fitness and aerobic endurance/capacity.

The aerobic system is by far the most adaptable. With the right training, we can see drastic changes in both aerobic capacity (how far we can run) and aerobic power (how fast we can run a 2-5km, for example). The lactate system is the second most adaptable. However, this pales in comparison to the aerobic system; rather than having many minutes and hours to work with, we only have a couple of minutes.

We are NOT going to increase our anaerobic capacity from two minutes to six minutes. Still, training anaerobically (above the threshold) will improve our ability to tolerate the stress the body is under and reprocess the waste products into more energy using the aerobic system (the aerobic system saves the day again).

Finally, the ATP-CP system, which is famous for the first few seconds of activity up to around ten seconds (usually less), is by far the least adaptable. Therefore, our aim is not to improve the power or capacity of this system by any real stretch but instead to improve our utilization of the energy we produce. For example, we referred to strength training and plyometrics as conditioning because we are conditioning the tissues to utilize the energy as efficiently as possible. When it comes to many activities (both short and long duration), it is not always a lack of energy that results in the regression or cessation of the activity, but things like coordination erosion, which can occur when operating at top speeds for more than a few seconds and the motor control systems start to break down and lose the ability to efficiently coordinate movement patterns. Or mechanical breakdown, where the tissues can no longer handle the stresses of the activity.

Energy utilization is heavily dependent on technique. For example, it would not be fair to have a runner perform a fitness test that involved rolling with a Jiu-Jitsu Black Belt for five minutes because they will be absolutely exhausted if they don't have the technique to move efficiently. This is also why cycling-based fitness tests can be great because cycling is not heavy on technique, even compared to running and rowing.

Improve Power, Capacity and Utilization!

Subjective Measures

Due to the ever-increasing accessibility of wearable fitness technology like smartwatches and heart rate monitors, it is easier than ever to quantify your training loads on an objective level. However, it can be easy to get swept up in the data. If you are someone who loves a bit of data, that's great, but it can create a barrier to entry to others, and it is key that you use methods that add to your training, not add stress to you.

Luckily enough, there are a variety of subjective measures that, with a little experience, can be incredibly accurate ways to quantify and manage your training loads (create training zones), and you don't need a Ph.D. in sports science to understand them.

In this section, we look at:

- The RPE Scale

- Reps in Reserve (RIR)

The RPE Scale

The simplest way to quantify the intensity of a set or training session is to use the RPE scale of 1-10 – Rating of Perceived Exertion.

Note: I have added a 12 to the Deadly Dozen RPE Scale as a rating for when the athlete goes beyond what is normally possible. And yes, it jumps from 10 to 12 because the Deadly Dozen RPE Scale is not going to finish on 11, is it?! (I do have an amp that goes to 11 though).

RPE	Description
1-2	Very Easy
3	Easy
4	Moderate
5-6	Somewhat Hard
7-8	Hard
9	Very Hard
10	Maximal
12	Supramaximal: Beyond what is normally possible

The RPE Scale can be used to quantify all modes of exercise, both strength training and conditioning. When someone is new to an activity, they are often unsure of what RPE to give to a specific activity. However, with experience, it becomes quite an accurate measure. For example, if an experienced athlete is working within a heart rate zone that should correlate to an RPE of around 8 out of 10, more often than not, when you ask what their RPE is, they will say 8.

Note: The RPE scale is NOT perfect, but it is an extremely useful tool considering how easy it is to implement – this manual will show countless examples of how I use it in programming.

RPE: Entire Session

Alongside getting RPE scores for all of the exercises performed in a strength training session, for example, it can be helpful to get an RPE rating for an entire session. Of course, this is extremely subjective once the session is over, especially if it included numerous forms of exercise, but with regular use, it can paint a brilliant picture of how an athlete feels throughout a training week or a specific part of a training phase.

I often use this number to gain an indication of the sessions an athlete enjoys or dislikes – I tend to see athletes give higher RPE scores to activities that, when asked, admit they don't like as much as others.

You can just give a session and RPE score from 1-10. However, you can also create a score for the Session Load:

- The session load is calculated by multiplying the duration of the session by the training intensity, as measured by session RPE

- Session load = duration of session (mins) x session RPE

- For example, if the session were rated by the athlete as a 6 and the session lasted 60 minutes, the session load would be 360 arbitrary units (AU): session load = 60 x 6 = 360 AU

Note: An Arbitrary Unit is just a relative or scale-free measurement without a specific, standardized unit of measurement. Instead of using a defined standard unit like meters, grams, or seconds, arbitrary units provide a way to express values in a scale that is convenient for a particular analysis or measurement, but without a precise and universally accepted reference

Reps in Reserve (RIR)

Reps in Reserve (RIR) expresses how hard a set is by estimating how many extra reps you could have performed.

For example, 0 RIR would mean that you could not perform any more reps and were, therefore, working maximally at RPE 10.

This subjective measure is more often used when it comes to strength training and performing reps of an exercise, but it can also be applied to an interval session. For example, "how many more 200m runs could you complete at that pace with just 30 seconds rest?"

When it comes to heavy strength training, our working sets would rarely be rated below an RPE of 5 (usually between 7 and 10). The same generally applies for RIR – any more than 5 RIR, and the intensity is low-moderate. Note: When we say, "could do 5 more reps," we generally mean "good reps" that are not an absolute grind. Especially when it comes to the legs, if pushed hard enough, we can usually do a fair few more than we think.

Just like the RPE scale, RIR is perceived by the individual and, therefore, requires some level of experience to estimate properly. However, as a whole, it is a very intuitive method and a great way to quantify the intensity of a set.

"Everything's destiny is to change, to be transformed, to perish. So that new things can be born." – **Marcus Aurelius**

Objective Methods

Objective methods use data such as our heart rate or a one-rep max (most we can lift for one rep) to establish training zones.

In this section, we look at the following:

- Maximum Heart Rate

- Lactate Threshold Heart Rate

- Functional Threshold Power (FTP)

- 5km + Time

- Maximum Aerobic Speed (MAS)

- Percentages

- INOL

- Volume Load

- Velocity-Based Training

Work to Rest Ratios (WRR)

Before we jump into the objective methods, there is a key concept that is vital when quantifying our training loads, and that is Work to Rest Ratios (WRR). WRRs refer to how long the athlete is working compared to how long they are resting. For example, the classic Tabata protocol of 20 seconds work and 10 seconds rest (for 8 rounds) has a 2:1 WRR. Whereas working for 30 seconds followed by 90 seconds break is a WRR of 1:3.

WRRs come into play more during interval training, and there are general guidelines on what these ratios should look like for different qualities. Generally, for aerobic intervals, we want a 1:1 WRR, meaning the athlete rests for as long as they have worked. In contrast, higher-intensity lactate intervals are more likely to see WRRs of 1:3-1:5.

"If you are pained by any external thing, it is not this thing that disturbs you, but your own judgment about it. And it is in your power to wipe out this judgement now." – **Marcus Aurelius**

Heart Rate

Heart rate can be effectively used to manage training loads in many sports and can be a useful tool even for the most novice of gym goers. However, it's important to understand that there are a variety of reasons why heart rates differ from person to person and why your heart rate may vary from day to day. Therefore, the various equations, numbers and percentages that are used by both the medical and sporting community are not an exact science but instead a guideline.

If you want to effectively use your heart rate to manage training loads, consider these points:

- Become familiar with what is normal on a day-to-day basis, at different times of the day and during and after different stimuli (the heart rate reacts differently to different stressors)

- Estimations are useful(ish), but direct testing is always optimal

Calculating Heart Rate Zones

Heart rate zones can be calculated from your Max Heart Rate (MHR) or Heart Rate Reserve (HRR).

A **ROUGH** estimate for your MHR is 220 minus your age:

Example: 220 – 30 = 190 MHR

Note: It is far more accurate to test your MHR – just test it, the famous equation above is far too much of a "guestimate."

MHR can be tested in a lab using a treadmill stress test. However, it can be effectively tested on a track or road run with a heart rate monitor – here's our **1-Mile MHR Test**:

400m warm-up – up the tempo for 400m – up the tempo again for 400m – max out the last 400m with an absolute sprint finish on the final 100m and record the highest heart rate during the session.

Heart Rate Reserve (HRR) is calculated by subtracting your Resting Heart Rate (RHR) from your Max Heart Rate (MHR).

For example, an athlete with a MHR of 190 and a RHR of 50 would have a HRR of 140.

From here, we can use the Karvonen formula to determine your target heart rate training zone. To do this, select a percentage of your HRR and then add your RHR to it.

Here's an example using a HRR of 140 and a RHH of 50:

80% of 140 (0.8x140) = 112

112 + 50 = 162

Basing training zones off the HRR is considered more accurate than basing training off your MHR alone because HRR considers both the MHR and RHR.

Heart Rate Zones

The table below shows heart rate zones that work off percentages of your max heart rate or heart rate reserve with the Karvonen formula – HRR is considered to be more accurate.

Zone	Percentage of MHR / HRR	RPE
Zone 1 (Active Recovery)	50-60%	RPE 2-3 – very low intensity
Zone 2 (Endurance)	60-70%	RPE 4-5 – low intensity
Zone 3 (Tempo)	70-80%	RPE 6-7 – moderate intensity
Zone 4 (Threshold)	80-90%	RPE 8-9 – high intensity
Zone 5 (VO2 Max)	90-100%	RPE 9-10 – very high intensity / maximal

Once you have tested your MHR, it will be updated on your smartwatch and app. You can find this in your setting on the app (search for a video for the brand/model you have if you are unsure). It is usually defaulted to be "based on % of Max Heart Rate." However, this can be changed to "% of Heart Rate Reserve," where you input your RHR (Resting Heart Rate).

Many apps will allow you to set heart rate zones for specific modes of exercise because they can elicit different heart rates. For example, running is load-bearing. Therefore, it will generally push your heart rate higher than cycling.

Note: Wearing a heart rate monitor around your chest is far more accurate than taking a reading from your watch alone (from the wrist).

Zone 2 is where we are going to spend A LOT of time building an aerobic base, with sessions that generally last 45 minutes to 3 hours. 90 Minutes is an ideal run time for me because it is long enough to elicit the adaptations I want without resulting in too much fatigue on my tissues.

The beauty of Zone 2 work is that it is scientifically proven to promote aerobic adaptations while not having the recovery demands of Zone 3 work, for example. This is why many endurance athletes will spend a lot of time in zone 2 (over 80% of their time) and then the rest of the time at the other end of the spectrum doing high-intensity work that builds speed, power and the ability to tolerate high metabolic stress.

Zone 2 works by developing the number and efficiency of Mitochondria, which are organelles found in cells that produce the molecule that provides us with energy: ATP (Adenosine Triphosphate). Mitochondria are often referred to as "energy-producing powerhouses within cells." Therefore, it is clear to see why working to develop them is critical for aerobic capacity and overall energy production.

Tip – Do these 3 things:

1. Spend time building an aerobic base – put the time into long, slow work.

2. Spend time working at a threshold pace – get used to being uncomfortable for longer durations.

3. Spend time working at maximal intensities – develop speed and power.

Lactate Threshold Heart Rate

Another effective tool for quantifying training loads is working off Lactate Threshold Heart Rate (LTHR) training zones, which is your heart rate (BPM) at your lactate threshold – this is my preferred method.

The lactate threshold (also referred to as the anaerobic threshold) is the intensity at which the body transitions from primarily using the aerobic energy system to using the anaerobic lactate system, and therefore, waste products build up, and performance diminishes – depending on genetics and an individual's fitness levels, the LT is generally around 75-90% of max heart rate but is most commonly described as 85% of max heart rate. However, we identify two distinct LTs.

Note: The lactate threshold heart rate essentially occurs at an intensity / pace that we could potentially sustain for up to an hour if we were well trained – I often refer to it as the ideal "Race Pace" for the Deadly Dozen.

As mentioned previously, different activities can elicit different heart rates, and therefore, the LTHR for cycling can be about 5-10 beats lower than your running LTHR.

The most common way to test your LTHR is to perform a maximal 30-minute time trial over a reasonably flat course and record your average heart rate during the last 20 minutes (Lap your watch after 10 minutes) – don't go too hard in the first few minutes of the time trial and burn yourself out.

Note: We can have our lactate threshold tested in a laboratory, which is the gold standard. Field-based tests like the one above only provide an estimation, but the estimation is more than accurate enough to provide useful training zones like the ones shown below.

The table below shows the common zones utilized with LTHR.

Zone	% of LTHR
Zone 1 (Active Recovery)	<85%
Zone 2 (Endurance)	85-89%
Zone 3 (Tempo)	90-94%
Zone 4 (Sub-Threshold)	95-100%
Zone 5a (Supra-Threshold)	100-102%
Zone 5b (VO2 Max)	103-106%
Zone 5c (Anaerobic Capacity)	>106%

Once you have established your LTHR zones, you can adjust your heart rate zones on your smartwatch (usually within the mobile app). It is usually defaulted to be "based on % of Max Heart Rate." However, this can be changed to "% of Lactate Threshold." You then input your LTHR and your MHR (Max Heart Rate – likely calculated on your watch already) / (you may have to change the top of zone 1 / bottom of zone 2 to 85%).

Note: Apps like Garmin Connect will have 6x boxes, with the 5th being 100% of your LTHR, then the 6th being your MHR.

Functional Threshold Power (FTP)

There are many training machines that can measure an athlete's power output (power is measured in Watts), and from this, we can work out an athlete's Functional Threshold Power (FTP).

Note: If a machine like a bike can measure power output, then you can perform a max/peak power test with a short maximal burst (a variety of work durations can be used).

FTP is the average power an athlete can produce over the course of an hour (essentially anaerobic/lactate threshold pace) – cyclists often perform FTP tests for 20 minutes and times it by 0.95 to estimate the hour value (subtract 5%).

FTP is expressed in Watts per Kg – Watts divided by the athlete's weight in Kgs: 320 Watts / 80kg = 4 Watts per Kg.

FTP can be done on Bikes, Rowers and Ski ERGs. However, it should be noted that FTP scores will vary depending on the equipment being used – a cyclist is going to perform better on a bike than a rower.

Power meter technology has also been adapted for running, with runners wearing small power meters on their trainers to work out their Running Functional Threshold Power.

Note: Running FTP (Functional Threshold **Pace**) can also be established by performing a 45–60-minute best effort time trial, establishing your average pace on your watch (your speed) and then using percentages of that pace to establish training zones.

Although FTP does not measure an athlete's blood lactate levels, because the test involves working for 20-60 minutes with the highest possible power output, the power output is likely to correspond with the athlete's lactate threshold – The goal is to approximate the power output that corresponds to the point just below the lactate threshold.

Of course, an FTP test and a Lactate Threshold Heart Rate (LTHR) test are two different tests that are based on different physiological measurements (heart rate for LTHR and power output for FTP) and, therefore, will have variability. However, they are both testing an athlete's ability to sustain high-intensity work and can be used in conjunction with each other to optimize training zones.

5km + Time

Similar to Functional Threshold Pace, where the athlete's average pace (data found on their watch) is used to establish training zones, we can also use the athlete's average pace during a 5km best effort.

This is a great way for athletes who have a GPS watch but are not using heart rate zones to monitor their pace during easy runs yet still want to be a little more objective than the RPE scale. For example, if their 5km time is 20 minutes, meaning their average kilometre pace is 4 minutes per kilometre, then for an easy run, I may program 90-120 seconds on top of their 5km average pace. So, for +120 seconds, I want them running 6-minute kilometres.

Note: When my athletes use any of the objective methods in this section, I still encourage them to record or at least think about the RPE score for the activity or session. By doing this, they become more familiar with how specific training modalities feel at different intensities and everything becomes a lot more intuitive.

Maximum Aerobic Speed

Recap: Maximum Aerobic Speed (MAS) is the slowest speed at which you reach your VO2 max. It is also referred to as velocity at VO2 Max (vVO2 Max) - Working at 100% or above of MAS is a critical factor in improving aerobic power.

VO2 Max: This is the maximal rate at which oxygen can be used by the body during maximal physical exertion involving large muscle groups – (V = Volume / O2 = Oxygen / Max = Maximum).

The MAS is used for measuring performance and to help set training zones depending on the volume of work. For example, an athlete may work at 120% of their MAS for short interval training with short passive rest periods – passive rest is rest that involves no activity, whereas active rest or recovery involves rest that is active (<40-70% of MAS).

Note: Anaerobic Speed Reserve (ASR) is the difference between MAS and MSS (Max Sprint Speed). In other words, ASR quantifies the additional speed an athlete can generate in a sprint beyond their aerobic capacity. ASR = MSS - MAS

The MAS can be measured with a VO2 max test in a lab or estimated off several fitness tests such as the multi-stage fitness test (bleep test). However, it is most easily tested with a maximal or a 1.5-2km run – I usually have the athlete run for 1600m: 1-Mile MAS Test.

If an athlete runs 1.6km in 6 minutes (360 seconds), it means their MAS is 4.4m/s (meters per second) – 1600 / time in seconds = MAS.

MAS can be applied to swimming, rowing, and various CV machines. However, these will create different MAS scores (meters per second). Athletes who compete in field-based sports or fitness races that involve a lot of running, performing a running-based MAS test is key.

The 1-Mile MAS test (4 laps of an athletics track) is part of the Deadly Dozen Testing Battery (DDTB), and I use it to gain an objective data point that I can then retest and see if improvements are being made. For the most part, I don't use MAS to establish training zones, simply because I like to use the RPE scale when performing short to mid-duration intervals (0-60 seconds and 1-6 minutes, etc). However, I use it when programming Aerobic Capacity Intervals and want a more tailored protocol or when working with a group of athletes (team sports for example) to ensure each athlete is working at the level that suits them.

Here is an example of how to run MAS interval session:

3x 10 Runs: 20 Seconds Work + 20 Seconds Rest (1:1 WRR) (2 Mins rest between sets).

For this example, the athlete has a MAS score of 4.5m/s. To work out the appropriate running distance for the athlete, you multiply the MAS score by the number of seconds they are working for: 4.5 x 20 = 90.

In this example, the athlete would aim to run 10x 90m intervals, with each one taking 20 seconds and the athlete having 20 seconds rest between the intervals. The athlete would then have 2 minutes off and repeat the process until they had completed the 3 sets.

If we wanted the athlete to run at 110% of their MAS score, we would add 10% to the distance (99m), or if we wanted the athlete to run at 120% of their MAS score, we would add 20% (108m).

If this were a team session, Athlete A (with a MAS score of 4.5) would be set to run 90m in 20 seconds, while athlete B (with a MAS score of 5.0) would be set to run 100m in the 20 seconds, and so on.

Objective Methods: Strength Training

In this section, we look at the objective methods used to establish training zones specifically for strength training. These methods are a little more specific to the BB. However, it can apply to other free weight training.

When it comes to using objective measures for Labour Fitness (lifting free weights for prolonged periods), it is best to quantify it using the subjective methods and the objective methods used for conditioning. For example, while performing station-only Labour Fitness training sessions (circuit-style training), we can track our heart rate to ensure we are in the desired training zone.

Percentages

Using percentages of a 1RM to calculate training intensities is not perfect, but with experience, it can be an extremely effective way to program – along with the RPE scale, this is how I program strength training for most athletes.

One of the major downfalls of percentages is that they can be a little daunting or confusing to those new to them in a training setting. However, with the guidelines in the table below, it can soon become the best way to quantify the primary lifts. Of course, it is fine to simply use the RPE Scale.

The coefficients in the table below have been rounded to simple percentages. Of course, this reduces the accuracy. However, they still create a good guideline for when programming – I commonly add 15% to a 5RM or 10% to a 3RM to estimate a 1RM to program off – the higher the rep range, the less accurate the 1RM estimate becomes.

Note: A coefficient is a numerical factor or constant that multiplies a variable in a mathematical expression or equation.

% Estimations	Coefficients
2RM = 95% of 1RM	2RM x 1.05
	ADD 5%
3RM = 90% of 1RM	3RM x 1.10
	ADD 10%
5RM = 85% of 1RM	5RM x 1.15
	ADD 15%
8RM = 80% of 1RM	8RM x 1.20 – 1.25
(LESS ACCURATE)	ADD 20-25%
10RM = 75% of 1RM	10RM x 1.25 – 1.30
(LESS ACCURATE)	ADD 25-30%

Note: Male athletes can often perform around 5 reps at 85% of their 1RM, whereas many female athletes will get close to 90-95% of their 1RM for 5 reps. This is because athletes who have greater slow twitch muscle fibres (endurance) tend to be able to perform more reps at higher percentages of their 1RM – female athletes often have lower max strength but recover much faster and have better strength endurance in relation to their max (these are typical finding across a broad selection of athletes and of course, male and female athletes lie on either side of this spectrum).

Novice lifters who have not yet mastered lifting techniques or honed their ability to produce maximal strength may also find they can achieve much higher reps at higher percentages of their 1RM.

Here are some rep range recommendations:

% of a 1RM	Recommended Reps Per Set
95%+	1-2 Reps
90%	1-3 Reps
85%	2-5 Reps
80%	3-6 Reps
75%	5-8 Reps
70%	8-10 Reps
65%	10-15 Reps
50-60%	15+ Reps

One of the most common questions I get asked in the gym is, "What is the best rep range?" This is usually related to their specific goal. For example, what is the best rep range for building muscle? What is the best rep range for building strength? What is the best rep range for endurance athletes?

Let's start with hypertrophy, which means building muscle: You can develop muscle mass using any rep range as long as there is sufficient overload, i.e., it is working you hard enough. This being said, I advise performing a wide array of rep ranges across your training program.

When it comes to strength, of course, lifting heavier loads will result in greater increases in strength (SAID: Specific Adaptation to Imposed Demands – if you lift heavy, you will increase your ability to lift heavy). However, lifting heavy all of the time can increase the risk of acute injuries (which happen suddenly) or chronic injuries (usually result from overuse and develop gradually). Therefore, it is beneficial for those who want to improve their strength to also perform higher rep ranges to help build tissue resilience and muscular endurance.

When it comes to endurance athletes, they tend to have the belief that because they are "endurance" athletes, they need to be doing high rep ranges to build endurance. But more often than not, they have great endurance and have come to the gym to build more strength. So why not work at the intensities that are going to elicit greater increases in strength?

Intensity x Number of Lifts (INOL)

Here's a great way to quantify the overall intensity of a strength session using percentages.

INOL = Intensity X Number of Lifts:

- Reps / (100 – Intensity)

- Intensity = Weight lifted as a percentage of your one rep max, i.e., 75%

- This is a simple formula that allows us to measure intensity across sets of different rep ranges

Example:

- Deadlift – 1RM = 140kg

- 5×5 at 80% = 25 reps of 112kg

- 25 / (100 – 80) = 1.25 (INOL)

Optimal INOL values per exercise for a single workout:

- <0.4 = Too easy

- <0.6 – 1.0 = Optimal range for most athletes

- – 2.0 = Tough workout

- >2.0 = Very tough, could lead to overtraining if performed regularly

"If we follow nature, all is easy and unobstructed; but if we combat nature, our life differs not whit from that of men who row against the current." – **Seneca**

Making the Plan

When it comes to programming exercise, most people think in terms of 4-6 or even 12-week blocks. However, if we really want to maximize our performance, we look at the BIG picture plan, which is usually a training year (365 days – the annual plan, aka the macrocycle) – for an Olympian, it would be a Quadrennial Cycle of 4-Years!

When we have a big plan that looks at what competitions we have coming up and how we are going to train for them (usually breaking the training down into cycles, phases, or blocks), we call it "Periodization." – I call the filling out of the subsequent training phases and sessions plans as "Programming," which essentially involves filling in the detail of the big periodized plan.

Where people go wrong is they believe the annual periodized plan has to be crazy detailed and dogmatic, and the athlete has to stick to it no matter what. But this is just silly because so much can change in any given week or month.

When I work with elite athletes, I have a big 12-month calendar on the wall, and we jot down all the major and minor events/competitions that are taking place during the year. I also jot down when the athlete is planning holidays or other miscellaneous events. I then plot the training phases that will help to elicit the greatest levels of performance at the times the athlete needs it, i.e., Important competitions. For example, if there is a long period at the start of the year where no competitions are taking place, this may be an ideal time to add more lifting and running volume to build muscle and strength and establish an aerobic base. From there, as the athlete approaches the major competition(s), training volume is reduced to allow for better recovery and more sport-specific training is incorporated.

Once the overall plan for the year (macro level) is established (see it as a rough draft that is always open to edits), it is time to start planning how training programs may progress over the coming weeks and programming on a micro level, building the session plans that form each training week.

Programming on a micro level should be dynamic and can be changed at any time. If an athlete walks into a session with an injury or just simply looks burnt out. The session is likely to be adapted, even if it is only slightly.

Training Period	Duration	Mode of Planning
Quadrennial Cycle	4-Years (Olympic Cycle)	Long-term
Macrocycle	12-Months / Several Months	
Mesocycle	2-8-Weeks	Medium-term
Microcycle	1-Week	Short-term
Training Day	Several Hours	
Training Session	Hours / Minutes	
Training Exercise	Minutes / Seconds	

Steps to Designing Macrocycles

1. Create a calendar that shows the entire year. This can be done on an Excel spreadsheet, etc.

2. Note down the major competitions (these can be triaged by importance with A, B and C competitions, etc). Also, input any holidays and any other important/miscellaneous events.

3. Work out the number of macrocycles within the plan – a macrocycle usually spans a year of training (annual plan), but a plan can be split down to 6-month macrocycles (double periodization) or 4-month macrocycles (triple periodization).

4. Subdivide the macrocycle(s) into preparatory, competition and transition periods/phases that relate to the competitions – you can use whatever titles you want for your phases – I explain the titles I use on the following pages.

5. Work out the length of general and specific preparatory and pre-competition and competition phases.

6. Note down key tapering phases.

Steps to Designing Mesocycles

1. Divide the plan into mesocycles.

2. Determine what the major goals in each mesocycle will be – what performance qualities are being targeted (these can become "Phase Titles") – phases don't have to be dogmatic, more often than not, we take a concurrent approach where key training modalities are practised regularly throughout the annual plan.

3. Program training volumes and intensities over the course of the mesocycles – this is an overview and includes preloads and deloads, etc.

4. Input where testing will take place.

Steps to Designing Microcycles

1. Program training frequency for the week (how many training sessions are taking place).

2. Program the modes of training to be used – resistance training and speed work, etc.

3. Program the volume and intensity of the training days/sessions – this is an overview.

4. Program rest days.

5. Ensure the microcycle is specific to the aims of the training phase.

"Freedom isn't secured by filling up your heart's desire but by removing your desire." – **Epictetus**

Preparatory, Competition and Transition Phases

The Preparatory Phase is used to prepare for the competition phase and is split into two phases:

1. General Preparatory Phase (GPP) aka General Physical Preparedness/Preparation

- Focuses on general physical training

- Often, higher volumes of training with an emphasis on strength and hypertrophy and building an aerobic base

2. Specific Physical Preparedness/Preparation:

- Higher training intensities

- More sport-specific training

Note: Coaches should be aware that trying to be overly sports-specific (often when strength training) can lead to negative transfer. For example, a boxer slowing down due to shadow boxing with heavy dumbbells.

The Competition Phase kicks in when competitions are close by and is split into two phases:

1. Pre-competition phase

- link between the preparation phase and the main competition phase

- Increase in sport-specific training

2. Main-competition phase:

- Working towards peaking the athlete for the main competition

- Workloads are varied throughout this phase when needed – tapers (programmed recovery prior to an event – usually involves greatly reducing training volumes), etc

The Transition Phase follows the major competition:

- This is the linking phase or period between either two annual plans or multiple macrocycles

- Significant reduction in volume and intensity

- Aim to maintain fitness and technical skills

- Time for athletes to recover

Note: Post-season, it is key to allow your athlete(s) to not only have physical recovery but also mental recovery from both competition and sports practise as a whole – have a deload and come back more motivated!

Deadly Dozen Periodization: FAIRR Periodization

Although "Preparatory" and "Competition" are brilliant titles for the various phases, I have adapted the terms used in the Block periodization model (we look at different models of periodization on the next page), and these are what I tend to use when working with the bulk of my athletes (from a variety of different sports) because they translate well to both short-term (6-12-weeks) and long-term programming (6-12-months+).

I call it **"Fairr" Periodization:**

Phase 1: Familiarization: This is the first phase following a Transition Period (Recovery Phase). It is usually quite short and is designed as a preload to ease the athlete back into higher volumes and intensities of training. This is a great time to test the optimal training splits.

Phase 2: Accumulation: This phase generally aims to increase the initial training volume to enhance the base of fitness. In this phase, we are looking to build aerobic and muscular endurance, build the overall conditioning of the muscles (get past the early stages of delayed onset muscle soreness DOMS – the muscle soreness you feel the days following exercise), and in many cases look to build more muscle or strip the excess fat that has been acquired during the transition phase.

Phase 3: Intensification: This phase is where training intensity is ramped up and usually becomes more sport-specific. The phase can be further broken down into Intensification 1 and Intensification 2, with the first intensification phase involving an increase in intensity of the same training modes used in the accumulation phase and the second intensification phase using more sport-specific exercises.

Phase 4: Realization: This phase is used to peak for important competitions and usually involves a decrease in volume leading up to the event. However, training intensities can remain the same or even increase. This phase includes the specific taper before a competition.

Phase 5: Recovery: This is the phase following the main season or the major competition. It is a time for the athlete to rest and recuperate. However, overall fitness is still maintained.

Note: Although each training phase has clear biases. My programming always takes a more concurrent approach where I ensure we are still stimulating qualities that we may have focussed on in previous phases or will be focusing on in future phases. For example, although the primary aim in the Accumulation phase is to build up training volumes, we still incorporate high-intensity training on a regular basis.

FAIRR Periodization is my go-to methodology for a wide variety of athletes. However, when working with fitness racers, I incorporate a variety of periodization models to suit the different training modes I am programming, but I always have the principles of the FAIRR approach in the back of my mind.

Athletes who are competing regularly are generally more suited to a plan that turns over the phases quite quickly, as they are required to taper and peak more often. However, athletes who have long periods between competitions can afford to stretch out phases to spend more time on specific qualities. Of course, phases may be stretched out during the off-season and then shortened during the season to allow for regular peaking.

Note: Peaking refers to an athlete training hard towards a competition to develop their abilities before tapering (reducing training loads) before the competition to ensure the athlete is physically and psychologically rested and in peak physical performance.

Periodization Models

There are many forms of periodization and even more terms for each type of periodization – as with all things S&C, semantics plays a huge role!

There are 3 fundamental periodization models:

- **Traditional** – commonly known as **Linear**

- **Undulating**

- **Block**

The **Traditional Model**, which we refer to as **Linear Periodization,** is described as a training plan that gradually increases intensity and decreases volume throughout multiple mesocycles (phases) in an annual training plan (macrocycle).

Reverse Linear Periodization, on the other hand, increases volume and decreases intensity as the training plan progresses.

Both linear models are ideal when there is more time to train for a competition. Generally, the longer we develop a performance quality, the longer it will last, and this is shown in endurance athletes who often spend a long time working at lower intensities to build an aerobic base. However, if a type of training stimulus is not revisited for many weeks or even months, then there is also bound to be some regression, hence why many coaches and athletes prefer a more "concurrent" model of periodization where specific performance qualities are revisited more often or worked in unison (the downside to that being there is only so much work you can get done it any given week).

Linear periodization is the default style for most gym goers. Their program starts with a higher training volume (higher rep ranges) then over the weeks they reduce the reps, increase the weight (intensity) and work up to a one rep max, etc. However, for a lot of runners, Reverse Linear periodization is often the default style, with shorter runs earlier in the program and working towards much longer runs. For example, a marathon program works towards the athlete running 20 miles before the race.

This all being said, periodization is quite simple when it comes to thinking about one training mode, for example, gym-based strength training. However, it becomes a little more nuanced when we have modes such as Gym-Based Strength Training, Road Running-Based Aerobic Training, Track-Based Speed Training and Circuit-Based Muscular Endurance Training – you will see how I do it when we get to the Deadly Dozen Annual Plan (DDAP).

The **Undulating Model** is described as a training plan that constantly changes the training stimuli either daily, weekly, or bi-weekly. This model is often described as a "Concurrent" model of periodization because specific training stimuli are regularly revisited within a given microcycle (week of training).

Common undulating models include Daily Undulating Periodization (DUP) and Weekly Undulating Periodization (WUP).

Undulating periodization is often better suited to athletes who have to compete more often. It also helps to ensure the athlete does not regress from the activities that may not be worked on for longer periods if following a linear model. Undulating different training volumes and intensities can also be more interesting and enjoyable.

Block Periodization breaks specific training phases into 2-4-week blocks of highly concentrated specialized workloads.

Block periodization usually incorporates three different stages:

- **Accumulation:** High volume, low intensity

- **Transmutation / Intensification:** Maintain a decent level of volume (moderate) and increase intensity

- **Realization:** Drop volume and increase intensity – peaking

These three phases are often followed by a short recovery phase.

The block periodization model could start with an accumulation phase, which consists of endurance and hypertrophy work. A transmutation / intensification phase, which consists of maximal strength work and a realization phase, which consists of speed and power work at high intensity (max speed and power), low volume.

This style of periodization involves concentrating on specific training stimuli for short-moderate periods to allow an athlete to peak more often.

When you think about it, the Block model is, in many ways, a shortened version of the linear model. However, much more emphasis is placed on developing specific qualities rather than just ramping up the intensity gradually.

Although we have defined three different periodization models, you do NOT have to follow one dogmatically and I often use elements of all three throughout the large plans I create using my FAIRR model – I regularly use a Linear model during the off-season and transition into an undulating model during the season.

For Deadly Dozen specific programs, I use FAIRR periodization. However, I use an Undulating Model as I like to vary the performance qualities that I target each week and like the contrast between high volume and high intensity days during any given week (microcycle).

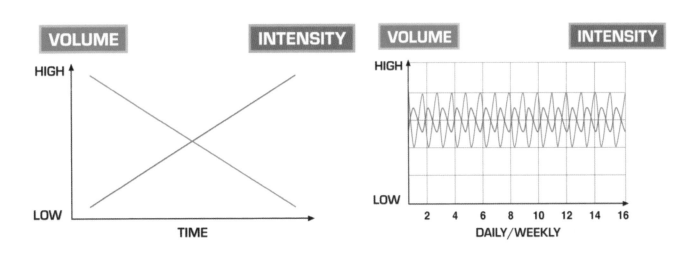

The Deadly Dozen Annual Plan (DDAP)

Now we understand how we approach creating a periodized plan, let's take a look at how I may develop a plan for a Deadly Dozen Race on the 22nd of June 2024 (the date of the first official Deadly Dozen Race).

For this example, the athlete has come out of their Recovery (Transition) Phase at the start of September 2023 and is going into the Familiarization Phase.

Note: The athlete has competed through the summer in several races and has taken a 1-month recovery phase at the end of July through to the end of August, where a more relaxed approach was taken to their training, and they also went on Holiday.

As Hybrid Athletes, our aim is to get Strong, Fast and Fit, and therefore, any good hybrid training program will lean into each of these areas to ensure optimal development. However, the ratios at which we lean into specific performance qualities (have a training bias towards them), is highly debatable.

As we have established in the needs analysis, the way in which we develop training programs is dependent on the needs of the sport and the need and goals of the athlete. However, it is not just about what an athlete may need; it is about what works for them, and this is something that has many variables.

Here's a question I ask a lot of my S&C students:

"If Program A will elicit greater improvements in performance than Program B, but Program B is more enjoyable to the athlete and long-term adherence is far more likely, which is the better program?"

Note: Program B still elicits increases in performance, just not as good as Program A.

Ultimately, you have to ask what is at stake? What is the athlete willing to sacrifice? How likely is the athlete going to adhere to the program? What compromises could be made to maximize performance while minimizing the risk of burnout?

Not only is it about what performance increases an athlete needs on an objective level and how they feel about the program on a subjective level, but it is also about how the athlete's body will handle a specific training program on a structural level.

Genetics, training experience and injury history all play a major role in how someone will respond to a program, and this is why the first program a coach writes for you is unlikely to be as good as the third one they write for you because at that point, the coach should have not just got to know you, but also got to know your body (how you respond to specific stressors). Any experienced coach knows that some people can handle more running volume while others can handle more heavy squats or bench presses, etc. We all have hotspots (points that tend to be a little more problematic than others), and the key is to build a program that understands how fast your body can progress with different activities.

All this being said, there are so many variables that you are NEVER going to create a perfect program. However, the aim is to consider all the variables and create a program that is as optimal as it can be.

"True happiness is to enjoy the present, without anxious dependence on the future." – **Seneca**

Most periodized plans come in the form of a large table on an Excel Spreadsheet or even a table on a Word document. However, sometimes, these can be a little confusing for people, so to start, I am simply going to lay out the year below.

I use the abbreviation **"FM" for "Frequency" (how many sessions) and "Mode" (type of exercise)**, and these are what I plan first – how many training sessions per week and what training mode is being used on each (at this stage there is no session detail beyond this).

I then use the abbreviation **"VI" for "Volume" (how long/how far/how many) and "Intensity" (how hard)**, and this can be a very rough overview of the entire phase, or it can be broken down into a block of a few weeks, each week (microcycle), or even differentiated between the different modes of training – it all depends to what detail you want to plan at this stage (there is plenty of time to get more detailed at the programming level, i.e., creating session plans to fill a week of training).

Finally, I have a small notes section to input relevant information such as competition dates, taper periods, holidays, etc.

September 1st – November 1st:

- **Familiarization:** The aim of this phase is to preload the athlete back up to a higher frequency, volume, and intensity of work – it can be described as a preload period

- **FM:** 4x Sessions per week: 2x Journey Fitness (Runs) / 1x Labour Fitness / 1x Strength Training

- **VI:** Moderate-low for both

- **Notes:** Aim for plenty of recovery between sessions to allow tissues to adapt

November 1st – March 1st:

- **Accumulation:** The aim of this phase is to ramp up the volume to establish an aerobic base, increase muscular endurance and build resilience ready for the intensification phase

- **FM:** 5-6x Sessions per week: 3x Journey Fitness (Runs) / 1x Labour Fitness / 1-2x Strength Training

- **VI:** Volume is increased in a linear fashion over the first two months of this phase while intensity decreases. Then, intensity increases slightly with more tempo runs during the second two months

- **Notes:** 1-week off during the Christmas break – 2x steady-state runs. Deloads are programmed

March 1st – May 1st:

- **Intensification:** The aim of this phase is to ramp up the intensity of exercise and the amount of race-specific work

- **FM:** 6-7x Sessions per week: 2x Journey Fitness (Runs) / 3x Labour Fitness / 1-2x Strength Training

- **VI:** Volume is maintained on 1 run while the other involves high intensities (tempo/intervals). Labour Fitness is increased to 3x per week and 1-2 of these involve running. Strength training VI undulates with a bias towards higher intensities

- **Notes:** Deload weeks are programmed once per month. There is NOT a cessation of training, just a reduction of various training variables depending on how the athlete is performing

May 1st – June 22nd:

- **Realization:** The aim of this phase is to peak for the competition and will involve the final race preparation leading up to the event and a taper prior to the event

- **FM:** 6x Sessions per week: 2x Journey Fitness (Runs) / 3x Labour Fitness / 1x Strength Training

- **VI:** 1x Tempo run and 1x interval session. Labour Fitness is still 3x per week and race sims are used regularly during the early stage of the realization phase. Strength training undulates with a bias towards high intensity and low volume

- **Notes:** The taper starts a couple of weeks from the event. However, major changes are not seen until the final week, with a cessation from any intense exercise 4 days out

June 23rd – TBC:

- **Recovery:** The aim of this phase is to recover from the competition and the final phase of training

- **FM:** 3x Sessions per week: 1x Journey Fitness (Run) / 1x Labour Fitness / 1x Strength Training

- **VI:** Moderate-low for both

- **Notes:** During holidays 2-3 low-intensity runs are advised

Below is an example of how I organise a Deadly Dozen Annual Plan on Excel. I will often triage competitions with colours. For example, Yellow = Not Important / Orange = Important / Red = Main Competition. However, in this example, I have just used dark blue to denote deload weeks and a lighter blue to denote the main comp (you can input the comp date and other info here).

Note: Don't overthink the Volume + Intensity Graph; it is an overview. Although during a single week, one training mode may be using high volume while another is using high intensity, ultimately, we are looking to illustrate the overall theme of that week (multiple graphs for each mode can also be added if you like) – in all honesty, I only use excel sheets to plan out the major competitions and miscellaneous events in the year. I don't go into huge detail on the variables, that all comes in when I program.

You can include as much info as you like in the mesocycle and microcycle boxes – when you click on these, you can easily read all the text.

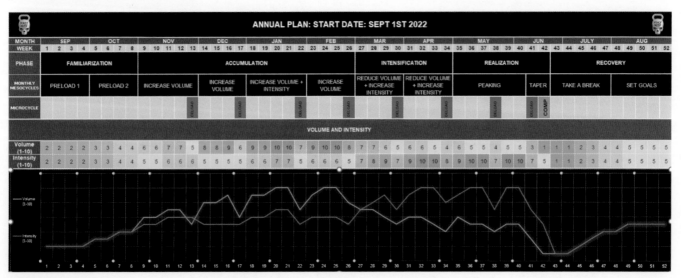

Over the last couple of pages, we have looked at an example of a periodized plan for an athlete working towards one Deadly Dozen event.

Having one main event makes things much easier as there is only one thing to peak for, and therefore, we can concentrate on a nice long progression towards it. We have plenty of time for a BIG accumulation phase before we start ramping things up on the intensity and specificity side of things.

However, what happens when we have multiple events/competitions/races in a year?

As briefly mentioned, it is best to triage the different events so we can establish which are the most important. Some events may be good warm-up races and don't require a peaking phase. They essentially act as a good training session and only require a couple of days of tapering before the event – I usually mark these as "Yellow" competitions.

Other events might not be the primary focus of the year. However, they are still important. Therefore, the plan is going to be restructured to allow for peaking towards these events. If there were two important events in a year, we could simply use "Double Periodization," where the 12-month program is condensed and duplicated to create two 6-month macrocycles.

If there are multiple important events leading up to a main event, then an initial Accumulation phase can be programmed prior to cycling through much shorter Accumulation, Intensification, and Realization phases prior to each competition. These shorter phases can also have an overarching progression towards the main competition.

I actually tend to program in 12-week blocks, and I consider each 12-week block a macrocycle (Quadruple Periodization).

Here's an example of how a periodized plan may look with multiple peaks within the training year.

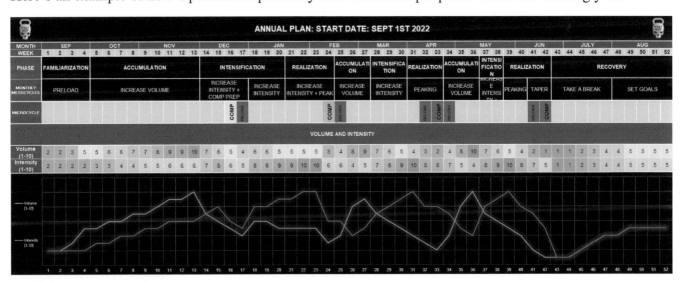

If you would like a **FREE** copy of this excel that can be edited, email **info@deadlydozen.co.uk**

"The greatest remedy to anger is delay." – **Seneca**

Programming

If Periodization is the development of a big plan, Programming is filling in the blanks.

In this section, we look at how we program using the Deadly Dozen Method (DDM), which is my go-to method for training Deadly Dozen Athletes (DDA's). We then look at how we build a week of training, a training day and individual training sessions.

When it comes to programming, there is no point in creating session plans months in advance because 1. It would take absolutely ages to do all in one go, and 2. Something could change, leaving all your programming obsolete; for example, the athlete tears their hamstring on week 2.

This being said, I tend to look at 4–6-week blocks, with a calendar month, making an intuitive mesocycle for us to program.

Once I have a month in front of me, I establish what my goals are and what I aim to achieve during that mesocycle, and I then start planning each microcycle (each week) – this should all fit in with the BIG picture plan.

In any plan or program, the first thing we establish is the frequency of training sessions (how many per week), and this is less about what we want to do and more about what we can fit in – I always tell my students not to "virtue program," which refers to writing a program that looks epic on paper but is never realistically going to be completed by the client or athlete.

Once we establish how many training sessions we can fit in during the week, we create a training split of different modalities that we believe will work to best achieve our goals for the mesocycle and the plan beyond.

The training split is where things get interesting because there are countless variables that will affect what is the optimal split to use, but this being said, the crux of a good training split is ordering the training sessions in a way that allows us to maximize the effectiveness of each individual session while ensuring they don't negatively impact on other training sessions throughout the week.

For example, if we have an interval session on the track programmed in for Tuesday, then having a heavy lower body strength training session on the Monday may result in the track session being a little harder than usual, or in other words, the athletes legs are written off for the track session.

Coaches need to use their expertise and experience to program effective training splits. However, they also need to discuss it with their athlete. Discussions with the athlete are important because people respond to things differently. Athletes can give feedback to the coach on how they feel throughout the training week and modifications can be made accordingly. In the initial stages of programming, this can be trial and error. An athlete can A/B test different training splits and see what works for them. For example, an athlete might respond better to having longer runs towards the end of the week or performing Labour fitness in the morning and strength training in the evening.

I can personally (in my own training) include a lot of high-intensity Labour fitness throughout the week and maintain high energy levels, etc. However, I generally like to have a day's rest (2 days if possible) between running sessions, as I feel it helps me to keep lower body overuse injuries at bay – my hotspots tend to be my shins and Achilles tendons when running a lot. However, I have never had a major issue in these areas because I listen to my body, manage my training loads, and have adequate recovery to allow my body to repair itself between bouts of hard work.

We will take a look at a few examples of how I would create different training splits in the next section on the Deadly Dozen Method (DDM).

The Deadly Dozen Method (DDM)

The crux of the Deadly Dozen Method (DDM) is the three key pillars of the training program, what we call the Deadly Dozen Triad (DDT).

The Deadly Dozen Triad:

1. **Strength Training:** Resistance training sessions (usually gym-based) that concentrate on low and mid-volume sets with higher training intensities (heavier).

2. **Labour Fitness:** Circuit training sessions that include some of, or all of the Labours (exercise stations) and other exercises performed at higher volumes (for high reps or time). These sessions can include or not include Journeys (runs).

3. **Journey Fitness:** Running (row, ski, cycle) training sessions that are usually split between long-duration work at lower intensities (steady state) or tempo and interval work at higher intensities.

Strength Training and Journey Fitness relate to the resistance training and cardio training modalities that are commonplace in training programs. However, although "circuit training" is the easiest way to describe Labour Fitness in layman's terms. There are a variety of principles that define exactly what it is.

Labour Fitness is defined as physical exercise that involves performing a variety of different movements and cardio activities for 1-6 minutes each (Goldilocks Zone: 2-4 minutes) with only 15-20 seconds of rest between exercises. These training sessions typically last between 20 and 120 minutes (Goldilocks Zone: 45-60 minutes). Note: Some exercises are grouped together in supersets, etc. Although exercises are performed back-to-back, the different nature of each exercise means higher intensities can be maintained. For example, going from a lower body movement to a cardio focussed movement, to an upper body movement, etc.

Labour Fitness sessions can or cannot involve Journey Fitness. For example, running, rowing, skiing, and cycling between each station, or these can be introduced as single stations within the circuit.

Just like how other forms of cardiorespiratory fitness activities are programmed with a spectrum of low to high-intensity sessions, Labour Fitness training sessions can also be performed at varying intensities.

Labour Fitness, as the name suggests, is laboursome; it is physically hard even when working at lower intensities and requires the athlete to be well conditioned if they don't want to be left with muscle soreness for days. Therefore, it is understandable why this style of training is often not utilized by strength and conditioning coaches working with athletes, simply because it may be too much stress for an athlete to handle within their busy training schedule. However, I have never seen a training methodology work so well with such a broad spectrum of people, and it is absolutely key for fitness racers.

I was an Army Physical Training Instructor, and I was very fit. However, I am over ten years older and 20kg heavier than I was while serving in the military and I can honestly say I have never felt fitter. In fact, every individual who has incorporated the above Labour Fitness principles into their training, even just one session per week, has reported quite drastic improvements in what can be best described as "work capacity" over a broad range of tasks, meaning they can get a lot more done. They also report huge increases in mental strength/toughness when it comes to arduous training.

From my personal experience of performing 2–4-minute round circuit sessions, my fitness has shot up immensely and regardless of how horrific a workout looks, psychologically, I am unphased by the thought of giving it a go – my body is used to performing arduous tasks for long durations.

A lack of physical stress both softens the body and the mind – hard training hardens the mind!

When it comes to working longer rounds above 2-3 minutes, many of the Deadly Dozen Labour stations are often best suited to be combined into micro-circuits within the main circuit. For example, rather than performing Goblet Squats for 3 minutes, you perform 10x KB Goblet Squats and 10x DB Push Press and cycle through them two exercises for 3 minutes before moving on to the next Labour station, which could be another micro-circuit, or a run, row or even an exercise like a sled push, etc.

We have Five tiers of micro-circuits:

- **Superset**: 2 exercises back-to-back (2-3 minute rounds)

- **Triset:** 3 exercises back-to-back (2-4 minute rounds)

- **Giant Set:** 4 exercises back-to-back (3-5 minute rounds)

- **Titan Set:** 5 exercises back-to-back (4-6 minute rounds)

- **HD (Half Dozen) Set:** 6 exercises back-to-back (4-6 minute rounds)

Journey Fitness activities like running, rowing, skiing, and cycling all work well with 1–6-minute rounds.

If you want to really develop your ability to perform a specific Labour (or any exercise), especially when in a fatigued state, you can perform 6-12 minute Supersets where you perform a Labour for a set number of reps/distance and then run (or perform another form of cardio) for a set distance repeatedly until the time is up – I call these Long-Duration Supersets.

Example: 40m Burpee Broad Jump + 400m Run back-to-back for 12 minutes.

Other exercises that I commonly include in my Labour Fitness sessions include:

- Sled Push

- Sled Pull

- Push-Up

- Inverted Row

- Battle Ropes

- Wallballs

- Boxing Bag Work

- Skipping (if proficient)

- Box Jump

I explain all of the above exercises + many more in full detail in the Bonus Exercise section.

The Half Dozen Week (HDW)

I consider the gold standard for experienced athletes to be a six-day or six-session* training week known as the Half Dozen Week (HDW) – *a Strength Training session and Journey Fitness session could take place on the same day (morning and evening, etc). However, not everyone has the time to train this much, and some athletes may respond better to more rest days or need to progress their strength and conditioning before working up to the six-day training week. Of course, elite (full time) athletes often do considerably more.

There are seven ways in which we can split each component of the DDT:

Sessions	Number of Sessions Per Week						
	TRIAD	SLJ	SJL	LSJ	LJS	JLS	JSL
Strength	2	3	3	2	1	1	2
Labour	2	2	1	3	3	2	1
Journey	2	1	2	1	2	3	3

If you are unable to fit in the six sessions, you simply drop off the sessions that you require least, and this may change throughout the duration of a training plan. For example, a plan may start Journey heavy and finish Labour heavy – a 3-5 session weekly training split is more than sufficient for most.

One of my favourite splits aside from the even Triad (222) is **LJS,** which includes 3 Labour Fitness sessions, 2 Journey Fitness Sessions and 1 Strength Training session.

How I split LJS:

- **3x Labour Fitness:** Two include no Journeys (running) and one includes Journeys (400m)

- **2x Journey Fitness:** One long steady-state run + one tempo or interval session

- **1x Strength Training:** One total body strength training session (or just upper body if it has been a hard week on the legs)

Note: Although the bulk of the exercises that I use in Labour Fitness sessions use low to moderate weights. I often include heavier lunges and sled pushes and pulls. Therefore, a lot of lower body strength is built on these sessions. Hence why I often get away with throwing in one upper body strength training session, which is usually focused on muscle building (bro sesh!)

I personally prefer programs that place a bias toward Labour Fitness (I love circuit-based training). Therefore, my choice if I wanted more strength would be **LSJ**.

How I split LSJ:

- **3x Labour Fitness:** One includes no journeys and two include journeys. However, I would drop the Journeys off one if it had been a heavy week on the legs

- **2x Strength Training:** This can be one upper body session and one lower body session. However, I prefer the training split: Squat and Upper Push (aka Lower and Upper Push) and Deadlift and Upper Pull (AKA Lower and Upper Pull) – I find working both lower and upper movement in a single training session minimizes DOMS

- **1x Journey Fitness:** One steady-state run (mid-long duration at a low intensity)

Split Examples for the Half Dozen Week

LJS (Version 1): 3x Labour Fitness / 2x Journey Fitness / 1x Strength Training

- **Monday Morning:** Labour Fitness (no running)
- **Monday Evening:** Journey Fitness (steady state run)
- **Tuesday:** Rest Day
- **Wednesday Morning:** Labour Fitness (with running)
- **Wednesday Evening:** Strength Training (total body)
- **Thursday:** Rest Day
- **Friday:** Labour Fitness (no running)
- **Saturday:** Journey Fitness (tempo run)
- **Sunday:** Rest Day

LJS (Version 2): 3x Labour Fitness / 2x Journey Fitness / 1x Strength Training

- **Monday Morning:** Journey Fitness (tempo run)
- **Monday Evening:** Strength Training (total body)
- **Tuesday:** Labour Fitness (no running)
- **Wednesday:** Rest Day
- **Thursday:** Labour Fitness (with running)
- **Friday:** Journey Fitness (steady state)
- **Saturday:** Labour Fitness (no running)
- **Sunday:** Rest Day

LJS (Version 3): 3x Labour Fitness / 2x Journey Fitness / 1x Strength Training

- **Monday:** Labour Fitness (no running)
- **Tuesday:** Journey Fitness (tempo run)
- **Wednesday:** Labour Fitness (no running)
- **Thursday:** Strength Training (total body)
- **Friday:** Labour Fitness (with running)
- **Saturday:** Rest Day
- **Sunday:** Journey Fitness (steady state)

JSL: 3x Journey Fitness / 2x Strength Training / 1x Labour Fitness

- **Monday Morning:** Journey Fitness (steady State)
- **Monday Evening:** Labour Fitness (no running)
- **Tuesday:** Strength Training (lower and upper push)
- **Wednesday Morning:** Journey Fitness (Tempo run)
- **Wednesday Evening:** Labour Fitness (no running)
- **Friday:** Strength Training (lower and upper pull)
- **Saturday:** Journey Fitness (intervals)
- **Sunday:** Rest Day

JLS: 3x Journey Fitness / 2x Labour Fitness / 1x Strength Training

- **Monday:** Journey Fitness (Intervals)
- **Tuesday:** Strength Training (total body)
- **Wednesday:** Labour Fitness (no running)
- **Thursday:** Journey Fitness (Tempo run)
- **Friday:** Labour Fitness (no running)
- **Saturday:** Journey Fitness (steady state)
- **Sunday:** Rest Day

SLJ: 3x Strength Training / 2x Labour Fitness / 1x Journey Fitness

- **Monday:** Strength Training (Total Body)
- **Tuesday:** Rest Day
- **Wednesday Morning:** Labour Fitness (with running)
- **Wednesday Evening:** Strength Training (lower and upper push)
- **Thursday:** Rest Day
- **Friday Morning:** Labour Fitness (with running)
- **Friday Evening:** Strength Training (lower and upper pull)
- **Saturday:** Rest Day
- **Sunday:** Journey Fitness (steady state)

The Deadly Dozen 2 & 3-Day Splits

Although I consider a 6-session training week to be the gold standard for myself and a lot of the athletes I work with, for some (even well-trained athletes), 6 training sessions a week is too much, or they simply can't fit it in.

Of course, as mentioned in the previous section, you can drop off 1 or 2 sessions to create a 4 or 5-session training week. However, some may only be able to fit 2-3 training sessions per week – I would generally advise 3 being a minimum to achieve a high level of fitness racing ability, but you can achieve a lot with 2.

A 3-day split could be split evenly between the Deadly Dozen Triad, with 1x Strength Training session (Total Body), 1x Labour Fitness session (with Journeys – act as interval work), and 1x Journey Fitness session (longer duration tempo of steady state).

Another way is to split the 3-day split into 2x Labour Fitness sessions with either both including Journeys (runs) or just 1, with the other having a Strength Training focus (using heavier weights), and then having a final Journey Fitness session which includes a longer duration tempo or steady state run.

My favourite strategy when I only have 2-3 sessions to work with is to program Labour Fitness sessions for each workout, with a bias on each:

- **Labour Fitness Strength:** This involves using much heavier weights (moderate rep ranges/time) to promote strength development. These sessions can include Journeys when it is used during a 2-day split. However, during a 3-day split, I would have this as the 1 session with less cardio (run, row, ski, cycle, etc)

- **Labour Fitness Speed:** This involves using race weights or lighter (moderate rep ranges/time) and including shorter duration Journeys (100-400m) to encourage speed and aerobic power development

- **Labour Fitness Stamina:** This involves using race weights or lighter (high rep ranges/time) and including longer duration Journeys (400m-2000m) to encourage muscular endurance and aerobic power and capacity development

One of the key benefits of working off a 2–3-day split is having 1-2 days' rest between training sessions, which usually allows adequate recovery for an athlete to go much harder on each session without risking overuse injuries or excessive fatigue: Remember, sometimes the aim is NOT to go hard.

I personally prefer to train hard on a Mondays, and even incorporate 2-3 training sessions within that day (I am fortunate to work in a gym), and then have the following day off as a full rest day. That is what works for me with my work schedule and how my body feels. However, others may prefer to train more frequently at lower intensities, and this reiterates the importance of the training principle of Individuality (training programs need to be individualised. However, we don't need to reinvent the wheel for everyone).

"If it is not right, do not do it, if it is not true, do not say it." – **Marcus Aurelius**

Structuring Performance Qualities

Now we understand how we design a week of training; we need to understand how to build a single training session.

When it comes to a 5km run, you warm up and then you go run 5km. However, when it comes to strength training, a lot more thought gets put into the order of the exercises that we are going to perform with the aim of getting the most out of the session.

Even more thought is put into the structure of a training session when it is what I define as a Strength and Conditioning (S&C) session, which potentially involves the athlete performing speed and power work, strength work and some form of metabolic conditioning (energy system development) all in one session.

Of course, you can structure a training session in a way that suits you. However, if our aim is to get the most out of each activity, we consider **fatigue sensitivity** (we tend to do strength training before cardio, but you don't have to do it that way).

Fatigue sensitivity refers to how fast a performance quality (a component of fitness) will deteriorate. For example, maximal (top-end) speed will start to deteriorate much faster than muscular endurance. Therefore, it makes sense to develop sprint ability towards the start of a session prior to long-duration muscular endurance or aerobic work that may negatively impact your performance on the sprints.

Of course, there is nothing wrong with performing specific qualities in a fatigued state (it often feels good lifting weights after cardio when you are very warm). However, the table below illustrates the way in which we would order different performance qualities to best optimize performance output.

Note: It also makes sense to have more complex activities towards the start of the training session (while you or your athlete is fresh). For example, the Olympic lifts. Before working on simple exercises towards the end of a session.

Fatigue	Quality	Example
More Fatigue Sensitive ↑ ↓ **Less Fatigue Sensitive**	Max Speed	Sprints
	Acceleration	Resisted Sprints
	Reactive Strength - SSC	Plyometrics – jumps
	Power	Ballistic Training – throws
	Max Strength	Resistance Training – Low Volume / High Intensity
	Hypertrophy	Resistance Training – Moderate Volume & Intensity
	Endurance	Resistance Training – High Volume / Low Intensity

Note: SSC = Stretch Shortening Cycle: Explained on Page-237

Here's an example of how to build an athletic gym session:

Phase	Example
Warm-Up	Raise / Activate / Mobilize / Potentiation (RAMP) / Running Drills / DROMEs / Potentiation (RDP)
Speed & Agility / Plyometric & Ballistic Training / Complex Lifts	Sprints & Change of Direction (COD) / Jumps & Throws / Olympic Weightlifting
Primary Lifts	Compound Lift – of most importance
Assistance / Accessory Lifts	Compound Lifts
Auxiliary Lifts	Single-Joint / Isolation Exercises
Metabolic Conditioning	Energy System Development
Cool Down / Mobility	Low-Intensity Cardio / Rolling & Stretching

Note: We cover warming up, speed & agility, and plyometric and ballistic training in the "Warming Up" section of this manual: Page-143.

Here's a little more information on the three different types of lifts:

- **Primary Lifts** are compound exercises. They are of utmost importance in terms of exercise selection as they usually work through the greatest ROM with the heaviest loads and, therefore, require the most effort, i.e., BB back squats, deadlifts, and press variations

- **Assistance Lifts** are often referred to as accessory (secondary) exercises and are also compound movements. They are chosen to develop specific movements or muscle groups that help you to perform the primary lift or specific sporting actions

- **Auxiliary Lifts** are single-joint (isolation) exercises. They are chosen to help develop your ability to perform the primary lift or specific sporting actions

When it comes to building a training session, it is key to consider Minimum and Maximum Effective Dose:

- **Minimum Effective Dode:** This refers to the smallest amount of training (or stimulus) required to elicit a desired physiological response or adaptation in an individual. It represents the threshold below which no significant improvements occur

- **Maximum Effective Dose:** This refers to the highest amount of training (or stimulus) that an individual can effectively recover from and adapt to, resulting in optimal improvements in performance and fitness

It is up to us to us to program the training loads that result in Adaptation NOT Maladaptation.

Example Weeks of Training

In this section, we look at an example week of training from each phase of FAIRR periodization and an example taper week prior to an important event:

- Familiarization
- Accumulation
- Intensification
- Realization
- Recovery

We also look at some example training session plans from different phases within the program.

Note: If the number of training sessions increases during the course of a training program, then it may make sense to rejig the session order to allow for better recovery between specific sessions, etc. However, if an athlete is used to doing their long run on a Sunday and that has become part of their weekly routine/lifestyle, then it can be detrimental to change it.

This being said, **I have designed each training week independently to best showcase a variety of training splits: Routine is key; therefore, I would usually aim to maintain a consistent training split that works.**

I list training times as Session 1 and Session 2. These session times are best performed hours apart and are generally split between a morning and an evening session. However, the evening session could be in the middle of the afternoon. If there is just one session, it can be performed at any time – it ultimately comes down to your availability to train.

"Rest" can involve full rest (normal daily activities), going for a walk or rolling and stretching, etc. Of course, specific flexibility and mobility sessions can also be programmed.

Familiarization: 4x Sessions: 2x Journey Fitness (Runs) / 1x Labour Fitness / 1x Strength Training

Day	Mon	Tue	Wed	Thu	Fri	Sat	Sun
Session 1	Strength Training: Total Body: 60 Mins: RPE 6-7	Rest	Steady State Run: 20 Mins: RPE 3	Rest	Labour Fitness: 30 Mins: RPE 6-7	Rest	Steady State Run: 20 Mins: RPE 3
Session 2	Rest	Rest	Rest	Rest	Rest	Rest	Rest

"Indifference to external events. And a commitment to justice in your own acts." **– Marcus Aurelius**

Accumulation: 6x Sessions: 3x Journey Fitness (Runs) / 1x Labour Fitness / 2x Strength Training

Day	Mon	Tue	Wed	Thu	Fri	Sat	Sun
Session 1	Strength Training: Upper Push: 60 Mins: RPE 7	Tempo Run: 30 Min: RPE 7	Labour Fitness: 60 Mins: RPE 7	Rest	Steady State Run: 60 Mins: RPE 3	Rest	Steady State Run: 90 Mins: RPE 3
Session 2	Rest	Rest	Strength Training: Upper Pull: 60 Mins: RPE 7	Rest	Strength Training: Lower Body: 60 Mins: RPE 7	Rest	Rest

Intensification: 7x Sessions: 2x Journey Fitness (Runs) / 3x Labour Fitness / 2x Strength Training

Day	Mon	Tue	Wed	Thu	Fri	Sat	Sun
Session 1	Labour Fitness: 45 Mins: RPE 10	Rest	Labour Fitness: 45 Mins: RPE 7-8	Rest	Labour Fitness: 60 Mins: RPE 9	Rest	Steady State Run 60 Mins: RPE 3
Session 2	Strength Training: Lower and Upper Push: 60 Mins: RPE 9	Rest	Tempo Run: 30 Mins: RPE 9	Rest	Strength Training: Lower and Upper Pull: 60 Mins: RPE 9	Rest	Rest

Realization: 6x Sessions: 2x Journey Fitness (Runs) / 3x Labour Fitness / 1x Strength Training

Day	Mon	Tue	Wed	Thu	Fri	Sat	Sun
Session 1	Tempo Run: 20 Mins: RPE 10	Labour Fitness: 45 Mins: RPE 8	Run Intervals: 30 Mins: RPE 10	Labour Fitness: 30 Mins: RPE 9	Rest	Labour Fitness: 45 Mins: RPE 10	Rest
Session 2	Strength Training: 60 Mins: Total Body: RPE 10	Rest	Run Intervals: 40 Mins: RPE 10	Rest	Rest	Rest	Rest

Taper Week: 6x Sessions: 2x Journey Fitness (Runs) / 3x Labour Fitness / 1x Strength Training

Day	Mon	Tue	Wed	Thu	Fri	Sat	Sun
Session 1	Steady State Run: 30 Mins: RPE 3	Rest	Steady State Run: 20 Mins: RPE 3	Rest/Walk	Rest/Short Walk	**Race**	Rest
Session 2	S&C Session: 45 Mins: Plyo / Ballistic / Speed Lifting: RPE 6	Rest	S&C Session: 35 Mins: Plyo / Ballistic / Speed Lifting: RPE 6	Rest	Rest	Rest	Rest

I start thinking about tapers 3 weeks out from the competition. In the third week out, I am thinking about peaking the final block of training before starting to reduce the training loads (specifically volume) on the second week out. In the last week before the competition, I don't like my athletes to cease all training because they just end up feeling lethargic. Instead, they include easy runs early in the week and perform Strength and Conditioning "Primer" sessions.

Primers aim to stimulate the neuro-muscular system while causing minimal fatigue, and this is best done with speed lifting, jumps, throws, and short sprints, etc – the next page shows example primers.

Note: The eccentric (downward: muscles lengthening) phase of a movement causes most of the muscle trauma that requires more recovery and most of the delayed onset muscle soreness (DOMS) we experience the days following a training session. Therefore, we can reduce this by limiting the range of motion of exercises or performing concentric (upward: muscles shortening) only exercises.

Recovery: 4x Sessions: 1x Journey Fitness (Runs) / 1x Labour Fitness / 2x Strength Training

Day	Mon	Tue	Wed	Thu	Fri	Sat	Sun
Session 1	Strength Training: 45 Mins: Total Body: RPE 7	Rest	Labour Fitness: 30 Mins: RPE 7	Rest	Strength Training: 45 Mins: Total Body: RPE 6-7	Rest	Steady State Run: 30 Mins: RPE 3
Session 2	Rest	Rest	Rest	Rest	Rest	Rest	Rest

The recovery phase is a great time to incorporate the training the athlete enjoys doing. For example, basic gym work at moderate volumes and intensities, etc.

Primer 1: 3-4 Days before a competition. (CM

Exercise	Sets/Reps	Intensity	Rest	Notes
KB Jump	5x3	RPE 5	1 Min	Jump as high as you can with a KB
Vertical Jump	5x1	Max Intent	15-20 Secs	Jump as high as you can
DB Floor Press	5x3	RPE 5	1 Min	Work at full speed
MB Chest Throw	10x1	Max Intent	15-20 Secs	Use a 3kg MB
MB Rotational Throw	5x1 ES	Max Intent	15-20 Secs	Use a 3kg MB

Primer 2: 3-4 Days before a competition.

Exercise	Sets/Reps	Intensity	Rest	Notes
KB Swing	5x5	RPE 5	1 Min	Work at full speed
Broad Jump	10x1	Max Intent	15-20 Secs	Jump as far as you can
Lateral Bound	5x2 ES	Max Intent	15-20 Secs	Bound from left to right
DB Push Press	5x3 ES	RPE 5	1 Min	Lift with maximal speed
MB Slams	5x3	Max Intent	30 Secs	Use a 5-6kg MB/Slam Ball

Primer 3: 1-2 Days before a competition.

Exercise	Sets/Reps	Intensity	Rest	Notes
Vertical Jump	5x1	Max Intent	15-20 Secs	Jump as high as you can
Broad Jump	5x1	Max Intent	15-20 Secs	Jump as far as you can
Bound	5x3 ES	Max Intent	15-20 Secs	Bound forward from one leg to the other
MB CM Rotational Throw	5x1 ES	Max Intent	15-20 Secs	Use a 3kg MB
MB Chest Throw	10x1	Max Intent	15-20 Secs	Use a 3kg MB

Primer 4: 1-2 Days before a competition.

Exercise	Sets/Reps	Intensity	Rest	Notes
Ankle Jump	3x10	Max Intent	15-20 Secs	Jump as high and as fast as you can
Pogo Jump	3x10	Max Intent	15-20 Secs	Jump as high and as fast as you can
Vertical Jump	5x1	Max Intent	15-20 Secs	Jump as high as you can
MB Chest Throw	10x1	Max Intent	15-20 Secs	Use a 3kg MB
MB Single-Arm Chest Throw	5x1 ES	Max Intent	15-20 Secs	Use a 1-2kg MB

Example Session Plans

In this section, we look at some different Strength Training, Labour Fitness and Journey Fitness (intervals, etc) Session Plans.

Note: I mix up the training loads on each program to demonstrate a wide variety of programming.

We also look at some Strength and Conditioning sessions where the emphasis is on overall athletic development.

When I program Strength Training sessions, I primarily use the RPE Scale, but I also use percentages of a 1RM for the primary lifts if the athlete finds them beneficial.

For both Labour and Journey Fitness, I use a combination of the RPE Scale and Heart Rate Zones to program training intensities – If the athlete prefers to just use the RPE Scale, that is fine.

Note: When programming, I have the following table printed out in front of me for reference.

Intensity	RPE Score	LT Heart Rate Zone
Very Easy	1-2	Zone 1 (Active Recovery) <85%
Easy	3	Zone 2 (Endurance) 85-89%
Moderate	4	Zone 3 (Tempo) 90-94%
Somewhat Hard	5-6	
Hard	7	Zone 4 (Sub-Threshold) 95-100%
	8	Zone 5 (Supra-Threshold) 100-102%
Very Hard	9	Zone 5b (VO2 Max) 103-106%
Maximal	10	Zone 5c (Anaerobic Capacity) >106%

Notes on the table above:

Zone 2 is where you are going to spend A LOT of time in Journey Fitness to build endurance (specifically during the Accumulation phase). You can spend a lot of time in zone 2 without placing too much strain on the body, which requires a lot of recovery – you should be able to hold a conversation while in zone 2.

It should be noted that working just above zone 2 can increase the need for recovery while eliciting little more physiological adaptations. Therefore, it is not always worth the extra recovery cost. This is one of the reasons why it is common to see endurance programs that place 80% of the work in zone 2 and the other 20% in the much higher zones that provide greater stimuli in contrast to the low-intensity work – the 80/20 model of training (80% easy runs / 20% hard runs), has been shown in various studies to provide better results than a 50/50 program that a lot of novice runners may instinctively gravitate to.

For Fitness Racing, we do a lot of work around the Threshold.

When it comes to short bouts of high-intensity work (<1 minute), there will be some lag in your heart rate reaching the targeted zone, especially in earlier sets of interval work, for example. Therefore, I primarily use the RPE Scale to quantify intervals, etc. Or, if I want to be more specific when quantifying training loads for intervals, I work off percentages of MAS (Maximum Aerobic Speed) scores.

Warm-up sets should be performed before working at the programmed intensity on a specific exercise. For example, before performing 4x8 (4 sets of 8 reps) Back squats at 60kg, you may perform 10x bodyweight squats, 10x goblet squats at 10kg, 8 reps with a 20kg unloaded BB, 8 reps at 40kg and then go into the "working" sets at the programmed intensity/the weight that feels right. This same protocol can be used when moving from a lower-body exercise to an upper-body exercise. However, if an exercise performed later in the sessions works a similar movement pattern and muscles as a previous exercise, fewer warm-up sets are required. You may just perform 1 or 2 lighter sets to "groove" the movement (get a feel for the exercise).

Of course, a full warm-up can be carried out before progressively loading the movement we are looking to work on – we will look at how we can get the most out of warm-ups in the Warming Up section: Page-143. Yes, progressively loading the movement you are going to work on is the most specific warm-up you can get, but we can also use warm-ups to stimulate other performance qualities and skillsets and potentiate (prime the muscles) for the session with explosive movements like jumps.

Due to the longer rest periods used during strength training sessions and the time it can often take for stronger athletes to ramp up to higher weights, just a few strength exercises can end up taking quite a long time to complete. Therefore, I always program the most important 3-5 exercises first and often state that additional exercises are optional if time and energy allow their completion. I also often have tables of core or specific isolation exercises (arm work, etc) for athletes to pick from if they have time for 1-2 more exercises at the end of the session.

Allowing optional exercises at the end of the session is great as it gives athletes flexibility. However, it should also be monitored as some athletes will choose to do so much. Remember, the whole idea of programming is to program the right exercise variations, volumes and intensities. However, I have also found that encouraging athletes to have some autonomy and teaching them to self-regulate is an approach that leads to more buy-in, long-term consistency and, ultimately, greater success.

Here are some of my go-to exercises that athletes can add at the end of the session if they have time:

- GHD Hip/Back Extension
- Single-Leg Calf Raise
- Ab Roll Out
- Hanging Knee Raise
- Band/Cable Rotation
- Wrist Roller
- Any Biceps Curl Variation
- Any Triceps Extension Variation
- Pull-Ups/Chin Ups
- Push-Ups

Note: If an athlete is not conditioned to exercises like the ab roll-out, it can leave them with some serious DOMS. Therefore, it is key that the athlete is well-conditioned, or is not adding the exercises in at the wrong time, i.e., a couple of days before a competition.

Core Exercise Table

Exercise	Sets/Reps	Notes
Ab Roll-Out	3x3-10	Increase the intensity by slowing the movement down or pausing at the bottom
GHD Back/Hip Extension / Dorsal Raise	3x10-20	Increase the intensity by adding weight
Shins / Toes to Bar	3x5-10	Increase the intensity by slowing the movement down
Hanging Knee Raise	3x10-20	Increase the intensity by slowing the movement down
Supine Leg Raise	3x10-20	Increase the intensity by slowing the movement down
Torture Twists	3x5 ES	Increase the intensity by slowing the movement down and/or adding weight
Russian Twist	3x10-20 ES	Increase the intensity by slowing the movement down and/or adding weight
Sit-Up / V-Sit-Up	3x10-20	Increase the intensity by slowing the movement down and/or adding weight
DB Press Sit-Up	3x10-20	Increase the intensity by slowing the movement down and/or adding weight
DB Woodchop / Band or Cable Rotation	3x10 ES	Increase the intensity by increasing the DB weight or band tension
DB Side Bend	3x10 ES	Increase the Intensity by adding weight and/or slowing the movement down
Dragon Flags	3x3-10	Increase the intensity by slowing the movement down
Pallof Press	3x5-10 ES	Increase the intensity by increasing band tension or slowing the movement down
Renegade Row	3x5-10 ES	Increase the intensity by slowing the movement down and/or adding weight
Front Plank or Push-Ups	3x30-90 Secs	Increase the intensity by engaging your muscles harder
Side Plank	3x30-90 Secs	Increase the intensity by engaging your muscles harder
Copenhagen Plank	3x5-10 ES	Increase the intensity by slowing the movement down

One of my favourite ways to work the core is by doing sit-ups with a medicine ball or slam ball between my legs. I squeeze the medicine ball with my legs to work my adductor/groin (inner thigh) muscles, while my abdominals and hip flexors are working to perform the sit-ups. Both the rectus abdominis (6-pack muscles) and many of the adductor/groin muscles attach to the pubis on the pelvis, and therefore, the sit-up with a medicine ball squeeze is a great combo – the abdominals, hip flexors and adductors are all incredibly important when running, squatting and lunging, so this is a great bang for your buck exercise to add to the end of a Strength Training or Journey Fitness session or within a Labour Fitness session.

"First say to yourself what would you be; and then do what you have to do." – **Epictetus**

Strength Training: Total Body Example V1

This program sticks to fundamental compound movements and does not add core or arm work in at the end, but it can be easily added.

The exercises in the strength programs can be found in the BB and Bonus Exercises sections of this manual: Pages-160+198.

Exercise	Sets/Reps/Distance/Time	Intensity	Rest
BB Back Squat	4x8	65% / RPE 7	2-3 Mins
BB RDL	4x8	RPE 8	1-2 Mins
BB Bench Press	4x8	65% / RPE 7	2-3 Mins
Incline DB Press	4x12	RPE 8	1-2 Mins
DB Single-Arm Row	3x12 Each Side	RPE 8	1 Min

Note: When it comes to relating percentages of a 1RM, the relative RPE is highly dependent on the rep range. For example, 4x8 at 65% could be described as RPE 7. However, 4x20 at 65% could be described as RPE 10.

Strength Training: Total Body Example V2

Exercise	Sets/Reps/Distance/Time	Intensity	Rest
BB Deadlift	4x5	75% / RPE 8	2-3 Mins
DB RFESS	4x8 Each Side	RPE 8	1-2 Mins
BB Strict Press	4x5	75% / RPE 8	2-3 Mins
Flat DB Press	4x8	RPE 8	1-2 Mins
Pull-Up	3x Max Reps	RPE 10	1 Min
Ab Roll-Out	4x5	RPE 8	30 Secs

Strength Training: Total Body Example V3

Exercise	Sets/Reps/Distance/Time	Intensity	Rest
BB Front Squat	4x3	85% / RPE 9	2-3 Mins
Hex Bar Deadlift	4x3	85% / RPE 9	2-3 Mins
BB Incline Press	4x3	85% / RPE 9	2-3 Mins
BB/DB Biceps Curl	4x10	RPE 8	1 Min
BB/DB Triceps Extension	4x10	RPE 8	1 Min
Hanging Knee Raise	3x15	RPE 7	30 Secs

Strength Training: Lower Body Example V1

Exercise	Sets/Reps/Distance/Time	Intensity	Rest
BB Back Squat	4x6	75% / RPE 8	2-3 Mins
DB RDL	4x12	RPE 8	1-2 Mins
DB Walking Lunge	4x6 Each Side	RPE 8	1-2 Mins
DB Lateral Lunge	4x6 Each Side	RPE 8	1-2 Mins
Single-Leg Calf Raise	3x Max Reps Each Side	RPE 10	30 Secs
GHD Hip Extension	3x15	RPE 8	30-60 Secs

Strength Training: Lower Body Example V2

Exercise	Sets/Reps/Distance/Time	Intensity	Rest
BB Overhead Squat	5x3	80% / RPE 8	2-3 Mins
Single-Leg Squat (On Box)	4x5 Each Side	RPE 9	1-2 Mins
DB Step-Up	4x6 Each Side	RPE 8	1-2 Mins
Heavy Sled Push	4x20m	RPE 9	1-2 Mins
Copenhagen Plank	3x10 ES	RPE 8	30 Secs
Pallof Press	3x10 Each Side	RPE 7	15 Secs

Strength Training: Lower Body Example V3

Exercise	Sets/Reps/Distance/Time	Intensity	Rest
BB Box Squat	3x2	90% / RPE 9	2-3 Mins
BB Sumo Deadlift	3x2	90% / RPE 9	2-3 Mins
DB RFESS	3x4 Each Side	RPE 9	1-2 Mins
DB Lateral Lunge	3x4 Each Side	RPE 9	1-2 Mins
Shins/Toes to Bar	3x5	RPE 8	30 Secs
DB Woodchop	3x10 Each Side	RPE 7	30 Secs

"To bear trials with a calm mind robs misfortune of its strength and burden." – **Seneca**

Strength Training: Upper Body Example V1

Exercise	Sets/Reps/Distance/Time	Intensity	Rest
BB Bench Press	4x8	65% / RPE 7	2-3 Mins
BB Strict Press	4x8	65% / RPE 7	2-3 Mins
Flat DB Press	4x12	RPE 7	1-2 Mins
DB Pullover	4x12	RPE 7	1-2 Mins
DB Single-Arm Row	4x12 Each Side	RPE 7	1 Min
Wrist Roller	3x Max Effort	RPE 10	30 Secs

Strength Training: Upper Body Example V2

Exercise	Sets/Reps/Distance/Time	Intensity	Rest
BB Push Press	5x2	90% / RPE 9	2-3 Mins
Standing DB Press	4x10	RPE 9	1-2 Mins
Pull-Up	4x5	RPE 8	1-2 Mins
Push-Up	3x Max Reps	RPE 10	1 Min
Sled Pull (Upper Only)	4x20m	RPE 10	1-2 Mins
Ab Roll-Out	3x5	RPE 8	30 Secs

Strength Training: Upper Body Example V3

Exercise	Sets/Reps/Distance/Time	Intensity	Rest
BB Floor Press	4x5	80% / RPE 8-9	2-3 Mins
Seated DB Press	4x8	RPE 8	1-2 Mins
Inverted Row	4x Max Reps	RPE 10	1-2 Mins
BB/DB Biceps Curl	4x10	RPE 8	1 Min
BB/DB Triceps Extension	4x10	RPE 8	1 Min
Cable Rotation	3x10 Each Side	RPE 7	30 Secs

"I made a prosperous voyage when I suffered a shipwreck." – **Zeno**

Strength Training: Bang for Your Buck Session

Here is one of my favourite strength training sessions. I often perform it when I am short on time and want to get the whole body working hard.

There are only 4 exercises in the session and the last 2 are completed as a superset:

- **BB Muscle Clean & Press:** No technicality, just muscle the BB from the floor and strict press it overhead (or use a push press)

- **BB Walking Lunge:** I often use an SSB (Safety Squat Bar)

- **Push-Up + Pull-Up:** Performed back-to-back. Near max reps on both – work until the reps start to break down a little (RPE 8-9)

Note: Single-leg strength is essential for a lot of fitness races, and a lot of fitness races include walking lunges. Therefore, it is highly beneficial to build up walking lunge strength with a BB or SSB.

Depending on time and energy, I perform 3-6 sets on all of the exercises. The BB Muscle Clean & Press is performed for 6 reps and the BB Walking Lunge is performed for 6 reps on each leg (12 lunges in total).

I work between RPE 7-10 depending on how I am feeling that day and the training sessions that are ahead of me.

Exercise	Sets/Reps/Distance/Time	Intensity	Rest
BB Muscle Clean & Press	3-6x6	RPE 7-10	2-3 Mins
BB/SSB Walking Lunge	3-6x6	RPE 7-10	2-3 Mins
Pull-Up + Push-Up	3-6x Near Max Reps	RPE 8-9	1-2 Mins

Other exercises I may add to this session if I have time:

- **Heavy Farmers Carry:** Try to go much heavier than you usually carry and walk for 30-120 seconds

- **Heavy Calf Raise:** Any Variation – aim to load the calves heavy

- **Biceps Curl + Triceps Extension Superset:** Use any variation

"Nowhere you can go is more peaceful, more free of interruptions, than you own soul." – **Marcus Aurelius**

Labour Fitness: With Journeys Example V1

We can vary the intensity (RPE Scale) of the work during Labour Fitness sessions. However, for all of the examples here, I have programmed an RPE of 6-8. RPE 6-8 means you are working hard but are not maximal. Some activities will bring you well above threshold if you push it, but you generally want to be working around your anaerobic threshold (LT2) with plenty of time spent sub-threshold.

When working with timed rounds, the standard changeover period for all Labour Fitness sessions is 15-20 seconds. However, when working for reps (most commonly when Journeys are included), the transition time is not timed and is generally done as quickly as possible.

Labour Fitness sessions can have a clear start and finish point. However, I tend to just run through as many rounds as possible (AMRAP) in the allocated time (this may be dependent on the time that I have available – often 45 minutes).

Deadly Dozen Race weights are programmed. However, these can be regressed or progressed depending on your ability level or goals – if you need to get stronger on specific activities, load them heavier.

Although we want a bias toward running, we can exchange runs for rowing, skiing, or cycling – I often program these as "Journey" if I am allowing the athlete to choose the cardio activity.

35-45 Minute AMRAP

Labour / Journey	Weight (Male / Female)	Time/Reps/Distance	Intensity	Rest
Run	BW	400m	RPE 6-8	N/A
KB Farmers Carry	M: 2x 24kg / F: 2x 16kg	120m	RPE 6-8	N/A
Run	BW	400m	RPE 6-8	N/A
DB Snatch	M: 1x 15kg / F 1x 9kg	30 Reps (Alternate)	RPE 6-8	N/A
Run	BW	400m	RPE 6-8	N/A
Burpee Broad Jump	BW	30m	RPE 6-8	N/A
Run	BW	400m	RPE 6-8	N/A
DB Push Press	M: 2x 12.5kg / F: 2x 6kg	30 Reps	RPE 6-8	N/A

Labour Fitness: With Journeys Example V2

35-45 Minute AMRAP

Labour / Journey	Weight (Male / Female)	Time/Reps/Distance	Intensity	Rest
Run	BW	400m	RPE 6-8	N/A
DB Devil Press	M: 2x 10kg / F: 2x 5kg	10 Reps	RPE 6-8	N/A
Run	BW	400m	RPE 6-8	N/A
Plate Overhead Carry	M: 1x 15kg / F 1x 10kg	120m	RPE 6-8	N/A
Run	BW	400m	RPE 6-8	N/A
Plate Clean & Press	M: 1x 15kg / F 1x 10kg	30 Reps	RPE 6-8	N/A
Run	BW	400m	RPE 6-8	N/A
Bear Crawl	BW	60m	RPE 6-8	N/A

Labour Fitness: With Journeys Example V3

This workout also includes non-Deadly Dozen exercises.

1-Round for Time

Labour / Journey	Weight (Male / Female)	Time/Reps/Distance	Intensity	Rest
Run	BW	400m	RPE 6-8	N/A
Row	BW	400m	RPE 6-8	N/A
Run	BW	400m	RPE 6-8	N/A
Plate Clean & Press	M: 1x 15kg / F 1x 10kg	40 Reps	RPE 6-8	N/A
Run	BW	400m	RPE 6-8	N/A
Ski	BW	400m	RPE 6-8	N/A
Run	BW	400m	RPE 6-8	N/A
Wallballs	M: 1x 6kg / F: 1x 4kg	40 Reps	RPE 6-8	N/A
Run	BW	400m	RPE 6-8	N/A
Cycle	BW	800M	RPE 6-8	N/A
Sled Pull	M: 120kg / F: 85kg	40m	RPE 6-8	N/A

Labour Fitness: Without Journeys Example V1

Timed Rounds: Keep going for 35-45 Minute

Labour / Journey	Weight (Male / Female)	Time/Reps/Distance	Intensity	Rest
KB Deadlift	M: 1x 32kg / F: 1x 24kg	2 Mins	RPE 6-8	15-20 Secs
DB Push Press	M: 2x 12.5kg / F: 2x 6kg	2 Mins	RPE 6-8	15-20 Secs
KB Goblet Squat	M: 1x 16kg / F: 1x 12kg	2 Mins	RPE 6-8	15-20 Secs
Burpee Broad Jump	BW	2 Mins	RPE 6-8	15-20 Secs
Plate Clean & Press	M: 1x 15kg / F 1x 10kg	2 Mins	RPE 6-8	15-20 Secs
DB Lunge	M: 2x 12.5kg / F: 2x 7.5kg	2 Mins	RPE 6-8	15-20 Secs
DB Snatch	M: 1x 15kg / F 1x 9kg	2 Mins	RPE 6-8	15-20 Secs
KB Farmers Carry	M: 2x 24kg / 2x 16kg	2 Mins	RPE 6-8	15-20 Secs

"Sometimes even to live is an act of courage." – **Seneca**

Labour Fitness: Without Journeys Example V2

Timed Rounds: Keep going for 35-45 Minute

Labour / Journey	Weight (Male / Female)	Time/Reps/Distance	Intensity	Rest
Plate Front Carry	M: 1x 25kg / F: 1x 20kg	2 Mins	RPE 6-8	15-20 Secs
KB Goblet Squat	M: 1x 16kg / F: 1x 12kg	2 Mins	RPE 6-8	15-20 Secs
Bear Crawl	BW	2 Mins	RPE 6-8	15-20 Secs
DB Devil Press	M: 2x 10kg / F 2x 5kg	2 Mins	RPE 6-8	15-20 Secs
Plate Overhead Carry	M: 1x 15kg / F 1x 10kg	2 Mins	RPE 6-8	15-20 Secs
KB Deadlift	M: 1x 32kg / F: 1x 24kg	2 Mins	RPE 6-8	15-20 Secs
Burpee Broad Jump	BW	2 Mins	RPE 6-8	15-20 Secs
DB Push Press	M: 2x 12.5kg / F: 2x 6kg	2 Mins	RPE 6-8	15-20 Secs

Labour Fitness: Without Running Journeys Example V3

This workout also includes non-Deadly Dozen exercises + Supersets on the Deadly Dozen stations

2-Rounds for Time

Labour / Journey	Weight (Male / Female)	Time/Reps/Distance	Intensity	Rest
Row	BW	3 Mins	RPE 6-8	15-20 Secs
KB Goblet Squat + DB Push Press	M: 1x 16kg / F: 1x 12kg M: 2x 12.5kg / F: 2x 6kg	3 Mins of 10 Reps on Each	RPE 6-8	15-20 Secs
Sled Push	M: 150kg / F: 1x 120kg	3 Mins	RPE 6-8	15-20 Secs
Ski	BW	3 Mins	RPE 6-8	15-20 Secs
KB Deadlift + Plate Clean & Press	M: 1x 32kg / F: 1x 24kg M: 1x 15kg / F 1x 10kg	3 Mins of 10 Reps on Each	RPE 6-8	15-20 Secs
Sled Pull	M: 120kg / F: 85kg	3 Mins	RPE 6-8	15-20 Secs
Cycle	BW	3 Mins	RPE 6-8	15-20 Secs
Wallball	M: 1x 6kg / F: 1x 4kg	3 Mins	RPE 6-8	15-20 Secs

"I judge you unfortunate because you have never lived through misfortune." – **Seneca**

Labour Fitness: Without Running Journeys Example V4

This workout also includes non-Deadly Dozen exercises + Supersets on the Deadly Dozen stations

2-Rounds for Time

Labour / Journey	Weight (Male / Female)	Time/Reps/Distance	Intensity	Rest
KB Deadlift + DB Push Press	M: 1x 32kg / F: 1x 24kg M: 2x 12.5kg / F 2x 6kg	3 Mins of 10 Reps on Each	RPE 6-8	15-20 Secs
Boxing Bag Work	BW	3 Mins	RPE 6-8	15-20 Secs
Skipping	BW	3 Mins	RPE 6-8	15-20 Secs
KB Goblet Squat + Push-Up	M: 1x 16kg / F: 1x 12kg BW	3 Mins of 10 Reps of Each	RPE 6-8	15-20 Secs
Row	BW	3 Mins	RPE 6-8	15-20 Secs
Battle Rope	BW	3 Mins	RPE 6-8	15-20 Secs
Farmers Carry + Burpee Broad Jump	M: 2x 24kg / F: 2x 16kg BW	3 Mins of 60m + 20m	RPE 6-8	15-20 Secs
Cycle	BW	3 Mins	RPE 6-8	15-20 Secs

Labour Fitness: Without Running Journeys Example V5

This workout also includes non-Deadly Dozen exercises + Supersets on the Deadly Dozen stations

3-Rounds for Time

Labour / Journey	Weight (Male / Female)	Time/Reps/Distance	Intensity	Rest
Cycle	BW	4 Mins	RPE 6-8	15-20 Secs
KB Goblet Squat + DB Devil Press	M: 1x 16kg / F: 1x 12kg M: 2x 10kg / F: 2x 5kg	4 Mins of 10 + 5 Reps	RPE 6-8	15-20 Secs
Ski	BW	4 Mins	RPE 6-8	15-20 Secs
DB Push Press + Push-Up	M: 2x 12.5kg / F: 2x 6kg BW	4 Mins of 10 Reps of Each	RPE 6-8	15-20 Secs
Row	BW	4 Mins	RPE 6-8	15-20 Secs
KB Deadlift + Plate Clean & Press	M: 1x 32kg / F: 1x 24kg M: 1x 15kg / F 1x 10kg	4 Mins	RPE 6-8	15-20 Secs

"You could leave life right now. Let that determine what you do and say and think." – **Marcus Aurelius**

Labour Fitness: Upper Body Bias

Although fitness races are often very leg heavy (meaning they involve a lot of lower body work), it is essential that you have good upper body strength and muscular endurance to complete the aspects that are upper body focused and to ensure that a lack of muscular strength and endurance in the upper body is not a limiting factor when performing total body movements. Therefore, it is beneficial to have Labour Fitness sessions that are biased towards building the upper body.

Due to the fact that fitness racing is leg-heavy, upper body focused sessions can provide respite and allow you to maintain a good level of training while the legs recover.

Of course, many of the movements performed in an upper body biased session may be compound in nature and work the entire body. The idea is that there is a clear emphasis on the upper body work.

Here are some of my favourite exercises to include in upper body biased sessions:

Note: This is a 12 Station Labour Fitness session I often perform: 2 Rounds – 2 minutes per station – 15-second transitions.

- Battle Ropes
- Push-Ups
- Sled Pull (Upper Only)
- Wallballs (Upper Only)
- DB Devil Press
- WP Overhead Carry
- DB Snatch
- WP Clean & Press
- Ski
- DB Strict Press
- DB Biceps Curl
- WP Triceps Extension

You can rest at any time. The aim is to complete as many reps as possible during the 2-minute rounds.

"It is the mind that makes us rich; this goes with us into exile." – **Musonius Rufus**

Labour Fitness: Labour Strength!

One of the best ways to develop muscular strength for fitness racing is to perform the specific movements within the race with much heavier loads: If you spend a bit of time working with heavier loads when you eventually go back to using lighter loads on activities, it will feel considerably lighter – I highly recommend people overload the movements they are required to perform on a race.

The Labour Strength Method is brilliant. However, it requires you to have access to a wider range of equipment (I often use my 40kg KB).

I use the Strength Labours method with Supersets (2 exercises) and Trisets (3 exercises), while performing 5-20 reps on each.

Examples:

Note: I have included the weights I often use. However, use weights that are suitable for your strength level.

- 6x 10x KB Goblet Squat at 1x 40kg + 10x DB Push Press at 2x 25kg

- 6x 20x DB Lunge at 2x 25kg + 10x DB Snatch at 1x 30kg

- 6x 40m Sled Push at 240kg + 20x Wallball at 1x 12kg

- 6x 20x KB Deadlift at 1x 40kg + 40m Sled Pull at 200kg

- 4x 20x DB Lunge at 2x 25kg + 20x Wallball at 1x 12kg + 20 Push-Up

- 4x 6x Pull-Up + 40m Sled Push at 240kg + 100m DB Farmers Carry at 2x 40kg

- 4x 10x DB Snatch at 1x 30kg + 10x KB Goblet Squat at 1x 40kg + 10x DB Push Press at 2x 25kg

- 4x 6x DB Devil Press at 2x 15kg + 15x WP Clean & Press at 1x 25kg + 15x Wallball at 1x 12kg

If you want to get used to running on tired legs, add some runs in between the sets of leg-heavy supersets.

When performing Strength Labour sessions, I perform the different exercises back-to-back. However, I tend to take as much rest as I feel I need between the sets. In strength training, when working with heavy loads, it is not uncommon for lifters to take 2-3 minutes rest between sets (often as much as 5 mins), but in general, I like to keep a little more metabolic stress while performing the above Supersets and Trisets, so I take about 30-60 seconds rest in between sets.

Note: If our aim is strength development, we don't want to reduce how effectively we can produce high force by leaving ourselves too fatigued. However, as the name suggests, "Labour Strength" is a combination of both Strength Training and Labour Fitness.

"If you want anything good, you must get it from yourself." – **Epictetus**

Journey Fitness: Intervals Example V1

This session can also be completed in reverse (starting with the 800m) which is a great way to get very warm before performing max sprint speed at shorter distances. However, if the aim is to get the highest quality of performance on the short sprints, you should start with them first.

Rest can be taken passively (static – shaking the legs off, etc) or actively with a walk (or slow jog). Usually, 100m will take about 60 seconds to walk at a slow/steady pace, around 50 seconds to walk at a fast pace and around 40 seconds to jog at a slow/steady pace.

On the track, I tend to refer to a 100m walk as a Short Rest, a 200m walk as a Medium Rest and a 300-400m walk as a Long Rest. Note: You don't need a track, just map out an ideal loop close to home.

Note: Although I tend to prefer to run a set distance on a track, it can be beneficial to program intervals for time, and this is especially useful when working with groups of individuals. For example, rather than everyone performing a 400m best effort, where running times may range from 55 seconds to 90 seconds, you could have everyone perform a best effort run for 75 seconds. Doing timed reps also allows you to run a group session where everyone is getting the same amount of rest simultaneously.

Sets / Distance	Intensity	Rest
4x 100m	RPE 10	2 Mins
Rest for 3 Mins		
3x 200m	RPE 10	2 Mins
Rest for 3 Mins		
2x 400m	RPE 9	3 Mins
Rest for 3 Mins		
1x 800m	RPE 8	3 Mins
Total Distance: 2600m		

Note: As the RPE scores show, the longer duration runs are not maximal, but hard-very hard.

Journey Fitness: Intervals Example V2

Sets / Distance	Intensity	Rest
2x 60m	RPE 10	2 Mins
Rest for 3 Mins		
3x 100m	RPE 10	2 Mins
Rest for 3 Mins		
4x 200m	RPE 10	2 Mins
Rest for 3 Mins		
3x 400m	RPE 10	2 Mins
Rest for 3 Mins		
2x 800m	RPE 9	3 Mins
Total Distance: 4020m		

Strength & Conditioning Session Example V1

The metabolic finishers in this session use the Tabata protocol: 8x 20 Seconds Work followed by 10 Seconds Rest (4 Minutes total) (2:1 Work to Rest Ratio).

Exercise	Sets/Reps/Distance/Time	Intensity	Rest
Box Jump	10x1	Max Intent	3-5 Secs
MB Chest Throw	10x1	Max Intent	3-5 Secs
Pull-Up	4x5	RPE 8	1 Min
BB Back Squat	4x5	RPE 8	2-3 Mins
BB Bench Press	4x5	RPE 8	2-3 Mins
DB Walking Lunge	3x6 Each Side	RPE 8	1-2 Mins
Hanging Knee Raise	3x15	RPE 7	30-60 Secs
Row	Tabata: 8x20 Secs	RPE 10	10 Secs
Ski	Tabata: 8x20 Secs	RPE 10	10 Secs
Mobility	10 Minutes	N/A	N/A

Strength & Conditioning Session Example V2

The metabolic finishers on this session use a 30 Second Work, 15 Seconds Rest protocol (2:1 Work to Rest Ratio).

Exercise	Sets/Reps/Distance/Time	Intensity	Rest
Ankle Jump	3x10	Max Intent	10-15 Secs
Broad Jump	5x3	Max Intent	20-30 Secs
Slam	4x5	Max Intent	20-30 Secs
Hex Bar Deadlift	4x3	RPE 9	2-3 Mins
BB Push Press	4x3	RPE 9	2-3 Mins
Sled Push	5x20m	RPE 9	1-2 Mins
Sled Pull	5x20m	RPE 9	1-2 Mins
Bag Work	Tabata: 6x30 Secs	RPE 10	30 Secs
Cycle	Tabata: 6x30 Secs	RPE 10	30 Secs
Mobility	10 Minutes	N/A	N/A

Note: You could also add 1 round of a Pantheon Labour to the end of an S&C workout – see the next page to download 2x FREE eBooks, which both include dozens of workouts.

"Leisure without study is death – a tomb for the living person." – **Seneca**

Pantheon Workouts

The Deadly Dozen has a ranking system for times achieved during the race. These are colour-coded and aligned to the various gods of the Greek and Roman Pantheons: We refer to this system as Pantheon Patches – what patch can you achieve?

Alongside the Pantheon Patches, each god has its own Deadly Dozen Labour (**Pantheon Labours**), which become progressively harder as you climb up the rankings – some are Labour only, others include journeys (runs).

There are three levels to each Gods Labour: 1. Hero Level 2. Demigod Level 3. God Level.

Pantheon Journeys on the other hand, are a variety of running workouts (intervals). However, they can also be performed on a Rower or Skier (same distances) or on a bike (double the distances).

Each God is also linked to a single distance, from 60m to 42km (26 miles – Marathon) – what time can you achieve on each of these distances?

Note: Exercises and weights can be scaled (s) to suit the athletes. You can also swap runs for the rower or skier (same distances) or cycle (double the distances).

You can grab FREE copies of both eBooks by clicking the links below:

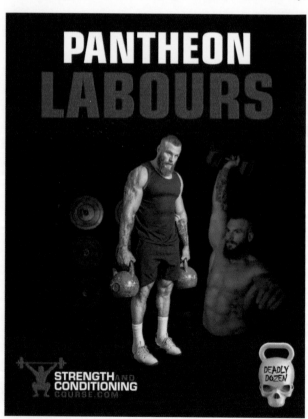
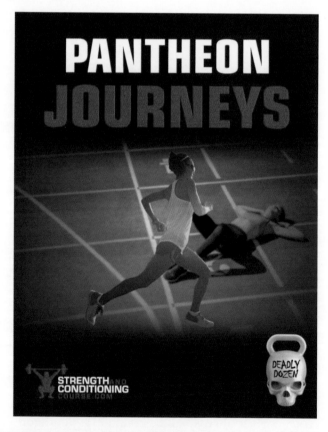

Pantheon Labours: https://courses.strengthandconditioningcourse.com/p/ddlabours

Pantheon Journeys: https://courses.strengthandconditioningcourse.com/p/ddjourneys

If you want Daily Dozen Workouts, follow our Instagram: @deadly.dozen

12-Week Deadly Dozen Triad Example

In this section, we look at a 12-week training program that works off the Even Deadly Dozen Triad:

- 2x Strength Training Sessions

- 2x Labour Fitness Sessions

- 2x Journey Fitness Sessions

The 2 Strength Training sessions work off the 12-1 Strength Program with both sessions working a total body split.

1 of the Labour Fitness sessions does not include running Journeys. However, the other does. Therefore, with the 2 Journey Fitness sessions, you essentially get 3x running sessions per week.

Note: Any of the running can be exchanged for rowing, skiing, cycling or swimming if needed, but running is the primary focus.

The 2 Journey Fitness sessions are split down between 1x interval session and 1x longer duration steady state or tempo session.

Although things can change from week to week in a training program, hence why you wouldn't want to program too far ahead, I find 12-weeks (3-months) to be a manageable amount of time where we create session plans while thinking about the long-term.

I see each 12-week block as a Macrocycle (Quadruple Periodization – 4x Macrocycles within a year) which is repeated 4 times to cover the year (evaluations and modifications are constantly being made to optimize the block as the athlete develops). 4x 12-week blocks = 48-weeks, then with various preloads, tapers, and short transition periods (holidays, etc), it makes up the full 52-week year.

The periodization and programming use a concurrent model where all performance qualities are developed during every phase/block of the program. As a whole the program has the backbone of the FAIRR Periodization model, where I am thinking about accumulating more volume to establish an aerobic base further away from the competition and upping the intensity closer to the competition. However, you will see how I have programmed each component of the DD Triad differently: Strength Training = Linear / Labour Fitness = Undulating / Journey Fitness Long Duration = FAIRR / Journey Fitness Intervals = Pyramid (work up to higher volume and then back down to low volume).

The Quadruple Periodization model (4x12 week macrocycles) allows athletes to peak for 4 big events each year, and if there is not a competition/race at the end of the 12-week block, it is usually used for testing (Deadly Dozen Testing Battery: DDTB), before recovering and starting a new block.

Note: Other small competitions can be included within the program, we just allow for short tapers before them: You can't be peaked all the time (at the peak of your fitness while also being well rested for a competition), but a true Deadly Dozen Fitness Racer maintains their fitness year-round – you should aim to be at a point where you can compete at a reasonable level at any time (perform well, but not necessarily hitting a PR – Personal Record). However, the aim of the program that works towards a peak (Realization phase) is to ensure you are at the very best you can be when you go into the most important competition for you.

The Paperback Program

If you want a physical copy of the Paperback Program which comes with logbook pages for each session to help you track your program, you can purchase a copy below.

Check out the Paperback Program below: Log your progress

Paperback on Amazon: https://mybook.to/ddtriad

PDF Download: https://courses.strengthandconditioningcourse.com/p/ddtriad

Check out some of my other Paperback Programs: www.jasoncurtis.org

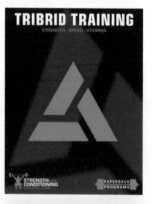

12-Week Strength Training Program: The 12-1 Program

This 12-week program is my personal program that I use to develop strength alongside my more specific fitness racing training sessions (Labour and Journey Fitness).

The program uses 4x lower body exercises and 4x upper body exercises (core work and additional arm work can be added).

Many of the exercises in this program are performed to a maximal range of motion (push it as far as possible – the aim is to create a loaded stretch). The eccentric (downward) phase is kept slow and steady; there is a slight pause of 1-2 seconds at the bottom, and then the concentric (upward) phase is performed as fast as possible. The exaggerated range of motion (ROM) and the slow eccentric and pause results in a much harder movement to achieve. Therefore, the weights lifted are generally a little lower. However, I believe this results in a far longer progression without plateau or injury (start light and build slowly – play the long game!)

Lower:

- **Squat** (I aim for a deep squat with emphasis on the quadriceps): This can be a BB back squat or front squat, or even a heavy KB/DB goblet squat. I often use a squat ramp to elevate my heels to allow for maximal depth with an upright torso. I also tend to use a narrow stance

- **Deadlift** (I often use a stiff-leg deadlift with emphasis on the hamstrings): This can be a BB conventional or sumo deadlift or a hex/trap bar can be used. Heavy KBs and DBs can also be used. To perform a stiff/straight-leg deadlift, I use a straight BB. The ROM of all the lifts can be increased by standing on a WP to create a 2-3inch deficit

- **Rear Foot Elevated Split Squat – RFESS** (Single-Leg): I perform this on a bench with a DB in each hand. The high rear foot position on a bench allows me to maximize the ROM and the stretch I can achieve through the rear quadriceps and hip flexors. You can also use a BB for this exercise. A walking lunge can be used as a race specific variation – I include heavy BB walking lunges in my training. However, due to the fact I do a lot of lunges in my Labour Fitness, I tend to use the RFESS is my main strength programming

- **Single-Leg Calf Raise** (Gastrocnemius and Soleus): I perform this on a thick WP, while supporting myself with one hand against a wall or squat rack and holding a DB in the other hand. The WP allows for a full heel drop to stretch the calves before performing the calf raise

Upper:

- **Bench Press** (Horizontal Push): I use a BB to perform this movement. However, a BB or DBs can also be used on a flat or incline bench

- **Strict Press** (Horizontal Push): I use either a BB or DBs to perform this movement and either perform it from a standing or seated position

- **Pull-Up or Lat Pulldown** (Vertical Pull): I usually perform max rep bodyweight pull-ups for multiple sets (they can also be loaded), or I vary it by performing lat pulldowns on a cable/pulldown machine – during either exercise, I pause when the arms are stretched overhead (bottom of the pull-up) to stretch out the lats and shoulders

- **Single-Arm Row** (Horizontal Pull): I perform this exercise with a single hand supporting me against a bench, DB rack, etc (3-point stance). I then use a heavy DB and allow my shoulder to protract and my torso to rotate slightly at the bottom of the movement, and then my shoulder to retract and my torso to rotate slightly at the top of the movement

There are many ways to split the program, as shown in the table below:

You can perform all 8 exercises in a 1-day split, but it would likely take a while. Therefore, it is often best to whittle it down to the exercises you need most.

I prefer using 2x total body days rather than having a lower body day then an upper body day: Spending a whole session on your lower body is far more likely to result in DOMS than working both your lower and upper body on the same session – I personally use the 2-Day Split V2.

1-Day Split V1	1-Day Split V2	2-Day Split V1	2-Day Split V2	2-Day Split V3
Squat Deadlift Bench Press Pull-Up Calf Raise	Squat RFESS Strict Press Lat Pulldown Single-Arm Row	Squat Deadlift RFESS Calf Raise	Squat Strict Press Pull-up Calf Raise	Squat Bench Press RFESS Single-Arm Row
		Bench Press Strict Press Pull-Up Single-Arm Row	Deadlift Bench Press RFESS Single-Arm Row	Deadlift Strict Press Pull-Up Calf Raise

During this program, you don't perform multiple sets at a programmed intensity when it comes to the top 2 lower body and upper body movements (Squat/Deadlift/Bench Press/Strict Press). Instead, you work up to a "Top Set" for the programmed reps – we call this "Top Set Training."

Top Set training results in you only performing 1 set at the programmed intensity. However, the additional volume is gained while working up to the Top Set (you should perform multiple warm-up sets) – all rep ranges in this program are programmed at RPE 8-9, meaning it should be hard to very hard (go off how you feel on the day – it is fine to work at RPE 6-7 if it feels best).

Rep Progression: Squat/Deadlift/Bench Press/Strict Press

- **Week 1:** 12 Reps
- **Week 2:** 11 Reps
- **Week 3:** 10 Reps
- **Week 4:** 9 Reps
- **Week 5:** 8 Reps
- **Week 6:** 7 Reps
- **Week 7:** 6 Reps
- **Week 8:** 5 Reps
- **Week 9:** 4 Reps
- **Week 10:** 3 Reps
- **Week 11:** 2 Reps
- **Week 12:** 1 Rep (this can be performed as a 1RM test)

On the remaining exercises, you perform 3-4 sets of the programmed reps at RPE 8-9

Rep Progression: RFESS/Single-Leg Calf Raise/Lat Pulldown/Single-Arm Row

- **Week 1-3:** 12 Reps
- **Week 4-6:** 10 Reps
- **Week 7-9:** 8 Reps
- **Week 10-12:** 6 Reps

Note: I either load my Pull-Ups or perform 3-4 sets of max reps at bodyweight – I often do the same with bodyweight Single-Leg Calf Raises.

The Program: 2-Day Split V2

During Top Set training, I highly recommend you use fractional plates (0.5-2.5kg – I call them biscuits) as they will allow you to add just that little bit more each week, even if you are only dropping 1 rep off – aim to add a little more to the BB each week, even if it is just a couple of biscuits.

Session 1	Week + Reps												RPE	Rest
Exercise	1	2	3	4	5	6	7	8	9	10	11	12		
Squat	12	11	10	9	8	7	6	5	4	3	2	1	RPE 8-9	2-3 Mins
Strict Press	12	11	10	9	8	7	6	5	4	3	2	1	RPE 8-9	2-3 Mins
Pull-Up	3-4x Max Reps			3-4x Max Reps			3-4x Max Reps			3-4x Max Reps			RPE 8-9	1-2 Mins
Single-Leg Calf Raise	3-4x12 Each Side			3-4x10 Each Side			3-4x8 Each Side			3-4x6 Each Side			RPE 8-9	1 Min

Note: If performing Lat Pulldowns instead of Pull-Ups, follow the same rep scheme as the Single-Leg Calf Raise.

Session 2	Week + Reps												RPE	Rest
Exercise	1	2	3	4	5	6	7	8	9	10	11	12		
Deadlift	12	11	10	9	8	7	6	5	4	3	2	1	RPE 8-9	2-3 Mins
Bench Press	12	11	10	9	8	7	6	5	4	3	2	1	RPE 8-9	2-3 Mins
RFESS	3-4x12 Each Side			3-4x10 Each Side			3-4x8 Each Side			3-4x6 Each Side			RPE 8-9	1-2 Mins
Single-Arm Row	3-4x12 Each Side			3-4x10 Each Side			3-4x8 Each Side			3-4x6 Each Side			RPE 8-9	1 Min

Here's an example of a 1-Day Split: For those that can't fit in the 2-day split

Session 1	Week + Reps												RPE	Rest
Exercise	1	2	3	4	5	6	7	8	9	10	11	12		
Squat	12	11	10	9	8	7	6	5	4	3	2	1	RPE 8-9	2-3 Mins
Deadlift	12	11	10	9	8	7	6	5	4	3	2	1	RPE 8-9	2-3 Mins
Bench Press	12	11	10	9	8	7	6	5	4	3	2	1	RPE 8-9	2-3 Mins
Strict Press	12	11	10	9	8	7	6	5	4	3	2	1	RPE 8-9	2-3 Mins
Lat Pulldown	3x12 Each Side			3x10 Each Side			3x8 Each Side			3x6 Each Side			RPE 8-9	1-2 Mins
Single-Arm Row	3x12 Each Side			3x10 Each Side			3x8 Each Side			3x6 Each Side			RPE 8-9	1 Min
Single-Leg Calf Raise	3x12 Each Side			3x10 Each Side			3x8 Each Side			3x6 Each Side			RPE 8-9	1 Min

12-Week Labour Fitness Program

This Labour Fitness Program Undulates. For example, on week 1, if session 1 has longer rounds, session 2 will have shorter rounds. Then on the following week (week 2), this is reversed, with session 1 having shorter rounds and session 2 having longer rounds – shorter rounds allow for more intensity.

Short, timed rounds are 1-2 minutes in length and short rep rounds use 20-40 reps on Rep Labours. You then reduce the Distance Labours by 1 third, 2 thirds or 3 thirds to match the rep range (you can do that with it being a Dozenal system) for example, 40 reps is 1 third less than the race reps of 60. Therefore, you would take off 1 third from the distance of the Distance Labour being performed. For example, if it was the 240m Farmers Carry, you subtract 1 third from the distance (80m) and perform a 160m Farmers Carry. The Running Journeys on the short rep rounds are usually 100-400m.

Long, timed rounds are 3-6 minutes in length and long rep rounds use 40-120 reps (remember we usually group Deadly Dozen Labours together during long rounds for sets of 10-20 each). The Running Journeys on long rep rounds are 400-2000m (the crossover point is 40 reps and 400m – we do 400m runs a lot!)

For the most part, you should be maintaining an RPE of 6-8. However, you can ramp it up to 9-10 on specific stations or when you are feeling good.

To maximize the intensity that can be sustained during Labour Fitness, stations are usually organised in a way where back-to-back stations work varying muscle groups or go from a strength focussed activity to a cardio focussed activity.

Labour Fitness Sessions without Running Journeys are all performed for time, whereas ones with Running Journeys are performed for reps. Although you could program 1 lap of the programmed exercises or 3 laps, aka "3 Rounds for Time," etc; I prefer to program both timed and rep rounds for a set period of time to create AMRAPS (As Many Rounds As Possible): I aim for 45-60 minutes of constant work during the bulk of my Labour Fitness sessions with 15-20 second change over periods – timed stations always use 15-20 second change over periods.

I find people pace themselves better when they know they are working for a set period of time rather than just trying to get the workout done as quickly as possible. This being said, any race simulations or workouts where I aim to test or set benchmarks will be best effort with no time cutoff – I like to perform a full race simulation every 4-8 weeks. However, have been known to do different race sims weekly.

You want to include Labour Fitness sessions that are shorter than your race time (how long it takes you to complete the fitness race), around the same time, and longer. Although I program a variety of different times for the Labour Fitness sessions, I understand many people may only get an hour in the gym. Therefore, just stick to the Goldilocks time of 45 mins of continuous work.

I use the official race weights on all Deadly Dozen Labours (these can be progressed or regressed) – I note the male and female weight when I program a non-Deadly Dozen exercise.

KB Labours	DB Labours	WP Labours
Farmers Carry **M:** 2x 24kg / **F:** 2x 16kg	**Lunge** **M:** 2x 12.5kg / **F:** 2x 7.5kg	**Front Carry** **M:** 1x 25kg / **F:** 1x 20kg
Deadlift **M:** 1x 32kg / **F:** 1x 24kg	**Snatch** **M:** 1x 15kg / **F:** 1x 9kg	**Clean & Press** **M:** 1x 15kg / **F:** 1x 10kg
Goblet Squat **M:** 1x 16kg / **F:** 1x 12kg	**Push Press** **M:** 2x 12.5kg / **F:** 2x 6kg	**Overhead Carry** **M:** 1x 15kg / **F:** 1x 10kg
	Devil Press **M:** 2x 10kg / **F:** 2x 5kg	

Warning: If you haven't trained Labour Fitness before, the first session is probably going to give you some DOMS: We DON'T want to chase DOMS, but there is nothing wrong with DOMS early in the program – we shouldn't be getting sore often during the later stages of the program.

Remember, if you are getting DOMS, it is a sign that there is a lack of frequency of the specific stressor that caused the DOMS – do things often and you don't get DOMS!

Note: Many of the Labour Fitness sessions include using a rower, skier, bike and equipment like sleds. If you don't have access to this equipment, just take them out and add in Labours that suit you.

Week 1	
Session 1 (No Runs)	**Session 2 (+ Runs)**
1 Min Rounds: Keep Going for 30 Mins **KB Deadlift** **DB Snatch** **Burpee Broad Jump** **KB Goblet Squat** **DB Push Press** **Bear Crawl** **DB Lunge** **WP Clean & Press** **KB Farmers Carry** **DB Devil Press**	**400m + 40 Reps: Keep Going for 30 Mins** **400m Run** **Plate Clean & Press** **400m Run** **KB Goblet Squat** **400m Run** **40m Burpee Broad Jump** **400m Run** **DB Push Press** **400m Run** **40m DB Lunge**

Week 2	
Session 1 (No Runs)	**Session 2 (+ Runs)**
3 Min Rounds: Keep Going for 45 Mins **10x KB Goblet Squat + 10x Push-Up** **Row** **Sled Push: M: 150kg / F: 100kg** **10x DB Push Press + 10x KB Deadlift** **Ski** **5x DB Devil Press + 10x WP Clean & Press** **Bike** **Wallball: M: 6kg / F: 4kg**	**300m + 30 Reps (50% of Race Reps): Keep Going for 45 Mins** **300m Run** **KB Deadlift** **300m Run** **DB Snatch** **300m Run** **KB Goblet Squat** **300m Run** **DB Push Press** **300m Run** **WP Clean & Press** **300m Run** **10x DB Devil Press**

Week 3	
Session 1 (No Runs)	**Session 2 (+ Runs)**
90 Sec Rounds: Keep Going for 45 Mins **Bike** **WP Overhead Carry** Ski **Bear Crawl** Row **WP Front Carry** Sled Pull: M: 100kg / F: 75kg **Burpee Broad Jump** Wallball **KB Farmers Carry** Sled Push: M: 150kg / F: 100kg **Bag Work**	**600m + 60 Reps (Split Between 2): Keep Going for 45 Mins** 600m Run **30x KB Deadlift + 30x Snatch** 600m Run **30x Goblet Squat + 30x Push Press** 600m Run **30x Plate Clean & Press + 10x Devil Press**

Week 4	
Session 1 (No Runs)	**Session 2 (+ Runs)**
4 Min Rounds: Keep Going for 45-60 Mins Ski **20x KB Deadlift + 20x WP Clean & Press + 20x DB Push press** Row **20x DB Snatch + 20x KB Goblet Squat + 5x DB Devil Press** Bike **60m Farmers Carry + 60m Front Carry + 60m Overhead Carry**	**200m + 50% of Distance Labours: Keep Going for 45 Mins** 200m Run **120m KB Farmers Carry** 200m Run **30m DB Lunge** 200m Run **30m Burpee Broad Jump** 200m Run **120m WP Front Carry** 200m Run **60m Bear Crawl** 200m Run **90m WP Overhead Carry**

"People who are excited by posthumous fame forget that the people who remember them will soon die too." – **Marcus Aurelius**

Week 5	
Session 1 (No Runs)	**Session 2 (+ Runs)**
2 Min Rounds: Keep Going for 45-60Mins DB Devil Press **Row** Sled Push: M: 150kg / F: 100kg Sled Pull: M: 100kg / F: 75kg WP Clean & Press **KB Goblet Squat** Ski **KB Deadlift** DB Push Press **Bike** KB Farmers Carry **Wallball**	**800m + 80 Reps (Split Between 2) / Full Distance Labours: Keep Going for 45-60 Mins** 800m Run **60m DB Lunge** 800m Run **40 DB Snatch + 40 KB Goblet Squat** 800m Run **120m Bear Crawl** 800m Run **40 DB Push Press + 40 KB Deadlift** 800m Run **60m Burpee Broad Jump**

Week 6	
Session 1 (No Runs)	**Session 2 (+ Runs)**
5 Min Rounds: Keep Going for 60-90 Mins Row **Sled Push: M: 120kg / F: 80kg** Bike **10x KB Deadlift + 10x DB Snatch + 10x KB Goblet Squat + 10x DB Push Press** Ski **Sled Pull: M: 75kg / F: 50kg**	**100m + 20 Reps / 1 Third of Distance Labours: Keep Going for 45 Mins** 100m Run **80m KB Farmers Carry** 100m Run **KB Deadlift** 100m Run **20m DB Lunge** 100m Run **DB Snatch** 100m Run **20m Burpee Broad Jump** 100m Run **KB Goblet Squat** 100m Run **80m WP Front Carry** 100m Run **DB Push Press** 100m Run **40m Bear Crawl** 100m Run **WP Clean & Press** 100m Run **60m WP Overhead Carry** 100m Run **10x DB Devil Press**

Week 7	
Session 1 (No Runs)	**Session 2 (+ Runs)**
2 Min Rounds: Keep Going for 45-60Mins DB Devil Press **KB Deadlift** WP Overhead Carry **KB Goblet Squat** DB Snatch **DB Lunge** Burpee Broad Jump **Bear Crawl**	**1000m + 100 Reps (Split Between 4) / Full Distance Labours: Keep Going for 60-90 Mins** 1000m Run **25x KB Deadlift + 25x DB Push Press + 25x KB Goblet Squat + 25x WP Clean & Press** 1000m Run **1000m Row** 1000m Run **60m Burpee Broad Jump + 240m KB Farmers Carry** 1000m Run **1000m Ski** 180m WP Overhead Carry + 240m WP Front Carry

Week 8	
Session 1 (No Runs)	**Session 2 (+ Runs)**
4 Min Rounds: Keep Going for 45-60Mins Sled Push: M: 150kg / F: 100kg **10x Burpee / 10x Wall Ball (6kg/4kg)** 10x Push Up + 20x DB Reverse Lunge (Alternate: 10 Each Side) **Sled Pull: M: 100kg / F: 75kg** 120m Farmers Carry + 60m Bear Crawl	**Full Deadly Dozen Simulation: 400m Run to Start and Between each Labour** 240m KB Farmers Carry **60x KB Deadlift** 60m DB Lunge **60x DB Snatch** 60m Burpee Broad Jump **60x KB Goblet Squat** 240m WP Front Carry **60x DB Push Press** 120m Bear Crawl **60x WP Clean & Press** 180m WP Overhead Carry **20x DB Devil Press** **1x Full Run Through: Best Effort – record you time**

"We are more often frightened than hurt; and we suffer more from imagination than from reality." – **Seneca**

Week 9	
Session 1 (No Runs)	**Session 2 (+ Runs)**
2 Min Rounds: Keep Going for 45-60Mins WP Overhead Carry **WP Clean & Press** Bear Crawl **DB Push Press** Plate Front Carry **KB Goblet Squat** Burpee Broad Jump **DB Snatch** DB Lunge **KB Deadlift**	**1200m + 120 Reps (Split Between 3) / Full Distance Labours: Keep Going for 60-90 Mins** 1200m Run **1200m Row** 40x DB Snatch + 40x KB Goblet Squat + 40x Push Press **240m WP Front Carry** 1200m Run **1200m Ski** 40x KB Deadlift + 40 DB Reverse Lunge (Alternate: 20 Each Side) + 40 WP Clean & Press **180m WP Overhead Carry** 2400m Bike

Week 10	
Session 1 (No Runs)	**Session 2 (+ Runs)**
6 Min Rounds: Keep Going for 60-90Mins 10x KB Goblet Squat + 10x Push-Up + KB Deadlift + 10x Burpee **Bike** 80m Farmers Carry + 80m WP Front Carry + 60m WP Overhead Carry **Row** 10x DB Devil Press + 10x WP Clean & Press + 10x DB Snatch + 10x DB Push Press **Ski**	**200m + 30 Reps / 1 Third of Distance Labours: Keep Going for 45-60 Mins** 200m Run **40m Bear Crawl** 200m Run **DB Push Press** 200m Run **20m DB Lunge** 200m Run **WP Clean & Press** 200m Run **20m Burpee Broad Jump** 200m Run **DB Snatch** 200m Run **80m Farmers Carry** 200m Run **KB Goblet Squat**

"For every challenge, remember the resources you have within you to cope with it." – **Epictetus**

Week 11	
Session 1 (No Runs)	**Session 2 (+ Runs)**
2 Min Rounds: Keep Going for 45-60Mins Ski **KB Goblet Squat** WP Clean & Press **Bike** Wall Ball: M: 6kg / F: 4kg **DB Devil Press** Row **Sled Push: M: 150kg / F: 100kg** Burpee Broad Jump **DB Lunge**	**1600m + 60 Reps: Keep Going for 60 Mins** 1600m Run **1600m Ski** WP Clean & Press **1600m Run** 1600m Row **DB Snatch**

Week 12	
Session 1 (No Runs)	**Session 2 (+ Runs)**
90 Sec Rounds: Keep Going for 45Mins Ski **KB Goblet Squat** WP Clean & Press **Bike** Wall Ball: M: 6kg / F: 4kg **DB Devil Press** Row **Sled Push: M: 150kg / F: 100kg** Burpee Broad Jump **DB Lunge**	**400m + 40 Reps (Split Between 2): Keep Going for 45 Mins** 400m Run **20x KB Goblet Squat + 20x Push-Up** 400m Row **20x KB Deadlift + 20x DB Push Press** 400m Run **20x DB Snatch + 20x Plater Clean & Press** 400m Ski **10x Devil Press**

If you like our Labour Fitness workouts, check out our Daily Dozen Workouts on Instagram:

12-Week Journey Fitness Program

This Journey program includes 2 distinct sessions: 1x Steady State or Tempo session and 1x Interval session.

The Steady State/Tempo program follows the FAIRR periodization model, where an initial familiarization phase is carried out with easy runs; it then progresses into developing high volume work before upping the intensity during the Intensification and Realization phases (long duration steady state work is undulated weekly with higher intensity tempo work at the later stages of the program).

Steady state (slow continuous pace) and tempo (faster continuous pace) runs are programmed for time rather than distance.

The Interval sessions, after an initial Familiarization phase, start with an initial speed block with shorter duration intervals. The interval durations are then increased in the middle block to develop speed endurance. Then, in the final block, the interval duration is gradually brought back down to peak for the competition, or just finalize the first Macrocycle (finish with testing, etc).

Steady State (Zone 2 / RPE 3) / Tempo Program (Pushing the Pace in Zone 3-4 / RPE 4-8):

Note: The longer the run is held at Zone 3-4, the higher the RPE will be. For example, running for 1-hour at zone 4 is going to be an RPE 9-10.

Week	Explanation
1	20 Minute Steady State (Zone 2 / RPE 3)
2	30 Minute Steady State (Zone 2 / RPE 3)
3	45 Minute Steady State (Zone 2 / RPE 3)
4	60 Minute Steady State (Zone 2 / RPE 3)
5	75 Minute Steady State (Zone 2 / RPE 3)
6	90 Minute Steady State (Zone 2 / RPE 3)
7	30 Minute Tempo (Zone 3 / RPE 5)
8	30 Minute Tempo (Zone 3 / RPE 6)
9	90 Minute Steady State (Zone 2 / RPE 3)
10	20 Minute Tempo (Zone 4 / RPE 7)
11	60 Minute Steady State (Zone 2 / RPE 3)
12	20 Minute Tempo (Zone 4 / RPE 8)

As stated previously, you can swap out running for rowing, skiing, cycling or even swimming. However, one of my favourite way to perform long duration work is to jump between rowing, skiing, and cycling (all on Concept2 machines in my gym). I call this the Concept2 Triathlon (Ski, Row, Bike) and I have 3 variations that my gym members compete in: (I also just work through 12 mins on each for 36-72 mins).

- **Full Triathlon:** 5km Ski – 10km Row – 20km Bike
- **Sprint Triathlon:** 2km Ski – 4km Row – 8km Bike
- **Sprinty Sprint Triathlon:** 1km Ski – 2km Row – 4km Bike (sorry about the name)

Interval Sessions:

This program starts with a 2-week familiarization phase where a mix of distances are worked at submaximal intensities. From there, the program progresses into a 3-week speed block, followed by a 4-week block where speed endurance is developed, then it finishes with a final 3-week speed block – I call this "Pyramid Periodization."

Note: I always use the RPE Scale for interval work that involves short sprints. The RPE Scale is a better option than working with your heart rate because there is always going to be a lag when it comes to your heart rate rising to where it needs to be to fuel the activity; hence why you shouldn't start off too quickly on longer duration work as you could create an oxygen debt you can't recover from.

After a proper warm-up (we look at warm-ups in depth from page-143), intervals will be programmed at RPEs of 10 (Maximal), 9 (Very Hard) and 8 (Hard) – 7 is a low hard.

Familiarization Phase:

Week 1: Sets / Distance	Intensity	Rest
4x 60m	RPE 8	2 Mins
Rest for 3 Mins		
2x 100m	RPE 8	2 Mins
Rest for 3 Mins		
1x 200m	RPE 8	N/A
Rest for 3 Mins		
1x 400m	RPE 7	N/A
Total Distance: 1040m		

Week 2: Sets / Distance	Intensity	Rest
3x 60m	RPE 8	2 Mins
Rest for 3 Mins		
3x 100m	RPE 8	2 Mins
Rest for 3 Mins		
2x 200m	RPE 8	2 Mins
Rest for 3 Mins		
1x 400m	RPE 8	N/A
Rest for 3 Mins		
1x 800m	RPE 7	N/A
Total Distance: 2080m		

Speed Block 1:

Week 3: Sets / Distance	Intensity	Rest
5x 60m	RPE 10	2 Mins
Rest for 3 Mins		
3x 100m	RPE 10	2 Mins
Rest for 3 Mins		
2x 300m	RPE 9	3 Mins
Rest for 3 Mins		
1x 400m	RPE 8	3 Mins
Total Distance: 1600m		

Week 4: Sets / Distance	Intensity	Rest
8x 60m	RPE 10	1 Min
Rest for 3 Mins		
8x 100m	RPE 10	2 Min
Rest for 3 Mins		
1x 200m	RPE 10	N/A
Rest for 3 Mins		
1x 300m	RPE 9	3 Mins
Rest for 3 Mins		
1x 400m	RPE 8	N/A
Total Distance: 2180m		

Week 5: Sets / Distance	Intensity	Rest
12x 60m	RPE 10	1 Min
Rest for 3 Mins		
12x 100m	RPE 10	1 Min
Rest for 3 Mins		
1x 200m	RPE 9	3 Mins
Rest for 3 Mins		
1x 400m	RPE 8	3 Mins
Total Distance: 2520m		

Speed Endurance Block:

Week 6: Sets / Distance	Intensity	Rest
6x 400m	RPE 10	2 Mins
Rest for 3 Mins		
2x 600m	RPE 9	3 Mins
Rest for 3 Mins		
1x 800m	RPE 8	N/A
Total Distance: 4400m		

Week 7: Sets / Distance	Intensity	Rest
6x 400m	RPE 10	2 Mins
Rest for 3 Mins		
4x 800m	RPE 9	3 Mins
Total Distance: 5600m		

Week 8: Sets / Distance	Intensity	Rest
6x 800m	RPE 10	3 Mins
Rest for 4 Mins		
2x 1200m	RPE 9	3 Mins
Total Distance: 7200m		

Week 9: Sets / Distance	Intensity	Rest
6x 800m	RPE 10	3 Mins
Rest for 4 Mins		
2x 1600m	RPE 9	4 Mins
Total Distance: 8000m		

"If a person gave away your body to some passerby, you'd be furious. Yet you hand over your mind to anyone who comes along." – **Epictetus**

Speed Block 2:

Week 10: Sets / Distance	Intensity	Rest
12x 400m	RPE 10	2 Mins
Total Distance: 4800m		

Week 11: Sets / Distance	Intensity	Rest
3x 100m	RPE 10	2 Mins
Rest for 3 Mins		
3x 200m	RPE 10	2 Mins
Rest for 3 Mins		
3x 300m	RPE 10	3 Mins
Rest for 3 Mins		
3x 400m	RPE 10	3 Mins
Total Distance: 3000m		

Week 12: Sets / Distance	Intensity	Rest
5x 60m	RPE 10	2 Mins
Rest for 3 Mins		
4x 100m	RPE 10	2 Mins
Rest for 3 Mins		
3x 200m	RPE 10	3 Mins
Rest for 3 Mins		
2x 300m	RPE 10	N/A
Rest for 3 Mins		
1x 400m	RPE 10	N/A
Total Distance: 2300m		

"Think of yourself as dead, you have lived your life. Now take what is left and live properly." – **Marcus Aurelius**

Beginner Program: Building Up to Full Triad

The 12-Week Deadly Dozen Triad Program is no easy feat. Therefore, I have developed a 6-week beginner program that is designed to build you up to the full 12-week plan.

The focus of the program is developing good movement technique, building muscular strength and endurance, and establishing a good aerobic base with progressive running.

The Training Split: Split the training sessions across the week in a way that suits you best

- **Week 1 & 2:** 2x Strength Training / 1x Journey Fitness (Run) / 1x Labour Fitness

- **Week 3 & 4:** 2x Strength Training / 2x Journey Fitness (Run) / 1x Labour Fitness

- **Week 5 & 6:** 2x Strength Training / 2x Journey Fitness (Run) / 2x Labour Fitness

The program uses the same training split as the full Triad program. However, during the first 4 weeks, many of the lifts are regressed slightly and the BB movements use DBs/KBs. The BB is then introduced during weeks 5 and 6 – all 6 weeks include 2x Strength Training sessions.

Weeks 1 and 2 include 1x Steady State Run and 1x Labour Fitness session that does NOT include runs.

Weeks 3 and 4 include 1x Steady State Run, 1x Interval session and 1x Labour Fitness session that does NOT include runs.

Weeks 5 and 6 include 1x Steady State Run, 1x Interval session and 2x Labour Fitness sessions, one without runs and one with runs.

Check out the Paperback Program below: Log your progress

Paperback on Amazon: https://mybook.to/ddbeginner

PDF Download: https://courses.strengthandconditioningcourse.com/p/ddbeginner

Strength Training Beginner Program

Session 1	Week + Reps				Rest
Exercise	**1**	**2**	**3**	**4**	
KB Goblet Squat	4x8: RPE 6	4x10: RPE 7	4x12: RPE 8	4x10: RPE 8	1-2 Mins
Standing DB Press	4x8: RPE 6	4x10: RPE 7	4x12: RPE 8	4x10: RPE 8	1-2 Mins
Band Pull-Up or Lat Pulldown	3-4x8: RPE 6	3-4x10: RPE 7	3-4x12: RPE 8	3-4x10: RPE 8	1 Min
Single-Leg Calf Raise	3x8: RPE 6 Each Side	3x10: RPE 7 Each Side	3x12: RPE 8 Each Side	3x10: RPE 8 Each Side	1 Min

Session 2	Week + Reps				Rest
Exercise	**1**	**2**	**3**	**4**	
KB Deadlift	4x8: RPE 6	4x10: RPE 7	4x12: RPE 8	4x10: RPE 8	1-2 Mins
Flat DB Press	4x8: RPE 6	4x10: RPE 7	4x12: RPE 8	4x10: RPE 8	1-2 Mins
DB Split Squat	3x8: RPE 6 Each Side	3x10: RPE 7 Each Side	3x12: RPE 8 Each Side	3x10: RPE 8 Each Side	1 Min
DB Single-Arm Row	3x8: RPE 6 Each Side	3x10: RPE 7 Each Side	3x12: RPE 8 Each Side	3x8: RPE 8 Each Side	1 Min

Session 1	Week + Reps		Rest
Exercise	**5**	**6**	
BB Back Squat	4x8: RPE 6	4x10: RPE 7	1-2 Mins
BB Strict Press	4x8: RPE 6	4x10: RPE 7	1-2 Mins
Pull-Up (Band)	3-4x Max Reps: RPE 10	3-4x Max Reps: RPE 10	1 Min
DB Single-Leg Calf Raise	3x8: RPE 7 Each Side	3x10: RPE 7 Each Side	1 Min

Session 2	Week + Reps		Rest
Exercise	**5**	**6**	
BB Deadlift	4x8: RPE 6	4x10: RPE 7	1-2 Mins
BB Bench Press	4x8: RPE 6	4x10: RPE 7	1-2 Mins
DB RFESS	3x8: RPE 7 Each Side	3x10: RPE 7 Each Side	1 Min
DB Single-Arm Row	3x8: RPE 7 Each Side	3x10: RPE 7 Each Side	1 Min

Labour Fitness Beginner Program

I use the official race weights on all Deadly Dozen Labours: The 2nd table shows regressed weights.

KB Labours	DB Labours	WP Labours
Farmers Carry **M:** 2x 24kg / **F:** 2x 16kg	**Lunge** **M:** 2x 12.5kg / **F:** 2x 7.5kg	**Front Carry** **M:** 1x 25kg / **F:** 1x 20kg
Deadlift **M:** 1x 32kg / **F:** 1x 24kg	**Snatch** **M:** 1x 15kg / **F:** 1x 9kg	**Clean & Press** **M:** 1x 15kg / **F:** 1x 10kg
Goblet Squat **M:** 1x 16kg / **F:** 1x 12kg	**Push Press** **M:** 2x 12.5kg / **F:** 2x 6kg	**Overhead Carry** **M:** 1x 15kg / **F:** 1x 10kg
	Devil Press **M:** 2x 10kg / **F:** 2x 5kg	

KB Labours	DB Labours	WP Labours
Farmers Carry **M:** 2x 20kg / **F:** 2x 12kg	**Lunge** **M:** 2x 8kg / **F:** 2x 5kg	**Front Carry** **M:** 1x 20kg / **F:** 1x 15kg
Deadlift **M:** 1x 28kg / **F:** 1x 20kg	**Snatch** **M:** 1x 10kg / **F:** 1x 6kg	**Clean & Press** **M:** 1x 10kg / **F:** 1x 5kg
Goblet Squat **M:** 1x 12kg / **F:** 1x 8kg	**Push Press** **M:** 2x 8kg / **F:** 2x 4kg	**Overhead Carry** **M:** 1x 10kg / **F:** 1x 5kg
	Devil Press **M:** 2x 6kg / **F:** 2x 3kg	

On all Labour Fitness circuits, take 15-20 second transition times (moving from 1 station to the next).

Week 1	Week 2
1 Min Rounds: Keep Going for 20 Mins with a 2 Min Break Every 10 Mins KB Farmers Carry **DB Devil Press** KB Deadlift **WP Overhead Carry** DB Lunge **WP Clean & Press**	**1 Min Rounds: Keep Going for 30 Mins with a 2 Min Break After 15 Mins** DB Snatch **Bear Crawl** Burpee Broad Jump **DB Push Press** KB Goblet Squat **WP Front Carry**

"Let philosophy scrape off your own faults, rather than be a way to rail against the faults of others." – **Seneca**

Week 3	Week 4
90 Sec Rounds: Keep Going for 30 Mins (No Break)	**90 Sec Rounds: Keep Going for 30 Mins (No Break)**
DB Push Press	WP Front Carry
DB Lunge	**KB Deadlift**
Burpee Broad Jump	DB Devil Press
DB Snatch	**WP Overhead Carry**
KB Goblet Squat	DB Push Press
Bear Crawl	**Burpee Broad Jump**
WP Clean & Press	KB Goblet Squat
KB Farmers Carry	**DB Snatch**

Week 5	
Session 1	**Session 2**
2 Min Rounds: Keep Going for 35 Mins	**200m + 20 Reps: Keep Going for 30 Mins**
WP Overhead Carry	200m Run
WP Clean & Press	**DB Push Press**
Bear Crawl	200m Run
DB Push Press	**KB Deadlift**
WP Front Carry	200m Run
KB Goblet Squat	**DB Snatch**
Burpee Broad Jump	200m Run
DB Snatch	**KB Goblet Squat**
DB Lunge	200m Run
KB Deadlift	**DB Push Press**

Week 6	
Session 1	**Session 2**
2 Min Rounds: 40 Mins	**400m + 50% of Distance Labours: 35 Mins**
KB Farmers Carry	400m Run
KB Deadlift	**120m KB Farmers Carry**
DB Lunge	400m Run
DB Snatch	**30m DB Lunge**
Burpee Broad Jump	400m Run
KB Goblet Squat	**30m Burpee Broad Jump**
WP Front Carry	400m Run
DB Push Press	**120m WP Front Carry**
Bear Crawl	400m Run
WP Clean & Press	**60m Bear Crawl**
Plate Overhead Carry	400m Run
DB Devil Press	**90m WP Overhead Carry**

Journey Fitness Beginner Program

Steady State Progression:

Week	Explanation
1	15 Minute Steady State (Zone 2 / RPE 3)
2	20 Minute Steady State (Zone 2 / RPE 3)
3	25 Minute Steady State (Zone 2 / RPE 3)
4	30 Minute Steady State (Zone 2 / RPE 3)
5	20 Minute Tempo (Zone 3 / RPE 5-6)
6	15 Minute Tempo (Zone 4 / RPE 7)

Interval Sessions: Week 5 and 6

Week 5: Sets / Distance	Intensity	Rest
2x 60m	RPE 8	2 Mins
Rest for 3 Mins		
1x 100m	RPE 8	2 Mins
Rest for 3 Mins		
1x 200m	RPE 8	N/A
Rest for 3 Mins		
1x 400m	RPE 7	N/A
Total Distance: 820m		

Week 6: Sets / Distance	Intensity	Rest
3x 60m	RPE 10	2 Mins
Rest for 3 Mins		
2x 100m	RPE 9	2 Mins
Rest for 3 Mins		
1x 200m	RPE 8	N/A
Rest for 3 Mins		
1x 400m	RPE 7	N/A
Total Distance: 980m		

Warming Up

A warm-up prepares you for the activity at hand, both physically and psychologically. It gets you ready to perform at your best and reduces your risk of injury – a warm-up usually lasts between 10-20 minutes.

Warm-ups can simply involve a few practice movements at moderate intensity before performing the main activity. However, in this section, we want to delve deeper into how we can optimize the warm-up protocol to minimize our risk of injury and maximize our performance in the subsequent session. We also want the warm-up to act as an important part of the session where various physical attributes can be developed long-term.

Let's face it, as we get older and as athletes push their bodies harder, there's an ever-growing need for a longer warm-up. A huge amount of an athlete's time is going to be spent warming up (athletes can spend an hour a week warming up), especially when they have a history of or are carrying various niggles and injuries. Therefore, the time spent warming up should be used as effectively as we can. It's not just about raising your heart rate and getting your muscles warm; it's about producing an aspect of the session that is developmental for the athlete (both movement and skill development).

By far, the most widely used warm-up protocol used by elite coaches is the RAMP warm-up developed by Ian Jeffreys, a world-class Strength and Conditioning coach from the UK – I highly recommend you purchase a copy of his book "The Warm-Up."

- **R**aise – heart rate and body temperature.

- **A**ctivate – key muscle groups.

- **M**obilize – key joints.

- **P**otentiate – prime the body for maximal intensity.

Although the RAMP warm-up is split into four clear categories (or three when you group activate and mobilize together), the warm-up should flow smoothly into the main session, with each aspect building on the next without a loss of previous benefits.

Outdoor Warm-Ups:

When it comes to outdoor, field-based (aka pitch-based) warm-ups, I often use a simple protocol I refer to as **RDP**:

- **Running Drills:** All sports that involve running will benefit from a high frequency of running drills (A-Skips and B-Skips, etc)

- **DROMEs: D**ynamic **R**ange **o**f **M**otion **E**xercises (just like dynamic stretches, but with more emphasis on working the muscles) – squats, lunges, inchworms, etc

- **Potentiation:** Sprinting and plyometric (jump) drills (sprinting is the fastest form of plyometrics)

Note: Dynamic stretches involve moving through the range of motion, e.g., leg swings. Whereas Static Stretches involve holding the stretch in place.

Indoor Warm-Ups:

When it comes to gym-based warm-ups, the running drills phase often turns into a simple raise phase, where the athlete spends 3-5 minutes warming up on a cardio machine (bike, rower, etc). However, DROMEs can also be effectively used to elicit all the raise phase benefits.

DP protocol:

- **DROMEs:** Greater volume of movement to elicit raise phase benefits.

- **Potentiation:** Gradually increasing the weight or using Plyometric and ballistic training (loaded jumps and throws).

If available, resistance bands are a great tool for "activating" (increase the intensity of muscle contractions) and potentiating key muscles and movements. Therefore, I have dedicated an entire chapter of this book to band exercises – I often add a "B" for (Bands) before the "P" of the above warm-ups (RDBP / DBP).

Running Drills

The initial stage of the warm-up (the "Raise" phase in the RAMP protocol) is designed to increase your heart rate, blood flow, and respiration rate. It should also increase core and muscle temperature, joint viscosity (reduces friction within the joint), and muscle elasticity. You want to feel your aerobic system working without inducing too much fatigue – having a slight sweat on is a good indicator that you are warm.

The warm-up should start at a low intensity and build up to a moderate intensity, usually around 60% of an athlete's VO2 max (maximum oxygen uptake). However, since we also want to prime an athlete's muscles and energy systems, we often peak the warm-up with short bouts of high-intensity work. For example, before a middle-distance run (5-10km), an athlete may perform 1-3 sets of 100m strides, where they work up to 80-90% of max speed/intensity for 10-20m (this is classed as potentiation), which will both physically and mentally prepare the athlete for the race. This being said, you only want to stimulate the body with short bouts of high intensity work as you don't want to fatigue the body.

The benefits we want from a warm-up can also be achieved using generic methods such as jogging, skipping, and using a variety of cardio machines (treadmills, bikes, rowers, etc.) However, the key to any good warm-up is to make it specific to the athlete, the planned session, and their sport. Not only should a warm-up increase in physical intensity but also in the level of skill and concentration required – an athlete's warm-up should consist of sports-specific movements and skills.

Suppose you are going into a running-based session. In that case, basic jogging and side shuffling drills are specific, just like skipping would be specific if going into a plyometrics session (jumping). There is nothing wrong with more generic methods of raising an athlete's heart rate and body temperature. However, be creative and formulate a raise phase specific to the athlete's sporting movements and the session at hand.

During the RDP warm-up, the emphasis is on running drills during the raise phase. This is because the raise phase is an ideal time to work on running drills before targeting more specific activities during the later phases. Of course, running drills might not be specific to every session. Therefore, a variety of raise techniques should be used as per the RAMP protocol.

Basic speed and agility drills performed at a moderate intensity are also ideal, with lots of emphasis placed on acceleration, deceleration, and change of direction (COD). Multidirectional speed is essential in many sports: We define Multidirectional Speed (MDS) as the ability to accelerate, decelerate, change direction, and maintain speed in multiple directions and movements.

We can also add more sports-specific skill development for team sports, such as throwing and catching or reacting to various stimuli, i.e., the ball drop drill. Reactive drills help to raise an athlete's alertness and are also great fun. Never underestimate the importance of fun in training sessions – enjoyment leads to better adherence and long-term consistency.

Before a gym-based strength session, especially when lifting maximally or performing a 1 rep max test (the most someone can lift for 1 repetition of a movement), the raise phase is usually kept short and straightforward to limit fatigue. It should emphasize psychological preparation, for example, listening to motivational music. Therefore, the raise phase might be seen as a simple pulse raiser to get the juices flowing. However, it is optimal to choose a pulse raiser that works and directs blood flow to specific muscle groups involved in the session, for example, using the Ski ERG before a session on the bench press because it works the shoulders and latissimus dorsi (yes, the lats are important for bench pressing).

On the other hand, an example pulse raiser for the squat could be using a bike, pushing a prowler, or merely performing some box step-ups to direct blood flow and warm the legs up.

Top 12 Running Drills

You can find videos to all of these drills on my personal YouTube: **@CoachJCurtis**

(Use the "@" symbol to ensure you find my handle)

DROMES: Dynamic Range of Motion Exercises

It's vital to understand the difference between flexibility and mobility. Flexibility is the muscle's ability to lengthen, so a test for this would be lying flat on your back while a partner lifts your leg to test hamstring flexibility (passive stretch).

On the other hand, mobility refers to a joint's ability to move through its full range of motion (ROM). Therefore, not only does it involve muscle flexibility but also joint structure, motor control, and stability – mobility involves muscle activity.

Traditionally, warm-ups included static stretches where various positions were held for 10-30 seconds. However, it has been argued (some studies back it up while others show no effect) that static stretching can reduce a muscle's contractile ability. Therefore, static stretches are usually carried out post-session during the cooldown or during separate flexibility sessions, where stretches may be held for 1-2 minutes to help develop flexibility.

On top of this, static stretches are, by nature, static. Therefore, they are not particularly progressive to the warm-up and can take up too much time – an athlete might cool down and get bored.

When it comes to mobility during a warm-up, we usually use dynamic stretches that involve actively moving through a joint's full range of motion in a controlled, fluid manner. These stretches can be as simple as swinging your arms or legs back and forth in any direction. Essentially, if a joint can move through a specific range of motion, you can work through that motion with some momentum to turn it into a dynamic stretch that targets the surrounding soft tissues.

Note: As the warm-up progresses, these dynamic stretches can be sped up to become ballistic stretches where a little more force is added to create an almost bouncing/springy stretch. When generating more momentum into the stretch, caution should be practiced to prevent injury. However, too much fear has been created around "bouncy" and "springy" actions when, ultimately, these are the types of forces that should be put on an athlete's body and help them to improve their speed and power.

I use the term **DROMEs** instead of dynamic stretches because it better describes these movements when there is just as much focus on activating/working muscles as there is on mobilizing the joints. The most effective DROMEs are movement complexes or flows (a series of movements performed in a fluid motion), where multiple bodyweight exercises and dynamic stretches are combined.

This section shows my top 12 DROMEs that can be effectively incorporated into a warm-up. But be creative and try to develop drills specific to the subsequent session and progressive to the athlete's long-term development. This is a great opportunity to develop balance and motor control (motor control refers to how the body uses multimodal sensory information to control movement).

Top 12 DROMEs

You can find videos to all of these drills on my personal YouTube: **@CoachJCurtis**

(Use the "@" symbol to ensure you find my handle)

Band Activation

The activation phase of a warm-up consists of exercises that are designed to activate (get the muscles contracting harder) key muscles that will be used during the session.

Note: The term "muscle inhibition" is often overused. Yes, things like nerve impingement can cause muscle inhibition (it doesn't contract). However, for the most part, people are just experiencing a lack of mind-muscle connection (struggle to feel the muscle working, or they want it to engage more). Therefore, when I say, "muscle activation," it refers to getting a muscle all fired up and ready to go (warmed up).

Resistance bands are an incredible tool for getting muscles warmed up, and progressively increasing the intensity of band exercises is a great way to potentiate the body. They are also useful when athletes are away from training facilities/equipment for extended periods.

I highly recommend buying a long resistance band set (yellow, red, black, purple, green) and a pack of small loop bands – all these are available on Amazon (colours will vary from different retailers).

Pump & Power

I categorize band activation into two categories:

- **Pump:** Higher rep ranges at lower intensities (8-20 reps) to get more blood flow to the muscle. This is often good to allow someone to really connect to the muscle (mind-muscle connection). However, during a warm-up, we obviously don't want excessive fatigue

- **Power:** Lower rep ranges performed at high intensities (1-6 reps) with far more speed and power. The aim here is to get the neuromuscular system firing. This is ideal band activation and potentiation to prime the muscles with minimal metabolic stress (fatigue)

Both forms are beneficial. It is a case of working out the needs of the individual.

Note: I generally stick to 1-3 sets on all exercises during warm-ups.

Top 12 Band Drills

You can find videos to all of these drills on my personal YouTube: **@CoachJCurtis**

(Use the "@" symbol to ensure you find my handle)

Pull Apart	Face Pull	Fly
Biceps Curl	Triceps Extension	Lateral Walk
Glute Bridge	Adduction	Good Morning
Psoas March	Spanish Squat	TKE

Potentiation

Potentiation is the progressive priming of the body for maximal intensity. Every muscle contraction is influenced by its previous activity, and there has been a lot of research done on Post-Activation Potentiation (PAP), where subsequent performance is improved after working at maximal intensity.

Of course, there will be physical, physiological (increased strength in nerve pathways), and psychological factors when it comes to potentiation. However, most of us have experienced weights feeling abnormally light after working with heavier loads.

Regardless of where the benefits are coming from, potentiation is the essential final phase of a warm-up that transitions the athlete into the session. This phase can also be repeated when progressing to different activities and exercises.

Just as with the previous stages of the warm-up, we want this phase to be specific to the session and include both the development of movement and skill and the athlete's final mental preparation.

The final prep for many field-based athletes may be increasing the intensity and complexity of the speed and agility drills they are performing (including jumping, kicking, throwing, and catching). A sprinter will gradually work up to a maximal sprint, while Powerlifters will progressively load the BB, adding another 10-20% of their 1RM to the BB each set. A Deadly Dozen athlete will perform running drills and jumps to potentiate themselves for the first 400m run. The key to specificity is often simplicity, i.e., the progressive loading of the activity we are looking to do. However, we can also be less direct and add exercises that maximize explosiveness in the plane or direction of the activity that is to follow. For example, a vertical jump prior to performing heavy back squats.

Most of the running drills within the earlier section can be incorporated into a potentiation phase when taken to much higher intensities (and many of the band exercises too). However, I usually include a selection of different running drills that are more explosive in nature, for example, power skips, and I call this the "secondary running drills phase." Therefore, a warm-up will often follow this protocol: *Primary Running Drills Phase – DROMEs – Secondary Running Drills Phase* (this usually includes more jumps/plyometrics).

On the next page, I have selected my top 12 potentiation drills.

Top 12 Potentiation Drills

You can find videos to all of these drills on my personal YouTube: **@CoachJCurtis**

(Use the "@" symbol to ensure you find my handle)

Example Warm-Ups

Mid-Long Duration Run Warm-Up

This warm-up is performed over a distance of 10-20m (running back and forth).

Phase	Exercise	Sets/Reps/Distance/Time	Rest
Running Drills	Gates	20m	3-5 Secs
	Jogging	40m	3-5 Secs
	High Knees	20m	3-5 Secs
	Heel Flicks	20m	3-5 Secs
	Fast Feet	20m	15-20 Secs
DROMEs	Walking Lunge	10m	15-20 Secs
Potentiation	Ankle Jump	1x10	15-20 Secs
	Fast Run	40m	1-2 Mins

Intervals/Track Session Warm-up

This warm-up is performed over a distance of 10-20m (running back and forth).

Phase	Exercise	Sets/Reps/Distance/Time	Rest
Running Drills	Jogging	40m	3-5 Secs
	A-Skips	40m	3-5 Secs
	B-Skips	40m	3-5 Secs
	High Knee Heel Flicks	40m	3-5 Secs
	Fast Feet	20m	15-20 Secs
DROMEs	Squat	1x5	15-20 Secs
	Lunge	1x5 Each Side	15-20 Secs
	Alternate Toe Taps	1x5 Each Side	15-20 Secs
Potentiation	Ankle Jump	1x10	15-20 Secs
	Power Skip	20m	15-20 Secs
	Bound	20m	15-20 Secs
	Stride	100m	1-2 Mins

"The blazing fire makes flames and brightness out of everything thrown into it." – **Marcus Aurelius**

Labour Fitness Warm-Up (With Journeys)

This warm-up is performed over a distance of 10-20m (running back and forth).

Phase	Exercise	Sets/Reps/Distance/Time	Rest
Running Drills	Jogging	40m	3-5 Secs
	A-Skips	40m	3-5 Secs
	Lateral Shuffle	40m	3-5 Secs
	Carioca	40m	3-5 Secs
DROMEs	Squat	1x10	5-10 Secs
	Lateral Lunge	1x5 Each Side	5-10 Secs
	Push-Up to Toe Tap	1x5 Each Side	15-20 Secs
Potentiation	Vertical Jump	4x1	3-5 Secs
	Broad Jump	4x1	3-5 Secs
	Bound	20m	15-20 Secs
	Scissor Kicks	20m	1 Min

Labour Fitness Warm-Up (Without Journeys)

Phase	Exercise	Sets/Reps/Distance/Time	Rest
Raise	Run/Row/Ski/Cycle	2-3 Mins	15-20 Secs
DROMEs	Squat	1x10	3-5 Secs
	Lunge	1x5 Each Side	3-5 Secs
	Inchworm + Push-Up	1x5	3-5 Secs
	Arm Circles	1x10 Each Direction	3-5 Secs
	Arm Swings	1x10	3-5 Secs
Potentiation	Vertical Jump	5x1	3-5 Secs
	Broad Jump	5x1	3-5 Secs
	Pogo Jump	1x10	15-20 Secs
	MB Chest Throw	5x1	1 Min

"If a man knows not which port he sails, no wind is favourable." – **Seneca**

Total Body Strength Training Warm-Up

Phase	Exercise	Sets/Reps/Distance/Time	Rest
Raise	Run/Row/Ski/Cycle	2-3 Mins	15-20 Secs
DROMEs	Squat	1x10	3-5 Secs
	Lunge	1x5 Each Side	3-5 Secs
	Inchworm + Push-Up	1x5	3-5 Secs
	Arm Circles	1x10 Each Direction	3-5 Secs
	Arm Swings	1x10	3-5 Secs
Potentiation	Vertical Jump	5x1	3-5 Secs
	Broad Jump	5x1	3-5 Secs
	Pogo Jump	1x10	15-20 Secs
	MB Chest Throw	5x1	1 Min

Lower Body Strength Training Warm-Up (With Bands)

Phase	Exercise	Sets/Reps/Distance/Time	Rest
Raise	Run/Row/Ski/Cycle	2-3 Mins	15-20 Secs
DROMEs	Squat	1x10	3-5 Secs
	Lunge	1x5 Each Side	3-5 Secs
	Lateral Lunge	1x5 Each Side	3-5 Secs
	Single-Leg RDL	1x5 Each Side	3-5 Secs
Band Drills	Spanish Squat	3x40 Secs	10-20 Secs
	Good Morning	1x20	10-20 Secs
Potentiation	Ankle Jump	1x10	3-5 Secs
	Pogo Jump	1x10	3-5 Secs
	Vertical Jump	4x1	3-5 Secs
	Broad Jump	4x1	1 Min

"How long are you going to wait before you demand the best of yourself?" – **Epictetus**

Upper Body Strength Training Warm-Up (With Band)

Phase	Exercise	Sets/Reps/Distance/Time	Rest
Raise	Run/Row/Ski/Cycle	2-3 Mins	15-20 Secs
DROMEs	Push-Up to Toe Tap	1x5 Each Side	10-15 Secs
	Torso Rotation	1x10 Each Direction	3-5 Secs
	Arm Circles	1x10 Each Direction	3-5 Secs
	Arm Swings	1x10	3-5 Secs
Band Drills	Band Fly	1x20	10-15 Secs
	Band Pull Apart	1x20	10-15 Secs
Potentiation	MB Chest Throw	10x1	3-5 Secs
	MB Rotational Throw	5x1 Each Side	3-5 Secs

Pre-Fitness Race Warm-Up

This warm-up is performed over a distance of 10-20m (running back and forth).

Phase	Exercise	Sets/Reps/Distance/Time	Rest
Running Drills	Jogging	40m	3-5 Secs
	A-Skips	40m	3-5 Secs
	B Skips	40m	3-5 Secs
DROMEs	Squat	1x10	5-10 Secs
	Lunge	1x5 Each Side	5-10 Secs
	Around the World's	1x5 Each Direction	5-10 Secs
	Alternate Toe Taps	1x5 Each Side	5-10 Secs
	Push-Up to Toe Tap	1x3 Each Side	5-10 Secs
Potentiation	Ankle Jump	1x10	5-10 Secs
	Very Fast Feet	20m	5-10 Secs
	Scissor Kicks	40m	5-10 Secs
	Shorts Sprints	3x20-40m	30-60 Secs

"He suffers more than necessary, he who suffers before it is necessary." – **Seneca**

Pre-Fitness Race Warm-Up (With Bands)

This warm-up is performed over a distance of 10-20m (running back and forth).

Phase	Exercise	Sets/Reps/Distance/Time	Rest
Running Drills	Jogging	40m	3-5 Secs
	Heel Flicks	40m	3-5 Secs
	Fast Feet	40m	3-5 Secs
DROMEs	Squat	1x10	5-10 Secs
	Lunge	1x5 Each Side	5-10 Secs
	Inchworm	1x5	5-10 Secs
Band Drills	Band Pull Apart	1x20	5-10 Secs
Potentiation	Pogo Jump	1x10	5-10 Secs
	Power Skip	20m	5-10 Secs
	Lateral Bound	1x5 Each Direction	5-10 Secs
	Stride	2x100m	1 Min

As you can see from the tables, these warm-ups are fairly detailed and involve quite a few exercises, and this may give the impression that these warm-ups are quite complex or take a lot of time. However, I suggest finding the warm-up protocol that works for you and drilling it prior to every session it is applicable to until it becomes second nature. Once the warm-up is second nature, you will roll through the drills in just a few minutes.

Remember, there is nothing wrong with throwing in a few running drills and jumps prior to an upper body session. Ultimately, the more often you incorporate these drills, the better – I am a big fan of micro-dosing running and plyometric drills (little and often).

Here's an example of a warm-up I perform regularly (usually in my gym over a 10m distance):

- A Skips: 20-40m
- B Skips: 20-40m
- Squat: 1x10
- Lunge: 1x5 Each Side
- Inchworm + Push-Up to Toe Tap (tap each foot once per rep): 1x5
- Ankle Jumps: 1x10
- Power Skips: 20m
- Scissor Kicks: 40m
- Short Sprints: 6x10m

Note: A and B Skips can be a little tricky at first, but with a little practice, you get used to them and they feel great – if they don't work for you, swap them for simple high knees and high knee heel flicks, etc.

Breathing for Performance

Before taking a deep dive into dozens of lifts that will help athletes build muscular strength and endurance, it is worth taking a detailed look at breathing methods, which are often overlooked.

It is important to breathe deeply "through your belly" using your diaphragm. This pulls your diaphragm down, expands your lungs, and allows you to take in more oxygen.

To practice diaphragmatic breathing, place one hand on your chest and one on your belly. Imagine a balloon in your stomach. From there, as you inhale through your nose or mouth, the balloon expands, and as you exhale through your mouth, it deflates. If your chest raises instead of your belly, your breathing is too shallow.

Many people breathe through the top of their chest, especially when mouth-breathing, and this can cause muscles that are not designed for respiration to overwork and create excess tension in the neck muscles.

Breathing at the top of the chest can also weaken the diaphragm through underuse and result in fatigue during exercise and a performance reduction.

Nasal breathing increases rib cage and diaphragm engagement during inhalation, and this is beneficial because it drives more oxygen into your lungs' lower lobes compared to mouth breathing. However, nasal breathing may not allow you to draw in enough oxygen when working at a high intensity.

Whether you use nasal or mouth breathing, the important thing is to maintain a constant rhythm rather than randomly mixing the two.

Biomechanical Breathing

During resistance training, we use a biomechanical breathing style that maximizes performance and minimizes injury risk.

When using biomechanical breathing, you match your inhalation with the exercise's eccentric (downward) phase and your exhalation with the concentric (upward) phase.

Most lifters inhale before or during the start of the eccentric phase and exhale during the latter stage of the concentric phase (concentric exhalation). However, the gold standard when lifting heavy loads is to hold your breath throughout the entire lift.

Biomechanical breathing is often coupled with the use of the **Valsalva Maneuver**, which is "a moderately forceful attempted exhalation against a closed airway" (like equalizing your ears on an airplane by blowing against a pinched nose).

The Valsalva maneuver, combined with braced trunk muscles, creates intra-abdominal pressure (IAP) and stabilizes the spine. To visualize this, imagine the rigidity of a sealed plastic bottle full of air compared to an open bottle.

Note: Using the Valsalva maneuver can cause a rise in blood pressure and dizziness. However, the performance benefits and reduced risk of injury generally outweigh the risks, barring other health considerations.

"If you accomplish something good with hard work, the labour passes quickly, but the good endures; if you do something shameful in pursuit of pleasure, the pleasure passes quickly, but the shame endures." – **Musonius Rufus**

Alongside the benefits of the Valsalva maneuver and IAP, wearing a weightlifting belt gives the lifter something to brace against (belly punch) and dramatically increases the amount of tension generated, which can improve performance.

Some lifters choose to develop strength and power without the use of aids such as belts and straps. We don't want to rely on these aids, but they have their benefits. It usually comes down to the coaches' and athletes' preferences as to whether they wish to utilize the tools or not. However, when individuals have dogmatic views on things like the use of belts, it is a little silly – a general rule of thumb in the health, fitness and nutrition industries is to avoid dogmatic and absolutist views.

Ultimately, if the aim is to develop strength in the legs and a belt allows the lifter to effectively work at heavier loads, there isn't an issue. But the general rule of thumb is that a lifter should feel comfortable belt-free with moderate-heavy loads (it should not be a crutch) and then utilize one as the weight creeps up (there isn't a golden percentage, but a coach may advise >80% of your 1 rep max).

Powerlifting belts are generally the same width all the way around (4 inches/10cm) and will usually be comprised of thick (1cm), rigid leather.

The thick buckles on Powerlifting belts can get in the way when Olympic weightlifting. Therefore, Olympic lifters usually choose belts that are thinner, often larger around the back, but minimal at the front in terms of locking system, i.e., Buckle.

Anatomical Breathing

Bracing and creating tension is a good thing when lifting heavy. However, during other forms of movement and physical training, excessive tension will cause fatigue and reduced speed and mobility.

This brings us to the **Force-Velocity Paradox:**

We need to produce force to create movement and speed. However, the corresponding tension that is created restricts speed. Therefore, there needs to be a balance between the contraction and relaxation phases.

Athletic performance is not just about the ability to produce force quickly (rate of force development). It's also about how fast a muscle can contract, relax (to maximize joint velocity), and re-contract – we often call this a double pulse.

When there is no need to create maximal total body tension, we instead aim to regulate our breathing in an optimal way for the activity we are doing – **anatomical breathing**.

For example, while running, an individual may inhale for 3 strides and exhale for 3 strides.

We can also consider the position of the body. For example, during a KB swing, we could exhale at the bottom of the movement while the body is bent over and inhale at the top of the movement while the torso is upright (opposite to the usual concentric exhalation used when lifting weights).

When it comes to the Deadly Dozen and other fitness races, there are a lot of transitions between activities, for example, going from a run to a KB deadlift. Therefore, it is key for the athlete to transition their anatomical breathing style for each activity. For example, the athlete regulates their breathing during the run. Then, as they approach the KB, they take a few forceful deep breaths in and out before lifting it and matching their breaths to the repetitions.

"The impediment to action advances actions. What stands in the way becomes the way." – **Marcus Aurelius**

Barbell Training

The Deadly Dozen primarily uses BW, KBs, DBs and WPs to train. However, the barbell (BB) is one of the best tools for developing strength. Therefore, in this section, we look at BB variations of the DD Labours.

The BB Half Dozen (BHD) exchanges the KB, DB and WP stations to BB variations.

- KB Deadlift – BB Deadlift

- KB Goblet Squat – BB Squat (Back or Front)

- DB Lunge – BB Lunge

- DB Push Press – BB Push Press

- WP Clean & Press – BB Clean & Press

- DB Snatch – BB Snatch

Bonus BB Lift: The Push-Up during the Devil Press (+Burpee Broad Jumps) – BB Bench Press

In this section, we will look at the BB lifts listed in the BB Half Dozen and some useful variations – much of this content has been taken from my 300+ Page Strength Training Manual and my Olympic Weightlifting Manual.

Note: These pictures were taken at the time when I was weighing over 109kg/240lbs, and you couldn't get a haircut that easily – the image of the hex bar deadlift is particularly unfortunate.

Key Lifts + Variations:
- Conventional Deadlift / Sumo Deadlift / Hex Bar Deadlift / Romanian Deadlift

- Back Squat / Front Squat / Box Squat / Overhead Squat

- Lunge / Lateral Lunge / Rear Foot Elevated Split Squat

- Bench Press / Floor Press / Strict Press / Push Press

- Snatch / Clean & Jerk

"Wealth consists not in having great possessions, but in having few wants." – **Epictetus**

Conventional Deadlift

The deadlift is the king of the hinge and pull movements and is fundamental to developing strong, powerful hips. The deadlift will build the posterior chain muscles that work to extend the hips and back (hamstrings, glutes, quadratus lumborum and erector spinae) and the quadriceps, which work to extend the knees – the quads are the strongest muscle in the body, so you want to use them.

Note: In a strength training setting, when a coach says, "strong hips," they are usually referring to the muscles that extend the hips, i.e., the gluteals and hamstrings – hip extension can be described as "the engine of athletic performance."

Please note that lifting a heavy weight off the floor can stress your back in a way that can cause injury. Therefore, optimize your technique and build strength progressively.

Injuries are not just a matter of technique or poor form. Regardless of whether you lift correctly or not, if your soft tissues haven't got the strength to handle the load (even with perfect form), injuries such as straining your lower back muscles can occur.

Remember, although we are using all the leg muscles to pull the weight off the floor, the lower back is the area that will take the brunt of the force. Therefore, it needs to be strong (working the lower back is a good thing).

Note: Even what could be considered a minor back muscle strain or sprain to the ligaments that surround the spine can cause significant discomfort and pain (most things heal on their own, but always seek advice from medical professionals when you are worried).

When it comes to the deadlift, many people are hell-bent on going as heavy as they can in every session, even if it's the first time they have lifted a BB off the floor. However, progressive programming is the key. Just because you have the strength to rip a heavy BB off the floor, it doesn't mean your structures have the strength to accommodate the stress.

It is essential to give your structures time to develop using submaximal loads over weeks and months. This is because tendons and ligaments do NOT develop as quickly as muscle tissue.

Technique Tip: Always drive your feet (specifically your heels but keep your toes down) into the floor when initiating the deadlift and create mind-muscle connection with your quads to break inertia. The knee transition will work the back intensely, so stay tight and once the BB crosses the knees, drive your hips/pelvis into the BB as fast as you can!

When starting the pull, it is vital to sit into the lift to maximize quad engagement. However, this is often overemphasized and results in a good morning fault. A good morning fault is where the knees extend prematurely before inertia is broken and the load is thrown onto the back (this is a common fault seen during a squat).

Remember, the deadlift is a deadlift, NOT a squat, and setting up with realistic hip and knee angles (not too low) ensures the muscles that extend the hips and knees work together, which will look like the hips and knees are in sync.

Note: The torso and the floor create the back angle, the torso and the upper legs create the hip angle, and the upper and lower legs create the knee angle.

Teaching Points:

1. Set the BB up on the floor with 45cm plates.

2. Approach the BB so that your midfoot is directly underneath it. Your shins should be an inch away from the BB.

3. Hinge with your hips and bend your knees until you can grab the BB.

4. Take a pronated (overhand) or alternated grip (one hand pronated, one hand supinated/underhand). Use a pronated grip as much as possible to develop your grip strength.

5. Sit back with your glutes and drive your chest up. This will bring your shins forward until they come into contact or are just off the BB.

6. Take a big gulp of air, brace your core, and use the Valsalva maneuver. As you do this, pull on the BB slightly to create total body tension and take the slack out of the BB and plates.

7. Drive your heels into the floor and pull the BB upwards and rearwards off the floor. Allow time for the inertia of the BB to be broken. You must produce enough force to break the weight off the floor, and this doesn't always happen as soon as you start pulling.

8. Engage your latissimus dorsi (lats – back muscles) to keep the BB within its vertical path.

9. Once the BB passes your knees, drive your hips into it and push your chest up. Your shoulders will fall naturally behind the BB. There is no need to shrug or throw your shoulders backward.

10. Once you have finished locking out your hips, sit back with your glutes and bend your knees slightly to allow the BB to track down your legs smoothly.

11. Once the BB passes your kneecaps, bend your knees until the plates touch the floor.

12. At the bottom, exhale and get ready for the next rep.

13. Don't bounce the plates off the floor to create upward momentum. When working with heavy loads, you must treat every rep as a single, perfectly performed movement.

14. Continue with successive reps.

Sumo Deadlift

Just like conventional deadlifts, sumo deadlifts involve pulling the BB off the floor. However, your stance is wider, and your arms hang down between your legs. This allows you to take a true shoulder-width grip (plumbline down through your shoulders, elbows, and wrists), which maximizes your arms' length, which, when combined with the wide stance, reduces the range of motion of the lift by 10-15% – some lifters have such long arms that the BB finishes just above the kneecaps.

- **Conventional:** Arms outside the legs

- **Sumo:** Arms inside the legs

The sumo stance position results in a deadlift that places a little more load on your quads and adductors rather than your back. However, it is still going to work your back intensely and some lifters find the sumo setup can encourage a little more rounding of the lower spine during the pull, so it needs to be strong.

During a sumo deadlift, you can take a wide stance where your toes are touching the plates, but the standard positioning for a sumo deadlift leaves the knees directly over the ankles while you are in the bottom position.

A lifter will usually turn their toes outwards to open up the hips, allowing for more mobility and greater engagement of both the abductor and adductor muscles. However, some lifters may find this stressful on the groin and choose to take a stance with their toes pointing forward, which reduces groin stress and places more load on the quads.

Regardless of whether your toes are forward or turned out, the cue "spread the floor/mats apart" is used. This cue is beneficial as during a sumo deadlift, not only are the lifter's hips extending through the sagittal plane as they are during a conventional deadlift, but they are also adducting through the frontal plane, hence the importance of strong adductors.

I suggest incorporating both the conventional and sumo deadlift into your training. However, many lifters will choose to concentrate on one.

Deciding which deadlift to use ultimately comes down to personal preference. We are all anatomically different. Some hip joint structures are suited to a wider stance, while others are suited to a narrower stance, so choose what works for you.

I recommend attempting a maximal lift (above 85%) with each variation and seeing which feels best for you. From there, you can consider that lift your primary deadlift. However, it works well to cycle in both because mixing up the way you perform a movement can help to iron out weaknesses due to more emphasis being placed on areas that may typically get less attention, and ultimately, it keeps things interesting.

Note: In Powerlifting, lifters can use either the conventional or sumo variation, whereas, in Strongman events, you can only use the conventional style.

The sumo deadlift is a great lift that is growing in popularity. However, it does get some hate as it is often seen as an easier lift.

As mentioned, the wide stance used during the sumo deadlift reduces the range of motion by around 10-15%, and therefore, there is an argument for it being easier. However, if the sumo deadlift were easier for everyone, all lifters would use it in competition.

Of course, some lifters see it as a matter of personal pride to perform the conventional deadlift. However, the truth of the matter is that although some lifters excel using the wide sumo stance, others cannot generate the same amount of force in a wide stance and are much better suited to a narrow stance.

My findings after years of working with Powerlifters at varying levels are that sumo is an easier lift when working at sub-maximal loads (<80%) and most can get more reps out in comparison to the conventional deadlift (reduced ROM), but when working at maximal loads (>85%), they are comparable for most.

This being said, when a lifter has the optimal anthropometrics (limb lengths, etc) for the sumo style, they tend to excel at the deadlift, and it can often far outmatch their other lifts. Essentially, if a lifter's anthropometrics are perfect for the sumo setup, it comes with huge advantages.

Note: I often see conventional lifters who can pull similar loads with a sumo style but don't like it. However, many sumo lifters cannot get close to their 1RM with the conventional style.

Teaching Points:

1. Set the BB up on the floor with 45cm plates.

2. Approach the BB and take a wide stance with your midfoot directly under the BB.

3. You can keep your toes pointing forward (it can be less stressful on your groin). However, most lifters will push their toes outwards (externally rotate their hips).

4. The width of your stance is ultimately dependent on the flexibility of your adductors (groin). Some lifters will take an extremely wide stance where their toes are touching the plates at either side. However, most lifters will take a stance where their knees are sitting directly over their ankles while in the bottom position.

5. Hinge with your hips and bend your knees until you can grab the BB on the inside of your legs – this allows you to take a narrow, shoulder-width grip.

6. Take a pronated/overhand or alternated (one overhand and one underhand) grip.

7. Sit back with your glutes and drive your chest/ribcage up. This will bring your shins forward until they come into contact or are just off the BB.

8. Take a big gulp of air, use the Valsalva maneuver and brace your core musculature. As you do this, pull on the BB slightly to create more tension and take away any slack between the BB and the plates.

9. Drive your heels into the floor and outwards as if you are spreading the floor apart. Pull the BB upwards and rearwards off the floor. Allow time for the inertia of the BB to be broken. You must produce enough force to break the weight off the floor, and this doesn't always happen as soon as you start pulling.

10. Once the BB passes your knees, drive your hips into it and push your chest up. Your shoulders will fall naturally behind the BB. There is no need to shrug or throw your shoulders rearwards.

11. Once you have finished locking out your hips, drive your glutes rearwards and bend your knees slightly to allow the BB to track down your legs smoothly.

12. Once the BB passes your kneecaps, bend your knees until the plates touch the floor.

13. At the bottom, exhale and get ready for the next rep.

14. Don't bounce the plates off the floor to create upward momentum. Treat every lift as an individual perfectly performed movement.

15. Continue with successive reps.

Hex Bar Deadlift

The hex bar (often referred to as the trap bar) deadlift is one of the best deadlift variations. It is considered by many to be superior to the conventional deadlift for athletic development. Studies have shown that individuals can lift heavier, with greater speed and power, while deadlifting with the hex bar.

Note: Many hex bars have raised handles, and therefore, this will reduce the range of motion, making for an easier lift.

Another benefit of the hex bar deadlift is the ease of the setup. Often, people struggle to perfect their conventional deadlift positioning with the weight held to the front of the legs. However, the hex bar allows the lifter to hold the weight on either side of their body, making for a much more intuitive setup with a straight back.

Bearing in mind all this information, you may question, why not just use the hex bar deadlift?

The hex bar does have huge benefits. However, it is an exercise in itself. The setup turns the exercise into more of a squatting movement with greater loads placed on your quads. (Some even refer to the movement as a hex bar squat).

On the other hand, the conventional deadlift places more load on your posterior chain, which is essentially the engine that drives strength development and athletic performance.

On top of all this, we must consider the accessibility of equipment. You can find BBs in most gyms, and you can squat, push, and pull them. Therefore, it makes sense that most strength development is centered around the BB. However, if you have access to a hex bar, I suggest using both variants because although they are both deadlifts, they do feel like different exercises. Therefore, it can be a great way to add more deadlift frequency and volume without it becoming monotonous.

Keeping things interesting is something I always recommend, as it helps to keep lifters motivated and encourages consistency. However, it is also key to get plenty of frequency on the same exercises to develop skill (the more you do a specific action, the better you become at it) and track your progress – find a balance that works for you.

1. Stand within the hex bar, with 45cm plates loaded onto it.
2. Squat down with an exaggerated hip hinge and grab the bars on either side – ensure you grab the center of the knurling (the grippy section on the bar), otherwise the hex bar will tilt forward or back.
3. Sit back to load your quads and drive your chest up.
4. Take a big gulp of air, brace your core and use the Valsalva maneuver. As you do this, pull on the hex bar slightly to create total body tension and take the slack out of the hex bar and plates.
5. Drive your feet into the floor and raise the hex bar up until your legs are fully extended.
6. Return the hex bar to the floor.
7. At the bottom, exhale and get ready for the next rep.
8. Don't bounce the plates off the floor. When working with heavy loads, it's important that you treat every rep as a single, perfectly performed movement.
9. Continue with successive reps.

Romanian Deadlift (RDL)

The Romanian deadlift came about when weightlifters in a gym in San Francisco saw the Romanian lifter Nicu Vlad performing the lift. They asked him what the lift was called, and he replied, "back strengthening exercise," so they named it the Romanian Deadlift, or RDL for short.

During a true RDL, the hips are not fully locked out (extended) at the top, which keeps the tension on the muscles and maximizes the need for a strong back. However, it is okay to lockout at the top to maximize glute engagement, and doing so in an explosive fashion is often referred to as a "Dimel deadlift," an exercise named after the late Matt Dimel, a renowned Powerlifter from Westside BB, an infamous gym in Columbus, Ohio.

As mentioned, weightlifters don't fully lockout during the RDL to keep tension on the back muscles. Instead, they develop explosive hip extension with snatch and clean pull variations.

The RDL is my lift of choice (alongside the rack pull) when progressing individuals from a bodyweight hinge and KB/DB deadlift to working with the BB, and it acts as the ideal prerequisite to the deadlift.

To perform the RDL, we hold the BB at the top of a deadlift, hinge at our hips, and allow the BB to tack smoothly down our thighs. Once the BB passes the kneecaps, we bend the knees slightly to bring the BB 3-4 inches below the knees before reversing the movement and returning to the starting position.

The slight bend in the knees slacks the hamstrings and places emphasis on the back and glutes – it is this prominent knee bend that differentiates the RDL from a stiff/straight-leg deadlift that starts at the hips.

When performing the RDL, the lifter must initiate the movement by pushing their glutes back and allowing their shoulders to come forward of the BB, enabling the BB to track smoothly down the thighs – if the shoulders are kept behind the BB and there is too much knee bend, the BB will get stuck on the thighs.

During an RDL, the lifter should turn their elbows into the plates, grip the floor with their feet (think heel, big toe, and the little toe), and push their knees out slightly to maximize the tension in the legs.

1. Start with the BB at your hips with a pronated (overhand) grip. Ensure you pick the BB up with good form, while maintaining a neutral spine.
2. Initiate the movement by driving your glutes back and bending your knees slightly. Allow your shoulders to come over the BB while it maintains contact with your legs.
3. Keep driving your glutes back to facilitate the hinge and allow the BB to track down your quads. If there is too much knee bend at this point, the BB will sit on your quads, rather than track down smoothly.
4. Once the BB passes your kneecaps, bend your knees slightly to bring the BB to about a palm's distance below your knees.
5. Engage your glutes and bring the BB back up your legs, following the same path it went down. Maintain a vertical bar path throughout (if someone were watching from the side, they would see the BB move in a vertical line).
6. Squeeze your glutes hard at the top to get them firing and continue with successive reps.

Back Squat

The back squat is considered by most to be the king of the squats because it allows for the most load to be lifted.

It is the first of three competitive Powerlifts (back squat, bench press, and deadlift) and is considered fundamental to most strength programs. However, there is no universal rule saying you have to BB squat to get strong.

During the back squat, the BB is held on your upper back. However, there are two distinct positions on the back that will affect the mechanics of the squat:

- **High Bar Position**

- **Low Bar Position**

There are pros and cons to each position and the various squat styles that are used for each. Therefore, the position you use comes down to your personal preference and your needs and goals – as I usually recommend, incorporate both if you can.

Note: The back squat is more often than not the backbone of strength programs, and I highly recommend you incorporate it into your training regime. However, if it isn't for you, you can still gain monstrous leg strength with deadlift and single-leg exercise variations, and you can also use a variety of lower body machines.

High Bar Position: The BB is held on the top of your upper traps, ensuring that it does not rest on the cervical vertebrae (distinct bony prominence on the back of the neck).

The BB should stay over your midfoot throughout the squat, and when the BB is high on your back, your torso requires less tilt to keep the BB over the midfoot compared to the low bar position, so it stays more upright and allows for more depth.

During the high bar squat, leverage is weakest as you come up past the parallel position (the point where your hips are furthest behind the BB). You can make a conscious effort to drive your hips back under the BB towards the end of the lift, which will bring you into a more mechanically efficient position. It maximizes quad engagement and prevents your torso from falling forward. However, this technique can place a little more stress on your knees.

The high bar position is usually the intuitive and comfortable position for most lifters and, therefore, the one I would introduce novice lifters to first.

Regardless of bar positioning, it is a steel bar across the back and therefore, it is not particularly comfortable if you are not used to it. To counter this, some novice lifters use a foam bar pad to provide cushion. It is not the end of the world to use a bar pad, and it is much better to squat with one than not squat at all. However, a bar pad can make the BB less stable on the back, and thick pads result in the BB sitting further back, which will affect squat mechanics, causing greater forward lean. Therefore, I encourage all my lifters to "dry their eyes" and get used to it (it doesn't take long to get used to the BB on your back).

Note: Things like bar pads and gloves come with some stigma in a more serious strength training environment and are often seen as only being used by novices. This being said, you really shouldn't care what other people think if you find weightlifting gloves or bar pads beneficial for you.

Low Bar Position: The BB is held 2-3 inches lower on your upper back, which will result in the BB sitting behind your rear deltoids (across the spine of the scapula).

The reduced distance from your hips to the BB can help maximize the weight lifted. Therefore, competitive lifters often use a low bar position.

The low bar position does require a decent amount of shoulder mobility and can be quite uncomfortable if you are not used to it.

During a low bar squat, lifters will often use a hip drive method, where rather than driving your hips back under the BB (which reduces the engagement of the hamstrings), you continue to drive upwards with your hips while maintaining a rigid back position (imagine driving upwards with your sacrum – upper buttocks).

Remember, the key to the back squat is to play with the different styles and find what works for you.

Note: When taking the BB off the rack in the low bar position, the BB needs to be set up on the rack 2-3 inches lower than it would be for the high bar back squat. I also cue lifters to keep their chin in, bring their elbows back, and look down to their front when taking the BB off the rack in the low bar position. This cue encourages the lifter to create a solid shelf for the BB to sit on; otherwise, it can feel like the BB is sliding down the back (Powerlifters will often chalk their t-shirt and appreciate a centre knurling for additional grip on the back).

Note: A centre knurling (grippy section of a BB) is great for the back squat as it provides extra grip (Powerlifters prefer this). However, during a front squat, it can rub on your neck.

Teaching Points:

1. Set the BB on the rack at upper chest height.

2. Grab the BB 1-2 palms wider than shoulder-width with a comfortable grip (either full or false grip).

3. A full grip will often feel more stable for the lifter. However, a false grip (thumbs on the same side as your fingers) allows your wrists to stay in a more neutral position (as your elbows are pointing backward). Take the grip that suits you.

4. Move your head under the BB, placing the BB into your preferred position on your traps – high or low bar position.

5. Walk under the BB so that your hips are directly underneath to ensure you don't lift the BB off the rack with your lower back.

6. Lift the BB up off the rack with your legs and take 2-3 short strides backward – a long walkout wastes energy and increases the risk of injury.

7. Adopt your squatting stance. Experiment with various stance widths and see what feels best for you (hip joint structure often dictates which stance width feels best for you).

8. Take a big gulp of air, brace your core, and use the Valsalva maneuver.

9. As you brace your core, pull down on the BB to help increase total body tension.

10. Initiate the squat with your hips, driving your glutes backward, and bend your knees.

11. Allow your knees to track directly over your toes (this will vary depending on limb lengths).

12. Sit back to the point where you break parallel, and your hip crease dips just below the top of your kneecaps or as deep as you can go while maintaining good form – go "ass to grass if it works for you."

13. Use the stretch reflex (involuntary contraction in response to a stretch in the muscles) to recoil out of the hole.

14. Drive your shoulders into the BB and your feet into the floor.

15. Pull down hard on the BB as if you are trying to bend it over your back. This helps to maximize total body tension and muscular engagement.

16. Drive back up out of the squat.

17. Once you reach the top of the lift, exhale and get ready for the next rep.

18. When working with heavy loads, you must treat every rep as a single, perfectly performed movement.

19. Continue with successive reps.

Front Squat

The front squat is often considered the "athletic" squat, partially due to its link to Olympic lifts, which are often described as the epitome of athletic prowess, but also because the front-loaded position results in a more upright back angle compared to the back squat because the BB is closer to the midfoot, which allows lifters to squat with greater depth, increasing ankle dorsiflexion and placing a little more load onto their quads – when the ankles are dorsiflexed, the shins are brought forward into what is called a positive shin angle, and this positioning is integral to countless athletic movements.

Many people struggle to achieve the front rack position and, even if they can, often find it quite uncomfortable. This is due to the mobility required in the latissimus dorsi, triceps, and forearms to hold the BB comfortably on the anterior deltoids.

Mobility dictates to what extent the hands stay on the BB. For a clean and jerk, maintaining as much grip as possible is ideal. However, it's not uncommon to see lifters have just their fingertips on the BB during a front squat, which is fine.

Some lifters may use a cross-armed position to hold the BB, which is an easy alternative if the front rack position is inaccessible.

Although the cross-armed technique is a great variation, it lacks a few areas as it doesn't allow for the same level of thoracic tension and can result in a lack of symmetry between the shoulder blades. However, I still often use it as a position for "backdown sets" (lighter sets after the main sets) or even use the "Zombie Squat" position where the BB is held across the front of your shoulders, and your arms are held straight out to your front (parallel to each other and the floor – how cartoon zombies are portrayed as walking).

My advice to all lifters is to work on your front squat; once you get used to the positioning, it often becomes a preferred squat for a lot of lifters. It just has a slightly higher barrier to entry than many others.

Some of my favourite cues for the front squat (in a front rack) are: "Lead with your elbows" (on the way up). "Get big," "push your elbows up and out," and "flare/spread your lats." These cues encourage a tall/strong torso and stop lifters from crunching up under the BB with their elbows pointing inwards and down.

Teaching Points:

1. Set the BB on the rack at upper chest height – I set the front squat up slightly lower than I do for the high bar back squat.

2. Grab the BB with your fingers slightly wider than shoulder width.

3. Take your elbows underneath the BB so that the BB sits in the crease that has been formed just behind the bulk of your anterior delts. Your elbows will be facing forward.

4. Walk under the BB so that your hips are directly underneath. This ensures you are not lifting the BB off the rack with your lower back.

5. Lift the BB up off the rack with your legs.

6. Take 2-3 short strides backward. Taking a long walkout wastes energy and increases the risk of injuries.

7. Adopt your squatting stance.

8. Take a big gulp of air, brace your core and use the Valsalva maneuver.

9. Initiate the squat by breaking at your hips, driving your glutes back. However, the front squat will not use as much of a hip hinge as the back squat.

10. Bend your knees almost simultaneously.

11. Especially when squatting specifically for the Olympic lifts, the cue "hips over heels" can be used to ensure the torso remains as upright as possible while the BB is kept over the midfoot – during a true Olympic squat, you do not sit right back with your hips. Instead, there needs to be a good amount of knee bend and dorsiflexion to get an ass-to-grass squat (full depth) with the torso as upright as possible, which will allow a lifter to receive a BB in a front rack for the clean or an overhead squat for the snatch.

12. Allow your knees to track directly over your toes.

13. Squat to a point where you break parallel, and your hip crease surpasses the top of your kneecaps or as deep as you can go while maintaining form. Full depth should be practiced if you Olympic lift.

14. Use the stretch reflex to recoil out of the hole.

15. Drive your feet into the floor and lead with your chest and elbows to ensure your elbows stay high and you maintain the rigidity of your spine – if your elbows drop, you will lose the BB to your front.

16. Once you reach the top of the lift, exhale and get ready for the next rep.

17. When working with heavy loads, it's important that you treat every rep as a single, perfectly performed movement.

18. Continue with successive reps.

Box Squat

The box squat is one of my favourite squat variations as it places more load on the posterior chain while minimizing the stress placed on the knees.

A lifter should aim to sit onto their hamstrings, and their shins should be vertical at the bottom of the movement. This positioning creates a hip-dominant squat.

Common Fault: Many lifters will sit back onto their glutes, which results in the lower back flexing slightly and the knees being pushed forward.

Hip-dominant squats will help build strong and powerful glutes and hamstrings. They are also an excellent exercise for those who find "standard squats" (without a box) stressful on their knees.

Box height can vary, and there are benefits to working at different depths. However, to maximize the benefits for Powerlifters and those that want to increase their overall squat strength, the box should be at a height that requires you to break parallel (just below parallel).

A box squat that breaks parallel is more challenging than a standard squat to the same depth. This is because squatting onto a box removes the stretch reflex, which rebounds lifters out of the bottom position (the hole).

An above-parallel box squat, on the other hand, will allow lifters to lift much heavier loads and, in many cases, heavier loads than can be achieved with a standard squat to an above-parallel depth. This is because the box provides a platform for the lifter to drive from in a very efficient position (without the box, more stability and control is needed to decelerate and accelerate).

A great cue for the box squat is "drive your shoulders into the BB." This cue helps the lifter to maintain tension in their torso and encourages the lifter to drive with their legs and get their hips back under the BB.

Technique Tip: Keep your heels down and your torso inclined at the bottom – exactly as shown in the 2nd image. Common faults include raising the heels and leaning back with the torso, which slacks the posterior chain muscles and releases tension – you never want to lose tension while lifting heavy loads.

Note:

- **Above Parallel:** More force and velocity can be produced, allowing you to lift heavier loads with a greater rate of force development. An above-parallel squat can be a good choice for athletes who want to work their neuromuscular system intensely while minimizing eccentric loading and, therefore, DOMS (Delayed Onset Muscle Soreness)

- **Below Parallel:** More mechanical stress and better transfer to standard squats below parallel, making them the best choice for Powerlifters or lifters who want carryover to a deeper squat

- Regardless of the box height, box squats can go from very easy to not being able to get off the box very quickly. It only requires you to lose your positioning (lose tension) or for you to sit on the box for a second too long for you to be unable to produce sufficient force to get the BB moving again. Therefore, caution should be practiced when working with heavy loads – if you throw a heavy BB off your back onto a wooden box, the wooden box usually survives, but the BB will bend massively

Teaching Points:

1. Set up a BB on the rack as you would for a back squat.

2. Have a box setup behind you – placed within a small walkout distance.

3. Take the BB off the rack on your back and walk backward towards the box.

4. Adopt a wide squatting stance.

5. Take a big gulp of air, use the Valsalva maneuver, and contract your core musculature.

6. As you brace your core, pull down on the BB to help increase total body tension.

7. Hinge at your hip and exaggerate the movement as you sit back with your glutes – you want your shins to be vertical once you sit onto the box.

8. Don't fall back onto the box. Sit down slowly onto your hamstrings, maintaining total body tension as you meet the box.

9. Keep your heels down, and don't lean back after you have sat on the box – maintain your torso angle to maintain tension through the posterior chain.

10. Once you have sat on the box for a second, keep the tension in your torso and drive your shoulders into the BB.

11. Once you drive your shoulders into the BB, your feet will drive into the floor, and your hips will start to raise upwards and forward underneath the BB.

12. Drive back up out of the squat.

13. Once you reach the top of the lift, exhale and get ready for the next rep.

14. When working with heavy loads, it's important that you treat every rep as a single, perfect movement.

Overhead Squat

The overhead squat with a BB is a lift that is inaccessible to many simply because they don't have the mobility to perform it.

If there is limited mobility, then even light loads can be incredibly stressful to the strongest of athletes – it's an eye-opening demonstration of how restrictions can make movements considerably harder.

A lot of people ask me what's the best way to learn how to overhead squat. Of course, release techniques and stretches (rolling the lats and thoracic spine, pec stretches, etc) are necessary if the movement is way off. However, the best way to develop your mobility (if you can manage a semi-decent overhead squat) is to overhead squat and progressively load the weight.

Nothing will free up your restrictions like overhead squatting with weight. So, start with a PVC pipe, add small fractional plates, use a technique BB, progress to a 20kg unloaded BB, add fractional plates, and so on.

Tip: Raising your heels by 1-2 inches (even 3-4 inches if needed) by standing on plates is a great way to get right into performing an overhead squat when mobility doesn't allow it, and many lifters will be able to take the plates away within a couple of sessions.

During the overhead squat, the lifter will take a snatch grip width, which, when stood up straight and holding the BB with straight arms (hanging down, not overhead), the BB should sit in the crease of the hips, running across the bottom of the abs just above the pubis.

From this position, if you were to take the BB (or PVC pipe) overhead and bring one arm to your ear, your arms should create a right angle.

Of course, lifters can choose to go a little narrower or wider with their grip width. However, if a lifter goes too wide (often compensating for poor shoulder mobility), it can cause wrist pain – a wide grip is necessary for a Snatch as it shortens the distance from the floor to overhead.

Note: A squat jerk involves a lifter receiving the BB in an overhead squat with a narrow clean/jerk grip width (usually slightly wider than shoulder width), which requires incredible mobility.

1. Take the BB off the rack on your shoulders/traps as you would for a back squat.
2. Assume your snatch grip and your squatting stance.
3. Press or push press/jerk the BB overhead and make a conscious effort to squeeze the upper inside edges of your shoulder blades together.
4. Squeeze your elbows to lock the BB out.
5. Take a big gulp of air, brace your core and use the valsalva maneuver.
6. Initiate the squat with your hips and knees to maximise depth and maintain an upright torso.
7. At full depth, hold the position for 1-3 Seconds to build stability.
8. Press your hands into the BB to maintain tension and positioning as your raise out of the squat.
9. Reset and perform successive reps.

Lunge

Lunges can be performed forwards, backwards, and laterally out to the side, either moving in one direction (walking lunge) or in an alternating fashion where you return to the same starting position each time.

A forward stride into a lunge is most often used because it is what comes naturally. During a forward striding lunge, you can choose to keep your front knee back from your toes (vertical shin) or allow it to come as far forward as possible to exaggerate the stretch and mechanical stress through the tissues. As we know, it often beneficial to work through a full range of motion. However, some individuals will find lunging with a vertical shin angle more comfortable. The reverse lunge (backward stride) encourages the front shin to stay vertical and stepping up from a reverse lunge is easier than stepping back up from an alternating front lunge.

During a lunge, the majority of the work is done by the front leg. However, you can push with the back leg to generate as maximal force from both legs.

There are a few foot placement variations that can be used during lunges. I suggest starting from a hip-width stance and lunging forward using a semi-inline lunge, leaving a slight gap between each foot (when looking from the front). It's OK to go wider than this if you require extra stability. However, an excessively straddled stance can apply stress to your groin.

Inline Lunge	**Semi-Inline Lunge**	**Straddled Stance Lunge**

1. Start with a hip-width foot placement.
2. During walking lunges, take a reasonably long stride forward with your left leg. This will allow your right knee to drop comfortably towards the floor while your left knee tracks forward slightly, or to a degree that suits you best – you can go knees over toes if you like (ask the question, do you want more load or more range of motion?)
3. If performing a reverse lunge, stride backward with your right leg and allow your right knee to drop towards the floor.
4. It is fine for the back knee to gently touch the floor. However, this is often avoided to ensure tension remains throughout your body and prevent the knee striking the floor – fitness races usually require your knee to touch the floor.
5. As you stride with the front leg and your knee bends, a slight hip hinge will ensure the movement maximises the engagement of not only your quads, but also your hamstrings and glutes.
6. During walking lunges, you can set the recovering leg down before striding out with it into the next lunge or pass it straight past the supporting leg and into the next lunge.

Lateral Lunge

The lateral lunge is a lunge variation where you stride out to the side, keeping the non-striding leg straight.

This variation both mobilizes and strengthens your adductors (inner thighs), which are often overlooked when training. They also work the glutes intensely.

The lateral lunge can be performed from a pre-set starting position where your legs are set at a distance required to lunge with good form, or you can start from a hip-width stance and stride sideways into the wider stance before dropping into the lunge.

I will be describing the lunge performed from the pre-set stance, as it is my preferred method of performing a lateral lunge (it could be described as a lateral split squat – during a split squat, the emphasis is on "squatting" with one leg).

A BB can be used with this movement, or a KB or DB can be used in the goblet squat position (held at chest height) or held with straight arms below your hips, which can aid stability.

The lateral lunge can also be performed on a "slider" (a flat plastic disk) on artificial grass or carpet or on a towel on smooth flooring (wooden/laminate). The "slider lunge" allows you to slide your leg out to the side (keeping it straight) while you squat and shift your weight onto the bent leg. If this is done correctly, you can smoothly slide your leg in and out of the lateral lunge and work the adductor muscles intensely.

Note: During a slider lunge, if you place too much weight onto the slider, it will not move as you try to pull it back in – you must shift all your weight onto the squatting leg.

During a lateral lunge, ensure you sit back onto the hip/glute of the bending leg. This will maximize the engagement of your posterior chain muscles and allow you to work with greater loads – when bending with the right leg. I often cue, "Sit back onto your right butt cheek" and "Sit back onto your left butt cheek" when bending with the left leg.

1. Take a wide stance that allows you to facilitate the lunge. This may need adjusting when you try the first rep.
2. Keep your toes forward facing and stay on the soles of your feet throughout the whole movement.
3. Bend your left knee and drive your glutes back to facilitate a hinge.
4. Full depth is achieved when you feel a full stretch on your adductors. Don't roll onto the side of your right foot.
5. Note: A Cossack squat involves performing a lateral lunge. However, as you lower, you roll onto the heel of the straight leg (point your toes to the ceiling), while keeping the sole of the bent legs foot flat on the floor. The Cossack squat puts more emphasis onto the hamstrings of the straight leg and requires great mobility to achieve the full range of motion.
6. Push hard with the foot of the bent leg and return to the starting position before continuing with successive reps – you can perform multiple reps on one side or alternate from right to left.

Rear Foot Elevated Split Squat (RFESS)

One of the most used split squat variations is the RFESS or Rear Foot Elevated Split Squat, aka Bulgarian Split Squat.

Note: I don't call it a "Bulgarian Split Squat" because they were never used in the infamous Bulgarian weightlifting system, which involves only 6 exercises (clean & jerk, snatch, power clean, power snatch, front squat, back squat). However, others suggest it was taken from Bulgarian track and field athletes – either way, it is a split squat with the rear foot elevated.

The RFESS involves a setup that places the rear leg on an elevation. This is usually done on a bench at knee or upper shin height. However, I often program this exercise using a 4-8-inch elevation (bumper plates are ideal). The smaller elevation allows for more weight to be loaded during the exercise. In comparison, the higher elevation (on a bench) requires a little more stability and allows you to work through a greater range of motion.

A greater range of motion increases the eccentric loading on the glutes as they stretch – a lifter will often find their quads tire during the lift, but their glutes feel it the most the next day.

When it comes to the optimal height for the rear leg, my recommendation is to try various heights and see what works well for you – a higher elevation will encourage your pelvis to tilt forward, and therefore, the lower erectors will feel more tension.

Once the height has been selected, you can position your rear foot as it would be during a split squat on the floor, so on the toes/balls of the foot. Or you can place the foot's dorsal side (top) onto the bench/plate, reducing the stress on the toes and encouraging you to concentrate the load on the front leg.

This exercise can be performed with a BB on your back or in the front rack or with DBs held at either side in a farmer's carry position.

Other variations include unilateral loading with a DB in one hand, or the weights can start and return to the floor each time to turn it into a rear foot elevated deadlift (the RFESS Deadlift works well with 1 or 2 KBs).

1. Stand in front of a raised platform (plates or bench) and take one long stride forward.
2. Place the non-working leg onto the raised platform. Either on your toes or by placing the laces of your trainers down – find what feels comfy for you.
3. If you are too close to the platform, the knee of your working leg will track too far forward, which will restrict your ability to drop the rear knee towards the floor. If you are too far forward, it will create too much of a stretch down the front of the rear leg and can also restrict depth – hop forwards or backwards to find the optimal position if needed.
5. Note: If you sit on the edge of a bench and straighten one leg and place your heel on the floor, this is usually a good distance for the front leg to be from the bench.
6. Squat down with the front leg until the knee of your rear leg is just off the floor.
7. Drive your heel into the floor and raise back up to the starting position before completing successive reps.

Bench Press

The bench press is by far the most used BB exercise in a commercial gym environment, with "What can you bench?" seeming to be the only judge of strength.

Unfortunately, the bench press has gained a reputation for being unfunctional, as you are lying on a bench. However, it is one of the most effective ways of developing your pushing muscles. Therefore, it is incredibly functional.

A great variation of the bench press is the close grip bench press, which emphasizes the triceps. This involves taking a much narrower grip but not to the extent where it negatively affects the wrists – slightly narrower than shoulder-width is usually ideal.

Other variations of the BB bench press include the decline bench press and the incline bench press.

The decline bench press is performed on a decline bench and dramatically increases the lats' engagement during the press, usually allowing heavier loads to be lifted.

The incline bench press is performed on an incline bench (between 35 and 45 degrees) and increases the upper chest and shoulders' engagement. The more you incline the bench, the more shoulder engagement, and less chest engagement there will be (there is also less lat engagement). The incline bench is harder than the flat bench in terms of the weight that can be lifted. Note: If you can't lift as much weight on an exercise, it is because less muscle mass is being recruited, or the movement is using a less efficient joint action.

Note: A common mistake is pulling the BB off the J-cups with too much force during the incline bench press. This is done during a flat bench press. However, the BB will often be thrown forward when on an incline bench and end up on the lifter's lap.

During a flat bench press, it is key that your glutes stay on the bench. Otherwise, you are essentially turning it into a decline bench press (lifting your glutes is not allowed in Powerlifting competitions). If you struggle to keep your glutes down, bring your feet back and push your knees out, and this will prevent it from happening. From there, arch your lower spine to bring your glutes as close to your upper back as possible. When you press the weight, you want to drive your feet into the floor (leg drive), which should almost feel like you are going to raise your glutes (this is when you know you are using the leg drive properly), but keep your glutes pinned down, drive your upper back into the bench and your palms into the BB.

Teaching Points:

1. Lie on the bench so that your eyes are under the BB – the BB should be between your eyes and chin (if your head is too far behind the BB, you will often hit the J-cups as you press the BB upwards).

2. Grab the BB 1-2 palms distance wider than shoulder-width apart. An ideal grip placement leaves your forearms perpendicular to the BB at the bottom of the lift.

3. Some lifters use a false grip (thumbs on the same side as the fingers, aka, a suicide grip). However, I recommend taking a full grip on the BB and squeezing it as tight as possible (squeezing the BB tightly will increase rotator cuff engagement) – there is more risk of the BB falling on you when using a false grip.

4. Pull your heels backward, push your knees out, and drive your soles into the floor. Some lifters come up onto their toes, and that's fine (there are many very specific Powerlifting techniques) – find what works for you.

5. Pull your shoulder blades inwards and down and drive your upper back into the bench. This will facilitate a slight arch in your lower back, leaving two points of contact on the bench (glutes and upper back) – aim to bring your glutes up towards your upper back.

6. Don't worry about having a slight arch in your lower back while holding the BB. The load is perpendicular to your spine and does not compress it as it would during a back squat.

7. If you suffer from lower back pain, exaggerating the arch can sometimes be stressful (back pain exacerbated by extension). If this is the case, simply reduce the extent to which you are arching or take it away completely (this is one of the reasons you see people with their knees up – it flattens the lower back) – some lifters also bench without using leg drive to place more emphasis on the upper body (the Larsen Press is a great example).

8. Take a deep breath in, brace your body, and pull the BB off the J-cups, ensuring you do not unset your position. If the J-cups are set too low or too high, it often causes you to unset your shoulder blades.

9. Hold the BB at the top, take a big gulp of air, brace your core, and use the Valsalva maneuver – a lifter may hold the initial breath that they took before pulling the BB off the J-cups. However, most will maximize the deep breath and Valsalva maneuver while under the load of the BB.

10. Lower the BB under control until it comes to your lower chest – this is the highest point of your chest while lying on the bench.

11. Use the stretch reflex without bouncing the BB off your ribcage (in Powerlifting competitions, lifters have to pause for a second with the BB on their chest).

12. Press the BB up while driving your upper back into the bench.

13. Once you reach the top of the lift, exhale and get ready for the next rep.

14. When working with heavy loads, you must treat every rep as a single, perfectly performed movement.

15. Continue with successive reps.

Floor Press

The floor press is essentially a bench press performed from the floor. Performing a press from this position has numerous benefits.

The floor press reduces the range of motion because the back of your arms touch the floor. Therefore, it places more emphasis on your anterior delts and triceps. This range of motion can allow you to lift heavy loads while reducing the stress placed on your shoulder joints.

The range of motion that the floor press works through is actually more specific to how you would push something or someone to your front. This is because it is unlikely that you would retract your arms right back with your elbows far surpassing your torso. Therefore, the floor press trains you to generate high force quickly (rate of force development) from a position where the upper arms are in line with the torso and is very task-specific.

Note: Although it is standard for lifters to touch their chest with the BB during the bench press, this results in lifters performing drastically different ranges of motion. For example, if a lifter has short arms and a barrel ribcage (large ribcage), then when the BB touches their chest, their upper arms might be in line with their torso, just like during the floor press. However, if a lifter has long arms and a slim ribcage (slight build), their upper arms are potentially going to go well beyond their torso. Of course, this disparity applies to all lifts, with limb lengths (levers) playing a huge role in how much weight an individual can lift – yes, levers play a HUGE role, hence why lots of short people are really good at lifting.

During the floor press, you can either keep your legs straight or bend your knees with your feet flat on the floor during the floor press.

If you perform a glute bridge while on the floor (extend your hips and raise your lower back off the floor), the floor press becomes a decline floor press. The decline floor press works the same range of motion (the back of the arms still touch the floor), but the increased lat engagement allows for a much stronger lift.

1. Set the BB up on a rack at a height that leaves it in the same position it would be in if you were lying on a bench (the floor being the bench) – around mid-thigh height.
2. Grab the BB 1-2 palms distance wider than shoulder width apart. An ideal grip placement leaves your forearms perpendicular to the BB at the bottom of the lift.
3. Keep your legs straight or bend your knees.
4. Pull your shoulder blades inwards and down and drive your upper back into the floor.
5. Take a deep breath in, brace your body and pull the BB off the J-cups ensuring you do not unset your position. If the J-cups are set too low or too high, it often causes you to unset your shoulder blades.
6. Hold the BB at the top and take a big gulp of air, brace your core and use the Valsalva maneuver.
7. Lower the BB under control (towards your lower chest) until the back of your arms touch the floor.
8. Press the BB up while driving your upper back into the floor.
9. Once you reach the top of the lift, exhale and continue with successive reps.

Strict Overhead Press

The Strict overhead press (known simply as the press or strict press) is by far the most underused BB exercise. This is because it's not one of the 3 Powerlifts (squat, bench, deadlift) and is not used in its strict form in Olympic weightlifting. However, I include it with all my Olympic weightlifters and commonly program it as an assistance exercise to the bench press for Powerlifters.

Many fitness races involve lifting and carrying weight overhead. Therefore, it is key for racers to build pressing strength.

The strict press is also one of the most challenging exercises to perform with any reasonable weight compared to the other primary lifts. Hence, some people shy away from it.

It takes an unbelievable amount of strength and stability to stand like a pillar and press a heavy weight overhead. Not only that, it requires good mobility and lifting mechanics to maintain a press that isn't placing vast amounts of stress on the supporting structures, such as your lower back.

Remember, if an individual doesn't have the shoulder and thoracic mobility (often caused by tight lats) to take the arms overhead. Then the lower back will compensate by hyperextending (you will lean back). Leaning back isn't bad if you have the strength to accommodate the stress (many strength athletes will lean right back while pressing hundreds of kilos overhead). However, lower back discomfort during overhead work can be quite common. Therefore, initially reducing any hyperextension of the lower spine while pressing/carrying weight overhead can be helpful (then build tolerance progressively).

The strict press (Olympic press) was the original lift performed by Olympic weightlifters after the clean. However, after the 1972 Olympics, it was removed and replaced by the jerk variations, which was due to the lifters leaning back so far and making it hard for them to judge.

The 4 Jerk Variations:

- Push Jerk
- Power Jerk
- Squat Jerk
- Split Jerk

The overhead press places more emphasis on the shoulders and triceps. We don't get as much muscle recruitment from the pectorals, making it a much harder press than the flat bench press. Not only that but as mentioned, individuals will also often have insufficient mobility to press overhead, causing compensations. However, this can often be down to poor technique and a lack of engagement of the right scapula mechanics or scapulohumeral rhythm (interaction of the scapula and humerus during movement).

When it comes to pressing overhead, you don't set your scapula; you need your shoulder blades to move throughout the movement to ensure shoulder health.

This movement is often described as a shrugging action. However, you don't want to elevate your shoulders; instead, you want your shoulder blades to rotate upwards. This action is facilitated by the serratus anterior and mid-trapezius.

Upwards rotation involves the upper, inside edge of the scapula (the superior angle/border) rotating upwards and inwards (look at the posterior view of the image below) – a common cue is to imagine the inferior angle (bottom point of the scapula) rotating upwards and outwards towards your armpit.

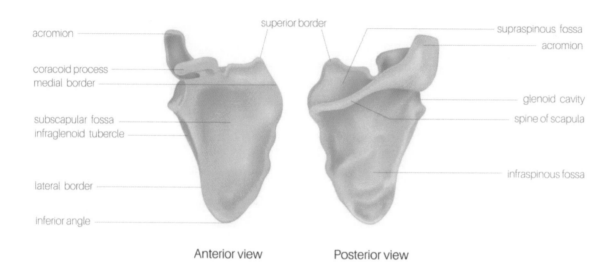

Anterior view   Posterior view

There are a few variations of the overhead press, each done with varying degrees of strictness.

The terms strict press or military press describe a pressing action that doesn't use the lower body in any way. It only uses upper body movement with no prior action to help generate upward drive, i.e., a knee bend.

In contrast, the push press uses a knee dip and drive, meaning the BB is propelled upwards using the lower body – this lift is best started from a rack position on the front of the shoulders.

Another variation of the overhead press is the behind-the-neck press (BTN press). This lift involves starting with the BB on the upper traps (back squat position) and pressing it overhead from there.

The BTN press is a staple exercise for Olympic weightlifters and works the delts intensely (weightlifters will perform the movement in both a clean and snatch grip). However, because the shoulders are heavily retracted, it is much harder for the shoulder blades to rotate upwards, which can make the lift a little harder on the shoulders (it is far more comfortable in a wide snatch grip).

Note: The Olympic lifts are explained on pages-187-193

Teaching Points:

1. Set the BB on the rack at upper chest height – I usually set the BB up slightly lower than I do for the high bar back squat (the same as the front squat).

2. Grab the BB slightly wider than shoulder-width apart. A false grip can be beneficial as it allows you to set the BB up on the base of your palms, which aligns your forearms directly under the BB. However, a full grip increases your rotator cuff's engagement – find which one works best for you.

3. Bring your elbows forward so they sit directly under the BB. While in this position, the BB should rest on your upper chest. However, if your forearms are long in relation to your upper arms, then the BB may not sit on your chest. This is not an issue; it just means you may have to hold all the load with your arms.

4. Note: A common fault involves having the elbows too far behind the BB – you want your forearms to act like pillars directly under the BB. I cue lifters to "get big" and "spread their lats." It is best to instruct them to bring their elbows slightly forward and outwards to do this. Otherwise, you often see a lifter's arms tucked into their sides, almost like they are being sunk in by the weight, which diminishes their strength greatly.

5. Stand underneath the BB and use your legs to lift it off the rack. Take 2-3 short strides backward and adopt a hip-shoulder width stance.

6. Squeeze your glutes, engage your core, and drive your chest upwards and your head back out of the way of the BB.

7. Take a big gulp of air, brace your core, and utilize the Valsalva maneuver.

8. Press the BB upwards without any leg drive (bending and straightening your knees).

9. Once the BB passes your head, consciously engage upward rotation of your shoulder blades to bring your torso and head underneath the BB.

10. The BB should travel upward in a vertical path (some lifters cue to push backward slightly). However, when your shoulder blades rotate upwards, it will bring your torso underneath the BB, so the BB will start over your upper chest and finish over the back of your neck.

11. Once you reach the top of the lift, lower the BB back to your upper chest, exhale, and get ready for the next rep.

12. When working with heavy loads, treat every rep as a single, perfectly performed exercise.

13. Continue with successive reps.

Push Press

The push press is an overhead press variation where a leg drive is used to propel the BB up off your shoulders, so there are a few setup differences.

The push press can be performed with the same setup as the strict press. However, it is beneficial to work from the front/jerk rack position to gain more benefit from the leg drive. A front/jerk rack setup is useful because the strict press setup creates too much tension in the arms and limits your ability to transfer force from your lower body into the BB.

The optimal rack position is often described as a "jerk rack position" (an Olympic weightlifting term), as it is beneficial to have your elbows lower than they would be during a front squat – from a standard front rack position, push your elbows downwards and outwards slightly while keeping your shoulders shrugged (you want as much of your hands on the BB as possible and this setup might require a slightly wider grip).

Pressing actions that use leg drive are a fantastic way to develop total body strength and power, producing force from your lower body and expressing it through your upper body.

The leg drive is not performed using a squatting action where you sit back with your hips. Instead, the key is to bend your knees and lower your body while keeping your hips under the load – this dip will usually be around 10% of a lifter's height, so around 7 inches (18cm) for a 6ft (183cm) tall lifter.

The initial *acceleration phase* of the dip (first two-thirds of the dip) is going to be smooth but performed with the intent to power the BB back up. The *deceleration* (braking) *phase* requires the lifter to decelerate before changing direction, reaccelerating, and driving up out of the dip. This needs to be even more explosive and should capitalize on the stretch reflex (involuntary contraction in response to a stretch).

As the lifter dips, the knees should stay in line with the toes. Therefore, if the knees tend to fall inwards (valgus), ensure they are consciously pushed outwards to counter this – I will usually cue lifters to "be bow-legged" to add torsion and tension through the legs.

1. Start in the jerk rack position.
2. Take a hip-width or slightly wider stance, with the weight balanced over your heels.
3. Take a big gulp of air, brace your core and use the Valsalva maneuver.
4. Dip smoothly at the knees to about 10% of your height and immediately drive back up – maximize the acceleration and deceleration phases of the dip.
5. Drive back up, propel the BB off the shoulders and push the BB up and back with the arms – ensure your head is back out of the way.
6. Keep your legs straight throughout the remainder of the lift.
7. As the BB elevates and passes your head, squeeze the upper inside edges of your shoulder blades together.
8. Make a conscious effort to lock your elbows out to secure the BB overhead.
9. Bring the BB back down to the starting position and continue with successive reps.

Snatch

The snatch is a one-part lift where the lifter takes a BB from the floor to overhead in one movement.

Teaching Points:

1. Set your starting position.

2. With a hook grip, take the slack out of the BB and plates by driving your chest up as you lower your hips.

3. Taking the slack creates total body tension before more force is produced to break inertia.

4. Push with your legs to break inertia and raise the BB off the floor.

5. Pull the BB smoothly and deliberately to the mid-hang position (lower thighs).

6. At the mid-hang, drive your feet into the floor, pull the BB up and back, and explosively extend your hips.

7. Keep the BB close with your lats and shoulders, and it will strike (brush past) the contact point as your hips extend. Your shoulders will be slightly behind your hips, which is facilitated by hip hyperextension, so squeeze your glutes!

8. Lift your feet up, shrug with your shoulders and pull your elbows upwards and outwards.

9. Keep the BB close to the body and turn it over as your feet transition (your feet do not have to transition).

10. Punch through the BB to receive it overhead as your feet land in the receiving position.

11. If not already there, continue sitting into a full depth squat and ensure you are stable before recovering to a standing position by pushing your hands into the BB and following with your body.

12. Drop the BB or catch it back at your hips.

Extended Teaching Points: For those who want a more in-depth explanation

1. Stand with the balls of your feet under the BB (the bottom of your laces) in a hip-width stance.

2. Bend over and grab the BB with a wide snatch grip, using the hook grip.

3. Sit back with your hips, drive your chest forward, look up to your front and extend your spine as much as possible – in this position, your shoulders will be directly over the BB.

4. Turn the points of your elbows towards the plates (internally rotate your shoulders).

5. Push your feet into the floor to lock your arms out and put tension through your body. This action also removes the slack between the BB and the plates.

6. Take a deep breath in, brace your trunk muscles, and use the Valsalva maneuver.

7. Start the 1st pull by driving your feet into the floor to extend your knees.

8. Keep your trunk under tension (your back and hip angle shouldn't change much, and your shoulders will come slightly in front of the BB) – the 1st pull is slow and controlled (don't rush this section of the lift).

9. The 2nd pull begins once the BB passes your knees, and they start to re-bend under the BB. This is when you need to accelerate – explosively extend your hips and pull the BB back into the contact point.

10. Explosively extend your hips and pull the BB back into the power position/contact point (this is the point where your shoulders come behind the BB) – for the snatch, this should be just above your pubis (bottom of your abs), right in the crease of your hips.

11. Extend up onto the balls of your feet and shrug your shoulders to ensure the BB remains within its vertical path – think, "Get tall and lift your shirt up with the BB."

12. As the BB elevates, lift and transition your feet into the receiving/squatting stance (you don't have to transition your feet).

13. As you drop, pull yourself under the BB (the 3rd pull), turn the BB over, and receive it overhead (the catch).

14. A parallel or above squat is considered a power snatch, and a deeper squat is a snatch, full snatch, or squat snatch (a muscle snatch involves receiving the BB with straight legs).

15. Hold the bottom position for a second or two before driving your palms into the BB (spread the BB apart with your hands) to drive out of the overhead squat.

16. Bring your feet back into a hip-width stance once you have recovered out of the squat.

Clean

The Clean and Jerk is a two-part lift where the lifter takes the BB from the floor to their shoulders (the clean) and then from their shoulders to overhead (jerk). On this and the next page, we look at the teaching points for the clean, then we will look at the teaching point for the jerk.

Teaching Points:

1. Set your starting position.
2. With a hook grip, take the slack out of the BB and plates by driving your chest up as you lower your hips.
3. Taking the slack creates total body tension before more force is produced to break inertia.
4. Take a big gulp of air, brace your core and use the Valsalva maneuver.
5. Push with your legs to break inertia and raise the BB off the floor.
6. Pull the BB smoothly and deliberately to the mid-hang position (lower thighs).
7. At the mid-hang, drive your feet into the floor, pull the BB up and back, and explosively extend your hips.
8. Keep the BB close with your lats and shoulders, and it will strike (brush past) the contact point (upper thighs) as your hips extend. Your shoulders will be slightly behind your hips, which is facilitated by hip hyperextension, so squeeze your glutes!
9. Lift your feet up, shrug with your shoulders and pull your elbows upwards and outwards.
10. Keep the BB close to the body and turn it over as your feet transition (your feet do not have to transition).
11. Catch the BB in the front rack position as your feet land in the receiving position – ensure the BB is caught right back at the neck to ensure the weight is held on your torso rather than your arms.
12. If not already there, continue sitting into a full-depth squat and use the stretch reflex to rebound out of the squat – lead with the chest and elbows.
13. Drop the BB or catch it back at your hips.

Extended Teaching Points: *For those who want a more in-depth explanation*

1. Stand with the balls of your feet under the BB (the bottom of your laces) in a hip-width stance.

2. Bend over and grab the BB with a narrow, clean grip using the hook grip.

3. Sit back with your hips, drive your chest forward, look up to your front and extend your spine as much as possible – in this position, your shoulders will be directly over the BB.

4. Turn the points of your elbows towards the plates (internally rotate your shoulders).

5. Push your feet into the floor to lock your arms out and put tension through your body. This action also removes the slack between the BB and the plates.

6. Take a deep breath in, brace your trunk muscles and use the Valsalva maneuver.

7. Start the 1st pull by driving your feet into the floor to extend your knees.

8. Keep your trunk under tension (your back and hip angle shouldn't change much, and your shoulders will come slightly in front of the BB) – the 1st pull is slow and controlled (don't rush this section of the pull).

9. The 2nd pull begins once the BB passes your knees, and they start to re-bend under the BB. This is when you need to accelerate – explosively extend your hips and pull the BB back into the contact point.

10. Explosively extend your hips and pull the BB back into the power position/contact point (this is the point where your shoulders come behind the BB) – for the clean, this should be towards the tops of your thighs (don't fire the BB off too early).

11. Extend up onto the balls of your feet and shrug your shoulders to ensure the BB remains within its vertical path – think, "get tall and lift your shirt up with the BB."

12. As the BB elevates, lift and transition your feet into the receiving/squatting stance (you don't have to transition your feet).

13. As you drop, pull yourself under the BB (the 3rd pull), turn the BB over, and receive it in a front rack position (the catch).

14. A parallel or above squat is considered a power clean, and a deeper squat is a clean, full clean, or squat clean (a muscle clean involves receiving the BB with straight legs).

15. The receiving position can be held for a second or two. However, lifters will often recoil out of the front squat position and use the momentum at the top to readjust their front rack position into a jerk rack position with more grip on the BB and lower elbows.

16. Bring your feet into a hip-width to shoulder-width stance once you have recovered out of the squat.

Jerk (Split Jerk)

The Jerk is the second part of the clean and jerk.

Teaching Points: Split Jerk

1. Stand in a hip-width to shoulder-width stance in a front rack or jerk rack position.

2. The BB must be held on your shoulders with the weight loaded down your spine.

3. Take a deep breath in, brace your trunk muscles, and use the Valsalva maneuver – elevate your shoulders as you do this.

4. Dip with your knees – push your knees out to drop your body vertically – around 10% of your height (approximately 7 inches for a 6ft athlete).

5. Drive upwards to propel the BB off your shoulders.

6. Lift and transition your feet, one forward and one back, and as you do this, push yourself under the BB (the foot transition and receiving position should be practiced with bodyweight alone before working with the BB).

7. Receive the BB overhead in a split stance.

8. Push back with the front leg to bring it back first, then step forward with the rear leg.

9. You should be back in a hip-width to shoulder-width stance within 2-3 strides.

There are four Jerk variations:

- **The Push Jerk** involves propelling the BB off the shoulders before pushing underneath it into a partial squat while keeping the feet in the same position

- **The Power Jerk** is very similar to the push jerk. However, as the BB is elevated off the shoulders, the feet are lifted and transitioned, and the BB is caught in a parallel or above squat

- **The Squat Jerk** is the same as the push or power jerk. However, the BB is received in a full-depth squat. Due to the narrow, clean grip, this requires incredible mobility

- **The Split Jerk** is the most used jerk variation in competition and involves splitting the feet forward and back as the BB elevates off the shoulders to drop underneath it and receive the BB overhead

Olympic Weightlifting Made Simple

As you can see from the teaching points for each lift, there is a lot to take in, and although this level of complexity makes the Olympic lifts incredibly fulfilling to learn, it can also discourage people from giving them a go.

We don't want to perform any movement with terrible technique, and we definitely don't want to ingrain bad habits by performing something incorrectly over and over again. However, technique isn't going to be perfect straight away, and the best way to get a feel for the lifts is to actually perform them, so don't be afraid to just give them a try – a martial artist would never learn to kick if they were worried the first few weren't going to be good enough.

I often program what I call a "Brute Strength" Clean & Press (I usually write it as "Muscle Clean & Press"), where the individual simply takes a BB from the floor to overhead with the sole cue of "keep the BB as close to you as possible". This technique builds brilliant strength, and it is amazing how, with just a few cues and technique tips, people will start to pull the BB up in the most efficient ways possible (the right ways).

Note: It is often best to drip-feed small cues and technique tips between each set rather than unloading a whole explanation of the entire lift.

Here's an example of how simply you can teach a muscle snatch where there is no bend in the knees when the BB is received overhead:

1. Stand under the BB and grab it with a wide grip.

2. Sit back with your hips and drive your chest forward to straighten your spine.

3. Lift the BB slowly off the floor.

4. Once the BB passes your knees, explosively extend your hips and pull the BB upwards, keeping it as close to your body as possible.

5. Turn the BB over and extend your elbows to receive the BB overhead.

Once the individual can perform a fairly decent muscle snatch, I have them practice lifting and transitioning their feet into a wider stance in a parallel or above squat without the BB. From there, I instruct them to perform the foot transition as they extend their hips and turn the BB over (elbows move under the wrists).

If they can receive the BB in a quarter squat, they can then continue to squat to full depth to build the confidence to receive the BB in a full-depth squat.

It all might be a little messy at first, but huge progress will be made in a short space of time, and especially with the snatch, a dowel or technique BB can be used. Therefore, there is minimal risk of injury.

"No tree becomes rooted and sturdy unless many a wind assails it." – **Seneca**

Loaded Carries

The Deadly Dozen includes three loaded carries:

1. **Farmers Carry:** Carrying weights at your sides.

2. **Front Carry:** Carrying a weight to your front.

3. **Overhead Carry:** Carrying a weight overhead.

During the race, these carries are performed with KBs or a WP. However, in the gym, we can use BBs and specialist equipment like farmer's walk handles or heavy sandbags to overload the movements. Of course, you can also use really heavy KBs to overload the farmer's walk – you can get 60kg+ KBs, but you tend to see more around 32-40kg in conventional gyms.

During loaded carries, not only are there different positions to support the weight (in your hands and on your shoulders, etc), but you can also grip the weight in different ways to help build strong forearm muscles and robust elbows, such as the full grip, hook grip (this is a different variation to the Olympic lifting hook grip), and pincer grip.

| **Full Grip** | **Hook Grip** | **Pincer Grip** |

"People are frugal in guarding their personal property; but as soon as it comes to squandering time, they are most wasteful of the one thing in which it is right to be stingy." – **Seneca**

Farmers Carry Variations

The farmer's carry is the most used carry during daily activities, as it simply involves picking an object up, holding it with straight arms at your sides, and walking with it – think shopping bags.

The suitcase carry is the name given to a farmer's carry/walk using one hand. This is one of the best core exercises as it works the obliques and quadratus lumborum intensely – the key is to keep your torso upright while having a heavy load on one side.

Farmer's walk handles, DBs, KBs, or any other objects can be used. You can also use a hex/trap bar. Having a separate weight in each hand maximizes the stability required, whereas a hex bar will allow you to work with heavier loads as it is far more stable.

As a Deadly Dozen athlete, it makes sense to spend a lot of time performing the Farmers Carry with KBs. However, it always makes sense to overload the movement using implements like farmer's walk handles and hex bars.

Front Carry Variations

The front carry, aka baby carry, is the second most accessible carry and is commonly used during daily activities when an object is too big or too awkward to be held in one hand.

The baby carry is usually practiced with a sandbag or Powerbag. However, it can be practiced with any heavy object – in the image with the red bag (45kg bag), I am doing a Bear Hug Carry where the aim is to squeeze the bag as hard as possible (it is horrendously hard).

You can also perform baby carries with a BB, which are referred to as Zercher carries (named after ED Zercher), as the BB is held in the Zercher position in the crooks of the elbows – I also perform Zercher carried with a strongman yoke.

Overhead Carry Variations

When it comes to building overhead stability, you can't do much better than an overhead carry, and it also works the core incredibly hard.

Overhead carries can be performed bilaterally with a BB (practise straight and bent arms carries), DBs, KBs, a weight plate, or a sandbag. They can also be performed unilaterally with a single DB or KB.

You can take a clean or snatch grip width during an overhead carry with the BB to add specificity to the Olympic lifts.

If you really want to challenge your overhead stability, you can try the Hanging Band Technique (HBT) where you hang weights on the BB using resistance bands.

Note: If the weight is going to fall, drop it to the front or rear and step in the opposite direction.

Bonus Exercises

In the last section, we looked at the BB equivalents of many of the Deadly Dozen Labours. In this section, I have selected a group of exercises that I feel are great additions to the program.

The strength exercises build key muscle groups that are worked during the Deadly Dozen, with the primary aim of building strength and resilience in the tissues and surrounding structures.

Although the core is developed while performing compound movements (exercises that work multiple joints and muscle groups), and the large movements should be prioritised, there is an optimal volume for any given exercise. Therefore, if we have the time and energy to isolate and focus on specific body parts like the core muscles or the arms, for example, then we absolutely should.

The core includes the muscles of your trunk/torso, and they play a key role in resisting and transferring forces while also facilitating flexion (bending), extension (straightening), lateral flexion, and extension (side bending and straightening from a side bend) and rotation of the spine.

Of course, there are dozens of core exercises to choose from. The ones in the table are the ones I find to be the most effective – I have also included my 360-core routine.

Strength Training	Core Training	Labour Fitness: Strength Emphasis	Labour Fitness: Cardio Emphasis
Calf Raise	DB Press Sit-Up	Sled Push	Row
Step-Up	Ab Roll-Out	Sled Pull	Ski
Single-Leg Squat: On Box	GHD Hip/Back Extension	Push-Up	Cycle
Pull-Up & Chin-Up	Side Bend	Inverted Row	Battle Rope
Pullover	Band/Cable Rotation		Wallball
Single-Arm Row	Woodchop		Boxing Bag Work
Biceps Curl	Coach Curtis Core Routine		Skipping
Triceps Extension			Box Jump
Wrist Roller			Slam

Each of the exercises is explained in the order listed in the table.

Note: Push-ups and heavy sled work clearly fit into the strength column. However, I primarily use this during Labour Fitness training sessions, so I have placed them there.

"The more we value things outside our control, the less control we have." – **Epictetus**

Calf Raise

The calves consist of two muscles, the gastrocnemius and the soleus. The gastrocnemius attaches above the knee; therefore, when the legs are straight and a calf raise is performed, the emphasis is placed on the gastrocnemius. However, when a calf raise is performed with bent knees, the gastrocnemius is slackened, and therefore, the emphasis is on the soleus, which attaches below the knee (both insert onto the calcaneus via the Achilles tendon).

Squats work the calves (especially full-depth squats) because the ankles are dorsiflexed as we lower into the squat and plantarflex as we extend the legs. However, to maximize the contraction of the calf muscles, we need to carry on plantarflexing the ankles to take our heels off the floor.

To maximize the range of motion, specifically the eccentric phase, we can add a heel drop where we stand on a step or platform with the balls off the feet and allow the heels to drop towards the floor.

Technique Tip: As you drive up into the top of a calf raise, ensure your drive through your little and big toe – it can be common to see the big toe lifted off the floor, which reduces stability and force production.

One of the best ways to work the calves and the Achilles tendon is with BB Calf Isometric Contraction as shown in the 3 images below (the BB is under the J-Cups): Straight Legs / Bent Legs / Single Leg – these are Overcoming Isometrics (pushing against an immovable object) rather than Yielding Isometrics (holding a static position).

1. Stand on a step with the balls of your feet (one or both legs can be used).
2. Keep your legs straight to keep the emphasis on the gastrocnemius or bend your knees to place more emphasis on the soleus.
3. Allow your heels to drop towards the floor to stretch your calf muscles.
4. Drive the balls of your feet and all your toes into the step to raise your heels.
5. Maximally contract your calf muscles at the top before lowering your heels to the bottom position under control and perform successive reps.
6. Note: A heel drop does not have to be used and calf raises can be performed from the floor and loaded with a weight in each hand.
7. Note: One of my favourite variations is the single-leg calf raise performed for maximal reps – this is an easy drill to add-in at home and it is much harder than most people think.

Step-Up

Climbing stairs is essentially a more powerful version of walking and requires far more muscular engagement. When we increase the height of the step (use a box) and add weight, it becomes one of the best exercises to build leg strength and stability in a way that couldn't be more functional to daily life.

Note: Any exercise that builds strength and conditioning is essentially functional (being fit is functional), but we tend to reserve the term for exercises that closely match everyday activities.

Step-ups can be performed with a BB but are most commonly performed with DBs or KBs in each hand. They can also be performed with a double or single KB front rack (pictured), with both, especially the unilateral version, being incredibly intense on your core.

Step-ups are usually worked at around knee height. However, the higher the step-up, the greater the glute engagement.

During step-ups, it is key that you place your full foot onto the box and drive it into the box to perform the step-up. Just like a lunge, your torso should come forward slightly to hinge your hips and maximize the engagement of your posterior chain muscles, i.e., hamstrings and glutes.

1. Stand a foot-length behind the box.
2. Stride upwards with your right leg, placing your entire foot onto the box.
3. Drive your right foot into the box and stride up with your left leg.
4. Once standing straight on the box, you can step back down, leading with your right leg.
5. A variation while leading with the right leg is to not place your left leg down onto the box but drive your left knee up to hip height instead (1st image below). This variation maximizes hip extension on your right side and requires more stability.
6. Once back on the floor, this constitutes as 1 rep.
7. Alternate the leading leg between each rep or lead with your right leg for half the reps, before completing the final half with your left leg.

Note: The KB Variations are incredibly taxing on your core muscles.

Single-Leg Squat: On Box

If you want to build strong and resilient legs/knees, then this is an exercise for you.

One of the key benefits of single-leg squats is that they allow you to overload the muscles of the working leg without having to apply much load (if any). This makes single-leg squats a great way to build leg strength outside of the gym or whenever you have limited access to weights.

My favourite way of performing a single-leg squat is on a high box (could be a low wall) that allows you to sit to full depth while the non-squatting leg is allowed to hang off the side of the box without touching the floor.

Although one of the key benefits of single-leg squats is the stability element, you can also use the foot of the non-squatting leg to push against the side of the box to add some stability and guide the movement.

To achieve a full-depth single-leg squat, you need good balance and good ankle mobility so that your foot can dorsiflex (toes towards shin), which will allow your knee to come forward as your torso lowers in a relatively upright position (too much lean in the torso will limit depth). And, of course, you need excellent leg strength, specifically in the quads, to drive back up out of the bottom of the squat.

People will often hit a sticking point on the descent of single-leg squats. However, the key is to trust your leg strength and push past the sticking point, usually by allowing your knee to push further forward. But remember, you don't have to go ass to grass (all the way down). You can also assist the movement by holding on to a sturdy structure or attaching a resistance band to a sturdy structure and holding onto that: Don't be afraid to regress an exercise right back and progress slowly. If you take the appropriate time to build your strength and conditioning progressively, your soft tissues will thank you for it!

I like to place the box between the two posts of a squat rack (my gym has a dozen squat racks, so I am not hogging the rack). I then start at the bottom of the squat (I use this position to mobilize my ankle) and hold the two posts to assist the movement for sets of 5-10 reps performed at a slow tempo (speed). Over time, you learn to use the post minimally, but some assistance from the posts allows you to create an incredible leg pump (it is a similar concept to a Hatfield Squat).

1. Stand on the edge of a box with one leg and ensure your heel, big toe and little toe are firmly down.
2. Initiate the squat by bending at your hip and knee and allow your knee to track forward (usually over your toes)
3. Go as far as you can go before driving your foot into the box and ascending out of the bottom position.
4. Complete successive reps.

Pull-Up & Chin-Up

Pull-ups involve pulling yourself up on a bar with your forearms pronated and your palms facing away from you.

Chin-ups involve the same action, but with the forearms supinated and your palms facing you. Therefore, there is far more biceps engagement, and with the narrow, supinated grip, individuals can easily lock their arms in and maximize lat engagement, making the chin-up easier than the pull-up.

Both variations are brilliant exercises. However, pulling from a pronated grip is generally more specific to real-life and sporting situations like climbing a wall or rock climbing. Therefore, the pull-up is often considered to be the primary variation.

I suggest using both variations and a neutral grip (palms facing each other), which are often built into various pull-up bar setups or rigs. You can also pull up with an alternate grip on a single bar and take your head to either side of the bar or use a V-bar grip to do the same action.

Pull-ups can be regressed using resistance bands or by supporting your weight with one leg on a box or progressed by adding weight with a dip belt or a DB between your legs.

1. Grab the pull-up bar with a pronated grip for pull-ups or a supinated grip for chin-ups.
2. As you take your weight, brace your core and push your feet forward slightly to take them off the floor. This position keeps your pelvis in a neutral position – having your knees bent with your feet to the rear, slacks your core which can result in you having less control of your body movement, but it is not a major issue, and it is often the ideal position for the legs when working on a low pull-up bar.
3. Use mind-muscle connection to ensure maximal engagement of your lats and biceps.
4. Pull hard with your back and biceps to bring your chin over, or your chest up to the bar.
5. Lower back down under control, keeping tension in your back at the bottom.
6. Perform successive reps.

Pull-Up	Chin-Up	Neutral Grip

Pullover

Pullovers are a great exercise for the latissimus dorsi and pectorals. They can be performed while lying on a flat or incline bench but are often performed with the lifter perpendicular to the bench with their upper back supported on it and their hips dropped slightly towards the floor.

During the pullover, you can maintain a more neutral spine or arch the back and expand the ribcage to exaggerate the range of motion and stretch through the muscles.

Pullovers can be performed with your elbows locked out or with a slight bend in your elbows. However, if there is an elbow bend, it should remain the same throughout the entire range of motion. Otherwise, it will turn the lift into more of a skull crusher (which brings the triceps into play).

Of course, you can create a hybrid exercise crossed between the pullover and skull crusher, adding as much or as little elbow flexion and extension as you like.

1. Lie on a flat or slightly inclined bench, or with your upper back supported on a bench.
2. Hold the DB with both hands over your chest. Your hands can be wrapped around the bar or you can cup your hands around the underside of the top bell.
3. Note: EZ or triceps bars are commonly used, or if you have the strength, the full BB can be used.
4. Your arms should be straight with a slight bend in the elbows (can be described as "soft elbows" similar to "soft knees", i.e., slight bend). During the pullover the arms stay straight throughout. Bending the elbows transfers more load to the triceps and turns the exercise into more of a skull crusher.
5. Flex your shoulder to bring the DB overhead to create a stretch through the lats and chest.
6. Engage the lats and chest to pull the DB back to the position over the chest.
7. Continue with successive reps.

Single-Arm Row

Single-arm rows are great for both single-arm pulling strength and overall shoulder and upper-back health.

Like most rows, the single-arm row can be performed strictly or with a jerking action.

When the single-arm row is performed strictly with no movement in the torso, it acts as a great anti-rotation and anti-flexion exercise because the core muscles work hard to maintain the positioning. Whereas, when more rotation is allowed through the torso, it increases the range of motion of the lift and therefore, the stretch through the back muscles. A jerking action can also be used, allowing a lifter to lift more weight, helping to build explosive pulling strength.

Single-arm rows can be performed in a wide or split stance, with one arm supporting you on a bench (3-point row – two legs and one arm). However, you can also place the same side's knee on the bench to provide more support.

There are pros to both variations (3-point row and kneeling supported). Having the extra support from the knee on the bench can allow you to concentrate more on the rowing action and maximize the back and biceps muscles' engagement. While only using the single-arm support requires you to create a stable base with your legs and puts more load onto the core and lower back muscles.

Single-arm rows can be performed from different back angles. The kneeling-supported version usually places your torso in a parallel position to the floor with your shoulders level with or slightly higher than your hips. Whereas the single-arm supported (3-point row) variation usually positions your shoulders higher than your hips.

The higher your shoulders during a single-arm row, the more the emphasis shifts from your rhomboids to your mid-upper traps.

A famous variation of the single-arm row is the Kroc row, named after an infamous Powerlifter. The Kroc row involves lifting a heavy DB (as heavy as you can) for high reps (20+) in a position where your shoulders are higher than your hips. This variation is unbelievable for building grip strength. However, it can also be performed with straps.

1. For the single hand supported/3-point row, hinge at your hips and bend your knees slightly, placing your right hand on the bench.
2. Your feet should be slightly wider than shoulder width apart, either side by side or in a split stance where the same leg of the rowing arm is to the rear which gives you room to row the DB.
3. Rows can be done with your torso parallel to the floor, or in a position where your shoulders are slightly higher than your hips which transfer more load onto the upper back.
4. Bend your knees to pick up the DB before raising it up 5-10 inches off the floor.
5. Pull the DB up to your side, ensuring you maximize mind-muscle connection with your lats, rhomboids, posterior delts and biceps. Also, squeeze the DB hard.
6. Lower the DB, keeping it under control, and allow your shoulders to protract slightly to stretch the muscles of your back.
7. Continue with successive reps.

Training Principles

Now we have established the components of physical fitness and the fundamental movement patterns. It is time to consider how we develop each quality. To start, we consider the Training Principles that underpin how physical training works.

Training Principle	Description
Individuality	Everyone responds to training differently. Some need more volume, while others need more intensity.
Specificity	Any changes or adaptations the body makes will be specific to the stress or stimuli it is exposed to. This is often described as the SAID principle (Specific Adaptation to Imposed Demands).
Adaptability	Over time, the body becomes accustomed to the stress or stimuli it is exposed to and, therefore, improves in several ways (specific to the stress), which is a good thing. However, we must also consider the law of accommodation, which states that our response to a constant stress will decrease over time. Therefore, we need to ensure our training is progressive and doesn't plateau (cease improving).
Overload	In order to elicit adaptations, the body must be put under additional stress (overloaded).
Progression	The additional stress that we put on our bodies to elicit adaptations needs to be progressive and gradually increased.
Recovery	The body needs time to repair. We need to overreach where possible to elicit the most results, but if we overreach too far and too often, we will overtrain, resulting in injuries and illness, etc.
Reversibility	If stressors are taken away or sufficient recovery isn't allowed, performance levels can be lost.

The training principles of overload and progression are combined to create the principle of **Progressive Overload** – Progressive overload simply means that training needs to get progressively harder.

We want to adapt and find things easier, but we also want to keep pushing forward without injury. Therefore, we overload the body with stress to invoke adaptations, but we do this progressively (little by little) to ensure we don't sustain injuries – Progressive Overload is the backbone of every training program.

Training Variables

Once we understand the Training Principles, we then look at the Training Variables. The acronym FITT (Frequency, Intensity, Time, Type) is a useful acronym to describe the training variables. However, these can be broken down further and ordered in a way that will systematically build a program.

Training Variable	Description
Frequency	How often? I.e., How many training sessions can be carried out each day, each week, each month, etc.
Exercise Type	What mode of training are these sessions going to include? E.g., Strength Training, Metabolic Conditioning, Speed & Agility.
Exercise Selection	What specific exercises will be used? E.g., Back Squat, Rower, Track Sprints.
Complexity	What is the complexity of the exercise? E.g., Olympic Weightlifting.
Exercise Order	What order will the exercises be performed in? (Consider fatigue sensitivity).
Intensity	To what intensity are the exercises performed? E.g., 90% of 1RM / Heart Rate Zone 4 / RPE 8.
Volume	How many sets and reps / how long (duration)?
Density/Rest	How long are the rest periods? Volume + Rest Periods = Training Density: 5x5 at 80kg done in 20 minutes is less density than 5x5 at 80kg in 15 minutes.

Note: Don't worry about any technical terminology in the descriptions. We will cover all of that in great detail in the Quantifying Training Loads section (Page-66).

The first variable we consider is training frequency, and that is because this is usually dependent on other factors like occupation and family commitments, etc. There is no use programming six training sessions a week if you can only fit in three 1-hour sessions.

From there, we consider what types/modes of exercise we want to fit into the time we have for training each week and how we are going to best split these sessions over the week (this is called a Training Split) and order the different activities/exercises in a way that makes sense.

Finally, we are going to decide the Volume and Intensity and the Rest periods we are going to be using – Volume and Intensity are the key variables that are modified during a training program.

This is a very broad overview, but we will look at this in more detail in the upcoming Making the Plan section.

Wrist Roller

The wrist roller is, in essence, a torture device for your forearm muscles. I can honestly say that I have never felt a more intense burn than this simple contraption elicits in the forearms. It is such a simple piece of equipment too – it is just a small bar with a long rope or cord that is attached to a small weight.

When it comes to physical training and activities like fitness racing, there are lots of activities that can be quite hard on your wrists and elbows. Therefore, it is key to strengthen the muscles that surround both of these joints, and these include the forearm muscles.

1. Grab the bar of the wrist roller with an overhead grip and your hands places on each end of the bar.
2. Hold your arms out to your front, with your elbows straight so that your arms are parallel to the floor.
3. Begin rolling the rope or cord around the bar by loosening the grip with one hand while gripping around the bar with the other and flexing the wrist to rotate the bar and alternate between your right and left hand with this action.
4. You can flex your wrist either way. For example, pulling your knuckles back and up towards the top of your forearms (primarily working the wrist extensors) or pushing your knuckles down so that your fingers are moved towards the bottom of your forearm (primarily working your wrist flexors)
5. Complete successive reps.
6. Note: You can also attach a weight to a resistance band and wrap the other end of the resistance band around the sleeve of a BB that is on a rack. You then use the same action as above to rotate the BB sleeve, which will wrap the band around the sleeve and gradually raise the weight.

Grip Strength is incredibly important for the Deadly Dozen, and it is easy to test with a Dynamometer, which is cheap to buy and incredibly easy to use (you just grip the handle and squeeze) – can you beat my score of 88.5kg?

Here's some Normative Data: (Our 1-12 System)

1. Male: 35kg / Female: 15kg
2. Male: 40kg / Female: 20kg
3. Male: 45kg / Female: 25kg
4. Male: 50kg / Female: 30kg
5. Male: 55kg / Female: 33kg
6. Male: 60kg / Female: 35kg
7. Male: 65kg / Female: 37kg
8. Male: 70kg / Female: 40kg
9. Male: 73kg / Female: 43kg
10. Male: 75kg / Female: 45kg
11. Male: 77kg / Female: 47kg
12. Male: >80kg / Female: >50kg

DB Press Sit-Up

The DB press sit-up is one of my favourite core exercises for fitness racing because not only does it build strong abdominals, but it also builds upper body power and muscular endurance, specifically in the shoulders – I often squeeze a slam ball between my legs to increase adductor/groin engagement.

The DB press sit-up can be performed bilaterally with a DB in each hand or unilaterally with a DB in one hand – I often call the unilateral version the DB Punch Sit-Up as I cue athletes to punch hard with the DB.

When it comes to abdominal training, people usually try to isolate the abs, whether it be minimizing the input from the hip flexors or preventing the rest of the body from working to generate momentum. However, during the DB press sit-up, the aim is to press the DBs explosively from the floor and use the abdominals and hip flexors to come all the way up to an upright seated position with the arms extended overhead – the movement can be performed with bent or straight legs.

It is often beneficial to isolate muscles, but we also want to get the body working as one complete unit (we want the abs and hip flexors to work hard together). The DB press sit-up allows you to use every muscle that assists you in the sit-up. Therefore, I usually incorporate high rep sets with weights that work me hard but allow me to perform the movement well.

Note: It is key to use weights that overload the movement, but don't place all the emphasis on the shoulders and restrict you from getting good abdominal engagement.

Because the explosive DB press is accompanied by a sit-up (the body moving with the DBs), there is little need to concentrate on decelerating. In actuality, people often don't produce enough acceleration to get them to the full seated position with the DBs overhead.

Lie on the floor with bent or straight legs. The DBs should be held in the position that you would perform a DB Floor Press (DB Bench Press). Press the DBs explosively and sit all the way up.

Sit all the way up and extend your arms overhead. Once at full extension, reverse the movement and return back to the starting position.

Ab Roll-Out

Ab roll-outs work your abs incredibly hard while requiring you to maintain the posture of your lumbopelvic region, making them one of the best core exercises in your arsenal.

The ab roll-out involves bracing your abdominal muscles to maintain the positioning of your lower spine (stop it from hyperextending) while you extend your hips and knees as you roll the ab wheel out to your front. This means that you are flexing and extending your hips while your abs maintain the positioning of your pelvis and lower spine, which is what your abs have to do while you squat and deadlift.

Caution must be practiced with the ab roll-out as form can easily be lost, causing the lower back to dip and, in some cases, resulting in strains in the abs. The intense eccentric phase can also cause severe DOMS – not many abdominal exercises involve such an intense eccentric phase. Hence, if you haven't performed them in a while, just a few sets of low reps can leave you sore for days (introduce them progressively).

Many of your adductors connect to your pubis on your pelvis, which is the same area that your abdominals attach. Therefore, combining the engagement of these muscles will increase your overall stability during the exercise.

To increase adductor engagement during the ab roll-out, simply place a medicine ball between your legs and squeeze your legs together as you roll out – this makes the ab roll-out a little easier.

On top of using an ab wheel, you can use a BB with WPs on, allowing you to take a much wider grip (shoulder-width), feeling more stable. The BB setup allows you to easily regress the movement with a resistance band by attaching it to a sturdy structure and looping it over the BB. From there, you roll away from the band attachment point (the band travels between your legs to the center of the BB), and the band tension will assist you on the way back in (some ab wheels have inner workings that assist you back in).

To increase the intensity of ab roll-outs, you can perform the movement from standing, which is incredibly intense. However, the standing variation can also be regressed by rolling up an incline (create a ramp to roll up) or by attaching a resistance band to the top of a power/squat rack, pulling it down around your hips, and using it to aid the movement.

1. Kneel with your hips stacked over your knees and grab the roller/BB.
2. Take a big gulp of air, brace your core and use the Valsalva maneuver.
3. Slowly roll the roller out to the front and allow your body to extend. Ensure your lower spine doesn't dip.
4. Note: A common fault is reaching forward with the arms but not allowing the hips to extend.
5. Once your hips are fully extended, or you have reached the furthest point your core strength allows, slowly return to the starting position and exhale.
6. Continue with successive reps.
7. Note: People often imagine that failing an ab roll-out to be quite catastrophic, with them falling to the floor and breaking their nose. However, you will likely just slump to the floor if unable to complete the movement – but still be careful.

GHD Hip/Back Extension

The most effective way to perform hip/back extensions is on a GHD (Glute and Hamstring Developer), a 45-degree hyper, or a Roman chair – a bodyweight alternative is dorsal raises on the floor (I program 3-4 sets of 10-20 dorsal raises for all my clients that sit for prolongued periods and complain of a stiff lower back – they work wonders: Don't just stretch a tense muscle, work it!)

Hip/back extensions will work your entire posterior chain (calves, hamstrings, glutes, and back muscles). However, making slight adjustments to the machine setup, the way you perform the movement, and the muscle you concentrate on working (mind-muscle connection) has enormous impacts on which muscles are working the hardest.

You can flex the spine slightly as you lower your torso to maximize the back muscles' engagement (erectors and quadratus lumborum). From there, you concentrate on extending your spine using the back muscles – you will be amazed how much your erectors switch on when you think about them working, especially if you hyperextend your spine at the top.

To maximize the engagement of the glutes, you can bend your knees to slack your hamstrings. Whereas ensuring your knees are locked out and dorsiflexing your ankles (toes towards shins) will maximize the engagement of your hamstrings, again, think about the hamstrings contracting and squeeze them hard at the top.

To maximize the calves' engagement, plantarflex your ankles and push the balls of your feet into the footplate.

Some coaches will cue to keep the spine neutral at the top, and this is fine as it facilitates great engagement of the posterior chain muscles without placing excessive stress on the lower spine. However, the notion that the spine shouldn't ever be hyperextended at the top is silly. The spine can absolutely be hyperextended at the top and this will allow lifters to maximize the engagement of the lower erector muscles.

Note: On many models, the back section of a GHD (the footplate) is adjustable (forward and back and up and down), and if unscrewed and without the bolt in one of the holes, it can come loose. Therefore, lifters should always check to ensure the GHD is set up correctly.

1. Set up the GHD so that with straight knees, your hips sit just to the front of the front pads.
2. Climb onto the machine, kneel on the front pads and place your feet between the supporting pads at the rear.
3. Hold the bars to the front for support and lie down flat, i.e., place your thighs onto the front pads and straighten your knees – many people will feel like they are going to fall forward off the GHD, but if their feet are between the supporting pads to the rear, they won't.
4. With your hands at your temples or with them crossed over your chest, allow your torso to drop forwards over and below the front pad.
5. Contract your posterior chain muscles to raise your torso back up in line with your legs – it is fine to hyper-extend at the top.
6. The movement can be loaded by holding a plate at your chest, looping a resistance band around the front pegs and over you back or even with a BB across your back.

Side Bend

Side bends involve bending to the side with a weight in one hand – you don't hold a weight in both hands as they will act to counterbalance each other.

During a heavy side bend, you must concentrate on the muscles you are trying to work (obliques and quadratus lumborum) rather than just bending at the spine and placing all the stress on the vertebrae.

You can emphasize the work on your obliques by standing up tall and emphasizing the mind-muscle connection to your obliques. To emphasize the quadratus lumborum and lower erectors, you can bend forward slightly.

Side bends are a brilliant way to build resilience in the lower back, as they will prepare the body for uneven forces around the spine. This is especially important for exercises like the deadlift, where both sides of the back should be working evenly to lift the weight. However, if there is a breakdown in form, the loading may become uneven, resulting in a higher risk of injury, such as strains to the back muscles or sprains to the ligaments that surround the facet joints of the spine.

Remember, injury prevention 101 is "build the strength to accommodate the stress," and side bends are an extremely versatile way to place positive/adaptive stress on the structures of the lower spine – if you can perform a movement, progress it by progressively loading it, and you will build resilience/robustness.

Ask the question, "if I can side bend and twist with 20kg and it feels great, but 50kg would likely result in injury, is it the uneven movement of the spine or the weight (inability to tolerate the load) that has caused the injury?" – Good technique simply spreads the load in the most optimal way, hence why it allows us to lift with a reduced risk of injury (we distribute the load in a way we can handle it).

Note: When it comes to the technique for any exercise, we may choose a technique that favours high performance over reduced injury risk and vice versa. It is all about what the priorities of the lifter are – always consider "Risk vs Reward."

1. Stand up straight with a DB in one hand.
2. lean to the side to allow the DB to track down the outer side of the leg.
3. Make a conscious effort to feel the obliques and QLs on the opposite side of the body stretching and holding the load.
4. Contract your obliques and QLs to raise back up to the starting position – mind-muscle connection is key.
5. You can lean over to the opposite side (towards the unloaded side) slightly to maximize peak contraction at the top of the movement.
6. Note: You can vary the angle of your decent down the leg to place emphasis on the obliques or QLs.
7. Continue with successive reps.

Band/Cable Rotation

Band/cable rotations are one of the most versatile ways to add rotational movements into your training.

Using a cable machine or attaching a band to a solid structure such as a post allows you to rotate in any direction or from any angle you like. You can isolate the rotation to your thoracic (upper) spine or pivot on your feet and incorporate hip rotation. You can perform the action from a standing (athletic or split stance), half-kneeling, or kneeling position. You can also perform the action from a bent-over position or even while in a high plank position.

Note: High plank = on your hands / Low plank = on your forearms.

Tip: Have a play with different positions and find what angles really work you hard or feel good.

1. Use a low-medium tension band. The tension can be varied by standing closer to or further away from the band attachment point if required.
2. Attach the band to something solid at chest height, looping the band through itself – the band can be attached low, up high, or somewhere in between.
3. Grab the band with both hands and stand side-on to the attachment point, holding your hands at your chest.
4. Sidestep away from the attachment point to add tension to the band.
5. Rotate away from the attachment point and vary the angles at which your rotate.

10. WP Clean & Press: Technique Variations & Tips

To start, you need to take a wide enough stance so you can comfortably touch the WP to the floor between your legs.

Only the edge of the WP needs to touch the floor. Therefore, you can rotate your thumbs down so the "top" edge of the plate touches the floor (pictured).

You don't want to reach too far between your legs (to the rear) as it will increase the range of motion, and often, people do not touch the floor, which is a no rep. Instead, as the WP comes down, bend your knees a little more and try to keep your torso a little taller as the WP touches down in line with your toes.

Make a conscious effort to think about the elbows extending at the top. Use as much force from the lower body to propel the WP upwards (just like you would during a snatch). However, ensure there is a real press at the end to get the full extension.

11. WP Overhead Carry: Technique Variations & Tips

The overhead carry can be done with bent or straight arms as long as the WP is held overhead and does not touch the head – I perform the entire Labour with bent arms.

When using bent arms, people can have a tendency of allowing the WP to fall back slightly behind their head. However, the centre mass of the WP has to remain directly over the top of your head, otherwise you will be stopped by the judge.

If you need to bring the WP down to your hips to rest, it is worthwhile sprinting to get to the end of the 30m lane before raising the plate back up and completing the next length of the lane.

Although you want to move fast to minimize the amount of time you need to keep the WP overhead, you also don't want too much vertical (up and down) movement that is going to make holding the WP overhead more difficult. Therefore, it is often best to use a shuffling technique, where there is less leg lift (knees stay low), but the feet are moving fast.

When performing loaded carries, it is generally best to use quick, forceful breaths – I exaggerate the exhale (blow the air out like you are blowing out candles on a birthday cake).

Bent Arms

Straight Arms

Sled Push

Sled pushing is one of the best ways to strengthen your legs, especially your quadriceps. It is brilliant for building resilience in your feet and calves, specifically, your soleus muscles, which work hard to plantarflex the ankle and drive the ball of the foot into the ground while the knee is slightly bent.

Note: Pound for pound, the soleus contracts harder than any other muscle during running.

The sled push has a low technical barrier to entry because you simply get behind the sled and push it, and often, people can either push a weight or they can't, meaning it has a low risk of injury. However, it should be noted that although we can throw heavy loads on a sled with far less risk than there would be when throwing weight on a back squat, the sled push is going to place a huge amount of stress through the calves and, therefore, the Achilles tendon, so it is key not to be reckless.

Too much sled work can over-stress the calves, which can be detrimental when running. Therefore, it is key to manage training loads effectively and to take this into consideration when going from sled pushes into a run in a fitness race setting.

There are many ways to push a sled, with the most intuitive being with the hands on the bars in either a bent arm or straight arm position. However, if your sled design allows it, one of the most effective ways to push a sled is with your forearms or the crooks of your elbows placed on the bars and pushing in that position (lean your full bodyweight into the sled).

During sled pushes, it is key to get low enough to maximize the drive from the legs. However, if the joint angles become too small (meaning the joints are fully bent), they will require more force to be produced to extend the joints – imagine the force required to perform a full-depth squat compared to a partial squat.

It is key when pushing the sled that your feet stay forward facing. It is not uncommon to see people angling their feet out in a way that creates instability.

1. Take your preferred grip on the bars of the sled.
2. Lean your bodyweight into the sled and drive your feet into the floor.
3. I will usually start the sled push with my feet side by side at hip width to distribute the force needed to get the sled moving (inertia) across both legs. However, you can take a split stance if preferred, but far more stress will be placed onto the rear calf and Achilles tendon.
4. Begin to walk the legs using short strides and driving the balls of your feet into the floor.
5. Regulate your breathing while pushing the sled – don't hold your breath.

Sled Pull

There are countless ways to pull a sled, all of which have huge benefits. You can pull a sled with emphasis on the lower body doing the work, with emphasis on the upper body, or a mix of both.

Pulling a sled with straight arms and walking backward is one of the best ways to strengthen your quadriceps while placing minimal negative stress on the knees. Whereas pulling the sled with a rope while standing in position and only using the arms and back muscles is a great way to build upper body strength, especially in the biceps, forearms, latissimus dorsi, rhomboids, and middle trapezius.

One of the most efficient ways to pull the sled is by leaning forward (far reach), grabbing the rope, and walking backward with the legs while also pulling with straight arms by leaning back with the body.

Walking Backward

Upper Only

Far Reach Method:
1. Take the rope and walk your hands down it as far as you can reach to take all the slack out of the rope.
2. In this position your knees are bent, your hips are quite high, and your torso is parallel or slightly above to the floor.
3. Drive your feet into the floor and pull with your lats as you extend your torso.
4. As your torso extends, start to walk a few strides backward. While doing this, your arms can remain straight, or you can work with the momentum of the sled and bring your biceps into play (pulling using the arm muscles).
5. Regulate your breathing while pulling the sled.

Push-Up

Push-ups, aka press-ups, are a simple exercise in theory, but they are an exercise people often struggle to get right. Not only do you need the chest, shoulder, and triceps strength to push yourself up, but you must have the core strength to maintain a rigid trunk.

Common mistakes include allowing the lower back to dip or raising the glutes high in the air. Other errors include placing the hands too far forward and flaring the elbows out to the side (this will elevate/shrug your shoulders), which can place a lot more stress on the shoulders.

Note: Pike push-ups, which are where the body is in an a-frame position, often involve having the elbows flared out to the side – it can be done.

A common misconception is that you must keep your upper arms locked into your sides while performing push-ups (how people perceive a soldier performing the action). Although this position is fine, some people find it hard to achieve due to their unique anatomy. It's optimal for your elbows to be anywhere from directly at your sides to around 45-65 degrees from your body.

A push-up can be performed while resting on the knees instead of the feet to regress the movement. Kneeling push-ups are fine to use during a fitness class but performing incline push-ups (hands on a raised platform) is a much better way to regress the movement if looking for specificity to the full movement.

Incline push-ups allow you to reduce the strength needed to push yourself up while keeping the movement identical to how it is performed on the floor (with your weight supported between your hands and feet). This setup emphasizes the need for a rigid torso and allows you to lower the incline to increase the effort progressively (I will often facilitate this by lowering J-cups down on a rack and performing the push-ups on a BB). Incline push-ups are the best way to progress into performing quality push-ups from the floor.

I often program narrow-handed incline push-ups to allow higher reps and create a colossal triceps pump.

Note: A muscle pump refers to the muscle swelling due to the muscle tissue being engorged with blood and the many substances that impact the development of hypertrophy.

1. Lie chest down on the floor and place your hands just under/slightly outside of your shoulders (tuck them into your arm pits).
2. Your feet should be hip width apart.
3. Keep your core braced and drive your palms into the floor, raising yourself up into an extended position.
4. Lower back down under control, until your chest is about 4 inches from the floor, or your chest softly touches the floor.
5. During the push-up, your core should remain rigid, and your upper arms should be anywhere from directly at your sides, to 45-65 degrees from your torso.
6. If performing a push-up from your knees, lie flat on the floor, raise your heels off the ground and perform your first rep from there. This ensures your hips are straight throughout the movement. A bent hip position often points the top of the head and shoulders towards the floor and doesn't allow you to maximize the engagement from the pectorals (chest muscles).
7. Continue with successive reps.

Inverted Row

Inverted rows are a fantastic exercise to build pulling and grip strength, and the BB version, when set up low on a rack, is much more difficult than most would expect.

Inverted rows can also be performed on suspension trainers (pictured) or even just a rope or towel looped around a sturdy structure (completing any form of pull-up or row with a towel is great for grip strength). One of the benefits of using a suspension trainer is you can easily tailor the intensity by adjusting your foot position to bring your body more horizontal or upright – you can have your knees straight (on your heels) or bent (on the soles of your feet).

To perform an inverted row with the BB, set the BB up on the J-cups or a set of spotter bars/pins around mid-thigh height. From there, lie underneath the BB so that your head is on the opposite side of the rack to the J-cups – setting yourself up in this way results in you pulling the BB back into the J-cups' uprights, which makes for a more secure position.

Positioning yourself so that your belly is directly under the BB and grabbing the BB with a slightly wider than shoulder-width grip will make for an efficient pull towards your lower chest.

To increase the intensity of a BB inverted row, you can elevate your feet on a box or bench.

1. Set the BB up on a rack at around mid-thigh height.
2. Lie with your belly underneath the BB.
3. Grab the BB with an overhand grip.
4. Bend your knees so your soles are flat on the floor and extend your hips. This will bring your body off the floor. You can also have your legs straight with the weight on your heels.
5. Squeeze your abs and glutes to keep your torso rigid.
6. Pull on the bar and bring your lower chest to the BB.
7. Lower down to the starting position and continue with successive reps.

Row

Rowing is one of the best forms of cardio because it is low impact and provides a total body workout, with it working the lower body, core, and upper body.

The rower is a great station to add during Labour Fitness session or can even be used instead of the runs: Dealy Dozen Row (400m Rows between Labours) – when it comes to rowing, skiing, and cycling, I use the Concept2 ERGs.

ERG is short for Ergometer, which is an apparatus that measures work or energy expended during a period of physical exercise. For example, the row ERG can track the metres you cover, how many calories you are burning (an estimate), and the number of Watts you are producing.

Note: Watts are a measure of the power you are producing (how much energy is needed to break inertia and make the row, ski, or bike go). The higher your Watts, the harder you are working (1 Watt = 1 Joule per second). Remember, Strength (Force) x Speed (Velocity) = Power. Therefore, for optimal power output, you need to produce force quickly.

You can work out your Watts per KG of bodyweight by taking your Max Watt score and dividing it by your bodyweight in KG. For example, an 86kg athlete who can achieve 500 Watts has a power-to-weight ratio of 5.8 Watts per KG (5.8W/KG) – you can also work this out with your Average Watts over a set time/distance.

One of the key metrics that I look at when rowing or skiing is the 500m split time: The PM (performance Monitor: The screen on the rower) shows you what your 500m time would be at your current rowing pace. For example, for a 1km row, I may aim to maintain a 1.45 pace, meaning I should complete the 1km in 3 minutes and 30 seconds. (The bike erg works off a 1000m split time).

Another key metric is Strokes Per Minute (SPM), which for a typical workout tends to be around 24-30spm. However, while racing stroke rates are generally a bit higher, but they are usually still below 36spm. (The bike erg works of RPM - Revolutions Per Minute).

When it comes to stroke rates, it is ultimately about hitting the Goldilocks zone between putting a lot of force into each stroke while also working fast enough to create the optimal power output and, therefore, cover the most distance in the given time – it is no good putting a huge amount of force into each stroke if you only achieve 10spm, while on the flip side, there is no use doing 100spm if there is hardly any force behind each stroke, in both examples, the number of meters racked up over a minute would be less than working within the Goldilocks zone. In short, if Rower A can sustain 300 Watts at 24spm and Rower B can sustain 280 Watts at 24spm, then rower A is winning the race.

The Home Screen	500m Split	More Metrics

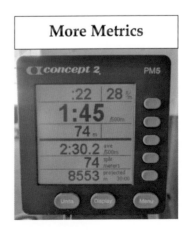

Damper settings: The damper is the lever on the flywheel. It controls how much air flows into the cage on each stroke.

Higher damper settings (the highest being 10) allow more air into the cage. The more air, the more work it takes to spin the flywheel, and the faster the air slows the flywheel down (drag factor) during the recovery (see the 4 phases of the row). Lower damper settings (lowest being 1) allow less air in and, therefore, make it easier to spin the flywheel.

Between each stroke, the PM measures how much the flywheel is slowing down. This rate of deceleration is called the drag factor. On the next stroke, the PM uses the drag factor to determine from the speed of the flywheel how much work you are doing. In this way, the effort is calculated regardless of the damper setting – a higher damper setting does NOT increase a row's intensity. The intensity is dictated by how hard you row.

Damper settings on an indoor rower are best compared to the gears on a bicycle, with a lower damper setting being comparable to low gears on a bicycle.

A higher damper setting will allow you to produce more Watts, which relates to covering more meters and burning more calories. However, it comes back to the Goldilocks zone for power output. Yes, a higher damper setting will allow for more Watts, but it may not allow the flywheel to maintain enough speed to beat the output of a lower setting.

Note: A damper setting of 5 on your home machine may feel like 6 on the machine at the gym. Differences in air temperature, elevation or how much lint is caught in the flywheel housing can all affect the drag factor from machine to machine.

Row	Ski	Bike
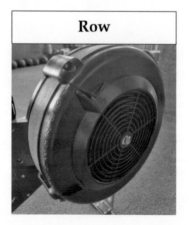		

You can test which damper setting provides the optimal drag factor on the PM.

- On the Main Menu, select More Options

- Select Display Drag Factor

- Begin rowing, skiing, or riding – you don't have to row at any specific pace

- The PM will display the drag factor after a few seconds

- You can adjust the drag factor by moving the damper lever on the flywheel

- As a rough guideline, adults generally want a drag factor between 100 and 140 – have a play and find what feels best for you

There are 4 Phases to Rowing:

The Catch: The name comes from the point at which, on a boat, the blade of the oar would 'catch' the water. During the catch, you are at the front of the machine with your knees bent and your shins vertical (perpendicular to the floor). In this position, your heels will be up slightly, but we want good dorsiflexion in the ankles to minimize this. At the catch position, it is important to keep a tall torso. However, your torso leans forward slightly as you perform a far-reaching movement with your arms (stretch your serratus anterior muscles). This far-reaching movement should bring your shoulders slightly in front of your hips (this is described as an 11 or 1 o'clock position, depending on which way you are looking at the rower). Your arms should be straight at shoulder-width on the outside of your legs and your hands should have a loose grip on the handle with your fingers on top and thumbs underneath (I like to use a false grip).

The Drive: Although rowing is a total body movement, the primary emphasis is on the legs. The drive phase is initiated by the legs extending, which pushes the rest of the body away from the front of the rowing machine. This action can be best compared to the start of a deadlift or an Olympic lift. A great cue is to think about extending the knees with your quadriceps (thigh muscles) while keeping the arms straight for as long as possible (as you would during an Olympic lift). Once your legs are about halfway extended, your hips should start to swing back, causing your torso to lean back, and then this is followed by the arms bending and pulling the handle into your torso to your lower ribs with your shoulders relaxed (don't shrug your shoulders) and your elbows neither flared out or tucked into your sides.

The Finish: The finish position is the point at which the legs are fully extended, the torso is leaning back slightly (the 11 or 1 o'clock position – depending on which way you are looking at the rower) and the handle has been pulled into the torso at the bottom of the ribs with the elbows back and out slightly.

Note: The cue for the drive phase is "Legs, Hips, Hands," aka "Legs, Back, Arms," and the cue for the recovery is the opposite, "Hands, Hips, Legs," aka "Arms, Back, Legs."

The Recovery: Once we have finished the drive phase, it is time to reverse the movement by letting the hands come forward first, following with the hips and finally the legs, and you are back to the catch again ready for the next drive phase.

Once the hands are released from the finish position, we cue to allow the handle to curve downwards (push the hands down) before the hips swing forward and when the handle passes the knees, it unlocks the knees, and they can bend to the position where the shins are vertical.

Note: Pushing the hands down ensures the shoulders and back are able to relax during recovery and are not overworked.

Before beginning the next drive phase, it is important to bring the chain back up in line with where it exits the front of the rowing machine.

 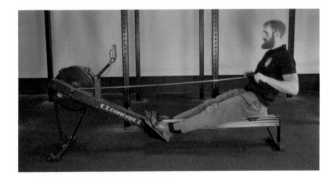

Ski

The Skier, like the rower, is an incredible machine for your cardiovascular fitness, and it also works the entire body, albeit in a different fashion.

The skier is a great station to add during Labour Fitness sessions or can even be used instead of the runs: Dealy Dozen Ski (400m Skis between Labours).

There are four phases to the ski:

The Start: You stand with your feet hip-width to shoulder-width apart, standing about 18-24 inches away from the flywheel. You grab the handles with and overhand/neutral grip so that in an upright position, your hands are slightly above your head, and your elbows are bent slightly.

The Drive: Drive the handles downward by engaging your abdominals, hip flexors, latissimus dorsi, and triceps and bending your knees (both your hips and knees flex). Maintain the bend in your arms and pull the handles down with your body, keeping them close to your sides.

The Finish: Finish the drive with your knees and hips bent and your hands down at your thighs. Your arms should still be slightly bent.

Note: It is absolutely fine to use more arm bend and triceps action if you feel it works for you.

The Recovery: Reverse the movement, extending your hips and knees and smoothly bringing your hands back up to just above your head with your elbows slightly bent.

Note: You can use an alternating technique on a skier where one arm pulls down as the other arm travels back up.

"The power of philosophy to blunt the blows of fate is beyond belief." – **Seneca**

Cycle

The bike is the third piece of cardio equipment that I utilize most alongside running. You can use a variety of different bikes, such as air bikes or spin bikes. However, my personal favourite is the Concept2 Bike ERG, along with the Row ERG and Ski ERG.

The bike is a great station to add during Labour Fitness sessions or can even be used instead of the runs: Dealy Dozen Cycle (800m rides between Labours) – cycling is a 1:2 run-to-ride ratio.

Note: We refer to completing simulations of the Deadly Dozen Run, Row, Ski and Cycle as completing the Deadly Dozen Quad (DDQ) – we could also incorporate Deadly Dozen Swim (swimming is a 4:1 run to swim ration, i.e., a 400m run and a 100m swim), and Deadly Dozen Climb, where an obstacle event is completed between Labours.

When using a bike, the first thing to do is set the appropriate seat height and handlebar position.

The seat should be set at around your hip height. If you stand side-on next to the seat and raise your leg up to 90 degrees, your thigh should be next to the seat. When sitting on the seat and the pedal is at its lowest point with your foot on it, your knee should be slightly bent and not locked out.

Once you have set your seat position, the handlebar position is more down to personal preference. Ideally, you want the handlebars to be at a height and distance away from you that leaves you in a comfortable position. For a more upright riding position, the handlebars should be higher than the seat. For a more aerodynamic and aggressive position, the handlebars may be lower than the seat. Choose the style that suits your riding goals and comfort.

"It never ceases to amaze me; we all love ourselves more than other people, but care more about their opinion than our own." – **Marcus Aurelius**

Wallball

Throwing a wallball at a target at a height of 9-10ft (9ft for females / 10ft for males) is a great way to develop overall conditioning.

The standard protocol for throwing a wallball is to stand underneath and slightly back from the target, perform a squat that breaks parallel before extending the legs and throwing the ball to the centre of the target.

As the ball descends, it is caught with the arms overhead, a squat is performed, and subsequent reps are completed.

For the most part, I will hold by arms overhead while waiting to catch the ball, and then as soon as I have caught the ball (the ball lowers to my upper chest), I quickly descend into the squat while keeping the ball up high to my front to assist me in keeping my torso upright while performing a below parallel squat.

If the ball drops forward, the torso will be pulled forward and a deep squat is then much harder to achieve – A more upright torso and a high ball position is also key because it will allow better force transfer from the legs into the upper body throw.

If I am performing a high number of wallballs with no rest, my shoulders may start to fatigue when holding the arms overhead, so sometimes, I lower my upper arms against my ribcage quickly after I have thrown the ball to give them a quick rest – I also like to perform upper body only wallballs (you can use a slight dip of the knees to generate a little more power). Upper body wallballs are great for building upper body strength, power and muscular endurance.

It is absolutely key on wallballs to take the time to accurately hit the target because, on fitness races that include them as an event, it is a no-rep if you don't hit the target.

A good weight for males is 6-9kg (12kg for strength focus) and 4-6kg for females.

Perform a deep squat with an upright torso and the ball held high.

Drive up out of the squat and throw the ball upwards and slightly forwards into the target – take the time to be accurate.

Battle Rope

Battle ropes are one of the best conditioning tools and are a great way to build muscular endurance in the upper body, especially the shoulders and biceps.

Fitness racing, by nature, is often lower body heavy. However, there are always one or two things that require the upper body to have great muscular endurance. Therefore, it is key to include drills in your conditioning that develop the upper body.

For upper-body muscular endurance with a strengthening emphasis, you can't go wrong with basic pull-ups and push-ups. For upper-body muscular endurance with a conditioning emphasis, you can't go wrong with battle ropes and boxing bag work (we will look at that next).

Technique Tip: When performing battle rope drills, it is best to keep the chest proud and regulate your breathing rather than slumping over the ropes and panting away.

Battle ropes can be performed in countless ways. Here are some of my favourites:

Double Wave

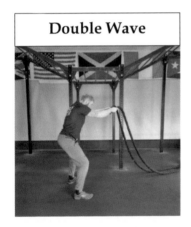

Alternate Wave

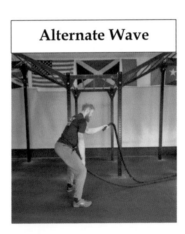

Lateral Wave

Power Slams

Reverse Grip

Deep Sumo Squat

"A good character is the only guarantee of everlasting, carefree happiness." – **Seneca**

Boxing Bag Work

Boxing bag work is one of the best ways to develop total body conditioning. Bag work specifically targets the upper body and core, but the footwork associated with boxing will also work the legs. Due to the rotational movement associated with throwing strikes, specifically hooks and uppercuts, it will work the trunk/torso muscles incredibly hard – heavy rounds on the bags can make your entire ribcage feel like it has muscle soreness.

Of course, the more boxing skill you have, the better the workout you will get. However, you don't need to be an experienced boxer to get a great workout on the bag. You just need to hit the bag sensibly with the appropriate power and technique until you develop the know-how.

When performing bag work, it is essential that you wear appropriate gloves (I tend to use 10+ ounce gloves) and strike with the well-padded area above your knuckles – this may sound obvious, but especially when performing bent arm shots like hooks, people can catch their thumbs, etc.

When performing bag work for fitness, I may program 4-12x 2-3 minute rounds with 1-minute rest between rounds and perform any techniques I like (I call these "free" rounds – you are free to do what you like), or I may take an approach where I am performing constant straight punches (left and right) for a full round of Tabata (20 seconds work, 10 seconds rest for 8 rounds).

I sometimes include boxing bag rounds into the Labour Fitness sessions I program. Yes, this means getting the boxing gloves on and off, but the standard 15-20-second change over time are more than sufficient.

Example: 2 Minute Rounds: Sled Push / Row / KB Goblet Squat + DB Push Press Superset (10 reps of each) / Ski / Boxing Bag / KB Deadlift + Push-Up Superset (10 reps of each) / Burpee Broad Jump / Bike.

Note: I always recommend having your own gloves because the smell of another athlete's old boxing gloves can be enough to knock out even the most resilient of fighters.

Skipping

Skipping with a rope is brilliant for cardiovascular fitness and is great for building reactive strength and resilience in the lower legs (calves).

This being said, while there is also a lot of running volume in a program, caution should be practised to not overdo the stress on the lower legs because too much impact can lead to shin pain, etc. Therefore, it is key to build resilience gradually.

Remember, the exercise isn't the issue, your inability to accommodate the stress is the issue (this is explained in great depth in the section on injury prevention: Page-232).

Skipping does require a little bit of practise to get it right. However, with a bit of work, it can be one of the best tools in your arsenal for warming up and incorporating high-intensity work.

When you are proficient at skipping, you can use it for high-intensity work. For example, I may do Tabata rounds (20 on, 10 off), but perform Double Unders (rope goes under the feet twice before you land from a single jump) continually for the 20 seconds of work.

A light, speed rope will also build muscular endurance in the shoulders and even the forearms. You can also purchase weighted ropes, with the best ones having the entire rope weighted. For example, the rope can be made out of a thicker plastic tube (like a hose).

I was first introduced to the tube skipping ropes when doing Muay Thai as a young lad, and it is fair to say they work you hard. They also absolutely punish your toes if you are skipping barefoot – you would learn to skip quickly!

"This is wholly up to you – who is there to prevent you being good and sincere?" – **Marcus Aurelius**

Box Jump

Box jumps are a great way to include jumps that have a low impact upon landing.

Any jump variation is going to require an explosive extension of the lower body, regardless of whether you are jumping onto a box or not. However, having the box gives the athlete something to aim for and requires more stability and confidence (increased psychological benefits). When jumping onto higher boxes, athletes will often land in a deep squat, which has benefits for mobility and stability. However, a high box is unnecessary as you can jump higher and land on a smaller box with only a slight bend in your knees to cushion the impact.

I tend not to include too much Plyometric (jump) training in a training session that is focused on developing metabolic conditioning. However, jumping onto a moderate-height box and stepping down between each rep is a great way to condition the legs, and it can act as a less intense station (on the cardiovascular system) between more intense stations – I will often perform single-leg box jumps (hops) to develop the calves.

I recommend soft plyo boxes (high-density foam) as they will cushion your landing if you fall.

1. Stand in a hip-width stance about a foot behind the box.

2. Swing your arms backward as you simultaneously sit back with your hips and bend your knees.

3. Swing your arms forward as you drive your feet into the floor and explode upward and forward.

4. Bend your knees upon landing to reduce the impact.

5. Step back down off the box before getting ready for successive reps.

Stand a about a foot away from the box to ensure that when you jump upward and forward, your toes don't clip the edge of the box – this is the number 1 reason why people fall and strike their shins.

When using a moderate height box, aim to land with soft knees – ensure you jump as high as possible regardless of box height.

Slam

Slams involve picking a weighted ball off the floor, taking it above your head and then slamming it down onto the floor.

A normal medicine ball can be used. However, if they bounce, they can come straight back up and hit you in the face (I have seen it happen a few times) – as you slam the ball, your body bends over, leaving your face as a target above the ball.

This being said, it is best to perform slams with no bounce slam balls – slam balls come in a whole range of weights from just a few kilograms to over 100kg (often used for strongman/woman training, etc).

Slams are a great exercise because they involve taking a weight from the floor to overhead, which in itself is a great exercise. They then involve an explosive throw onto the floor that works the latissimus dorsi, abdominals and hip flexors intensely.

Usually, when it comes to incorporating throws, you have to retrieve the ball (unless you are working with a partner or against a wall or rebounder). However, throwing the ball straight down onto the floor allows you to complete numerous reps in quick succession, and therefore, slams are a great exercise to use within conditioning work (Labour Fitness).

Note: Although I use "no bounce" slam balls, when working with 5-15kg slam balls, if you slam them hard enough, they will bounce slightly upon the initial contact with the floor and if you are fast enough, you can catch it on that bounce (you don't get a second bounce).

Take the slam ball overhead and come up onto the balls of your feet.

Slam the ball down as hard as you can.

"A consciousness of wrongdoing is the first step to salvation." – **Seneca**

Mobility & Flexibility

This manual has covered all things strength training and metabolic conditioning. However, it hasn't yet covered mobility and flexibility in any real depth.

Rather than adding hundreds of more pages to this manual, you can download a FREE copy of my 300+Page Mobility & Flexibility eBook.

The eBook includes over 45 Release Techniques and over 100 Stretching Techniques – static, dynamic, ballistic, PNF, band distraction, etc.

https://courses.strengthandconditioningcourse.com/p/mobility-flexibility

If you do want a Paperback or Hardcover copy of the Mobility & Flexibility book, you can also purchase a copy on Amazon using the link below:

https://mybook.to/mobility

Total Body Routine (20 Drills)

This routine can be done daily (aim for 1-2 times per week) – work from bottom to top or top to bottom. You can solely perform the lower body drills post-run or just the upper body drills following an upper body session, etc. Or choose the drills that work for you.

All of the drills in this table can be found in the Mobility & Flexibility eBook.

Technique	Sets/Reps/Time
Heel Drop Calf Stretch	1x 1 Minute Each Side
Standing Bilateral Hamstring Stretch	1x 1 Minute Each Side
Deep Squat Adductor Stretch	1x 1 Minute
Couch Stretch	1x 1 Minute Each Side
Figure-4 Glute Stretch	1x 1 Minute Each Side
Lying QL Stretch	1x 1 Minute Each Side
Side-Lying Thoracic Rotation	1x 5 Reps Each Side
Kneeling Rhomboid Stretch	1x 1 Minute
Kneeling Lat Stretch (Childs Pose)	1x 1 Minute
Cobra Stretch	1x 1 Minute
Medial-Posterior Deltoid Stretch	1x 1 Minute Each Side
Standing Pec Stretch	1x 1 Minute Each Side
Biceps Wall Stretch	1x 1 Minute Each Side
Standing Triceps Stretch	1x 1 Minute Each Side
Back Scratch Stretch	1x 30 Second Each Side
Floor Wrist Flexor Stretch	1x 30 Seconds
Floor Wrist Extensor Stretch	1x 30 Seconds
Deep Neck Extensor Stretch	1x 20 Seconds
Standing Trapezius Stretch	1x 20 Seconds Each Side
Scalenes and Sternocleidomastoid Stretch	1x 20 Seconds Each Side

"Doctors keep their scalpels and other instruments hand for emergencies. Keep your philosophy ready too."
– Marcus Aurelius

Injury Prevention

When it comes to injury prevention, the first thing people think about is exercise technique, and this is because "good technique" refers to distributing the loads of a specific activity across different structures in a way that both maximizes performance and minimizes the risk of placing too much stress on any individual structure.

Note: The right amount of stress is "Adaptive" (positive) stress and results in progressions. Whereas too much structural stress and it becomes "Maladaptive" (negative) stress and injuries occur – we want Eustress (Eu = good), not Distress!

Although technique is very important, I consider there to be three key pillars when it comes to injury prevention: **The 3 L's**

- **Load Tolerance**

- **Load Management**

- **Listen to Your Body**

- **Technique gets an honorary mention**

A key component of **Load Tolerance** is **Mechanical Strength,** which refers to the inherent capacity of the body's structures (such as bones, muscles, ligaments, and tendons) to withstand forces without breaking or failing. It encompasses the structural integrity and resilience of these tissues. For example, strong bones can resist fracture when subjected to compressive or impact forces, and strong muscles can generate and sustain force during movements and activities.

Load tolerance extends to how the body responds to and adapts to different types and magnitudes (sizes) of loads. Load tolerance considers not only the inherent strength of tissues but also factors like neuromuscular coordination, joint stability, and the body's ability to distribute and manage forces effectively (technique). It involves the body's capacity to handle various loads without experiencing pain, injury, or dysfunction.

In physical training and sports, improving load tolerance often involves enhancing mechanical strength, but it also encompasses aspects like flexibility, balance, proprioception, and endurance. For example, a well-rounded training program for an athlete might include strength training to improve mechanical strength and agility drills to enhance load tolerance by improving coordination and stability.

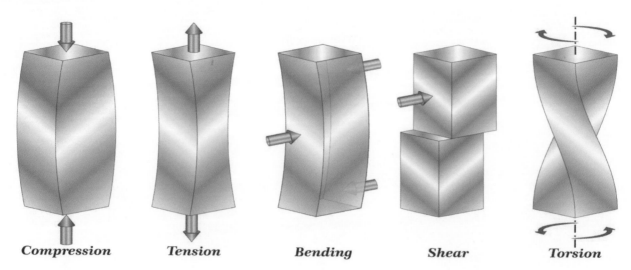

Compression   *Tension*   *Bending*   *Shear*   *Torsion*

A person's mechanical strength is influenced by a combination of factors, including genetic predisposition, lifestyle choices, nutrition, and physical activity. Although genetics can play a role in an individual's baseline mechanical strength, many of the factors listed below are modifiable through lifestyle choices and interventions. Regular exercise, a balanced diet, and other healthy habits will help improve and maintain mechanical strength throughout one's life, even in the presence of genetic predispositions or aging-related changes.

1. **Genetics**: Genetics play a significant role in determining a person's baseline bone density, muscle fibre composition, and the overall structural integrity of their musculoskeletal system. Some individuals may inherit genes that make them naturally more predisposed to having strong bones and muscles.

2. **Physical Activity**: Regular physical activity, particularly strength training and weight-bearing exercises, can significantly improve mechanical strength. Activities like resistance training and bodyweight exercises help stimulate muscle growth, increase bone density, and improve joint stability.

3. **Nutrition**: Proper nutrition is essential for maintaining and building mechanical strength. Adequate intake of essential nutrients, including calcium, vitamin D, protein, and other vitamins and minerals, supports bone health, muscle growth, and tissue repair.

4. **Hormones**: Hormones, such as testosterone and estrogen, directly impact muscle growth and bone density. Hormonal imbalances can affect an individual's ability to develop and maintain mechanical strength.

5. **Age**: Mechanical strength tends to peak in early adulthood and gradually declines with age. Aging is associated with a decrease in bone density, muscle mass, and muscle strength. However, regular exercise (especially load-bearing exercises) will mitigate some of these age-related declines.

6. **Gender**: Gender can also influence mechanical strength. Generally, men tend to have greater muscle mass and bone density than women, which can result in differences in overall mechanical strength. However, both men and women can improve their strength through training – women can also experience a large reduction of bone mineral density (BMD) during the menopausal transition.

7. **Injury History**: Previous injuries or medical conditions can impact mechanical strength. Injuries to bones, muscles, or joints can lead to weakness or reduced functionality in affected areas. Proper rehabilitation and physical therapy are often essential for recovery and restoring strength.

8. **Lifestyle Choices**: Lifestyle factors such as smoking, excessive alcohol consumption, and poor dietary choices can negatively affect mechanical strength. These behaviours can contribute to bone loss, muscle weakness, and reduced overall physical fitness.

9. **Medications and Medical Conditions**: Certain medications and medical conditions can impact bone health and muscle function. For example, long-term use of corticosteroids can lead to bone loss, and conditions like osteoporosis can weaken bones.

10. **Environmental Factors**: Environmental factors such as exposure to high levels of pollution or toxins can have adverse effects on health, including bone and muscle health.

As we can see from the list, countless factors influence an individual's ability to tolerate stress and the forces placed through the body when walking, running, jumping, and lifting, and many of these factors can be hard to quantify. However, one data point that gives us a lot of insight into someone's load tolerance is their training history (Training Age) and current training state.

Training age is a concept used in sport and fitness to describe the number of years an individual has been consistently engaged in structured training or physical activity. It's a way to measure an athlete's or fitness enthusiast's experience level in their chosen sport or exercise regime. Training age is a more relevant indicator of an individual's readiness and ability to handle certain training loads and intensities compared to their chronological age.

1. **Chronological Age vs. Training Age**: Chronological age refers to the number of years a person has been alive. In contrast, training age focuses specifically on the number of years an individual has been actively participating in training or sports. Two people of the same chronological age can have vastly different training ages, depending on their athletic backgrounds.

2. **Beginner vs. Experienced**: Individuals with a low training age are typically beginners or novices in their chosen activity. They may have recently started training or have limited experience. On the other hand, individuals with a high training age have been training consistently for many years and have accumulated a wealth of experience and adaptations from their training.

3. **Training Adaptations**: Training age is closely related to an individual's physical adaptations and improvements. As someone trains consistently over time, their body undergoes various physiological changes, such as increased strength (**Mechanical Strength**), endurance, flexibility, and skill development. These adaptations contribute to their overall training age.

4. **Training Readiness**: Training age is important when designing training programs. It helps coaches to gauge an individual's readiness for more advanced training techniques and higher-intensity workouts.

5. **Plateaus and Progression**: Individuals often experience faster progress and adaptation in the early stages of their training age. As training age increases, progress may slow down, and individuals may encounter training plateaus. This is when more advanced programming and training strategies become crucial to continue improving.

6. **Injury Risk**: Individuals with a low training age are generally at a higher risk of injuries when exposed to intense or advanced training protocols prematurely. Training age should be considered when assessing an individual's injury risk and designing injury prevention strategies.

7. **Sport-Specific Training**: In sports, training age can be used to identify athletes who have spent considerable time developing their skills and fitness for a particular sport. This can be a factor in talent identification and athlete selection.

8. **Individual Variation**: It's important to recognize that individuals may progress at different rates, even with the same training age. Genetics, dedication, training quality, and other factors can lead to substantial variation in training outcomes.

Why Technique is Important:

Now we have established what mechanical strength and load tolerance are; it is easy to explain why technique is important. Ultimately, the aim of technique is to distribute the work across multiple structures in a way that facilitates the best performance while not overworking a single structure. Of course, if that structure has the load tolerance to pick up the slack, then it will likely be fine, but if someone who can lift 200kg spreading the load across almost every structure in the body suddenly tries to do it with far more emphasis on the back, the back may not be able to tolerate the additional load and therefore, the said structure might sustain an injury.

To create a program that is suitable for an athlete, it is key to understand their training history and training age, as well as their current training state, which relates more to the present conditions.

An athlete's training state refers to their current physical condition, including their fitness level, readiness for competition, and overall preparedness to perform at their best. This term encompasses a wide range of factors that coaches and athletes consider when planning and assessing training programs. An athlete's training state can be dynamic and can change over time as a result of training, recovery, and other lifestyle factors.

Key elements of an athlete's training state include:

1. **Fitness Level**: This is a measure of an athlete's physical capabilities, including strength, endurance, speed, agility, and flexibility. It reflects the training they have undergone and the adaptations their body has made in response to that training.

2. **Fatigue Level**: Athletes experience varying degrees of fatigue as a result of training and competition. Monitoring fatigue is important to prevent overtraining and to ensure that athletes are adequately rested and recovered before important events.

3. **Injury Status**: The presence of injuries or niggling issues can significantly affect an athlete's training state. Coaches and medical professionals need to consider an athlete's injury status when planning training programs and competition schedules.

4. **Nutrition and Hydration**: Proper nutrition and hydration are essential for maintaining energy levels, supporting muscle recovery, and overall performance. An athlete's diet and hydration status can impact their training state.

5. **Mental Preparedness**: An athlete's mental state is critical to their performance. Factors such as confidence, focus, and motivation can all influence an athlete's training state. Mental skills training and psychological support may be used to enhance mental preparedness.

6. **Recovery**: Adequate rest and recovery are crucial for maintaining an optimal training state. This includes factors like sleep quality and duration, active recovery techniques, and the management of stress.

7. **Training Progress**: Coaches and athletes monitor an athlete's progress over time to assess their training state. This involves tracking improvements in performance, such as strength, speed and aerobic fitness.

8. **Competition Schedule**: An athlete's training state must align with their competition schedule. They need to peak at the right time to perform at their best during important events.

9. **Periodization**: Training programs are often organized into periods or phases, with varying intensity and volume. The athlete's training state should align with the specific phase of training they are in.

10. **Environmental Factors**: Environmental conditions, such as climate and altitude, can also affect an athlete's training state and performance.

Once we have established an athlete's training history and their current training state, **it is all about managing the loads that we place on the athlete**.

Of course, we can't eradicate all injuries because accidents happen. Sometimes things just don't go to plan, and there isn't always a clear reason for that. However, we can take an educated approach to managing the frequency, volume, and intensity of training to ensure we create a training program that minimizes the risk of injuries.

Injuries and niggles are often caused by doing a little too much and overreaching a little too far in a session (a spike in training intensity) or doing a little too much of the same thing causing repetitive strain injuries (a spike in frequency/volume). Therefore, the management of these training variables is, in my opinion, **by far the most important thing to consider when it comes to injury prevention.**

Disclaimer: Rule 1 when it comes to injuries: Don't risk making it worse. If you are not qualified to diagnose the issue, refer to a doctor or physical therapist (there might be exercises that are initially contraindicated), and of course, there could be other underlying issues that need to be addressed.

The final "L" is Listen to your body, and this one is absolutely key!

Ultimately, when it comes to most injuries, **time is key**. The human body is amazing and works to heal itself and fix little niggles and injuries all the time. In fact, most of the injuries people worry about will heal all by themselves given time, and this is especially true if the injury has not been compounded by the individual NOT listening to their body and refusing to give the specific structure time to rest and heal.

More often than not, giving a specific structure time to heal doesn't mean a complete cessation of activity. It simply means an adaptation of some of the activities you are doing. And this brings me to my TAB Method.

The TAB Method

The TAB method is a protocol I created after years of working with general clients and athletes and mentoring numerous personal trainers and coaches. The TAB method may seem like the common sense approach and that's because it is; it makes absolute sense. However, when people get injured, they tend to worry, and that's normal. But it is key to understand that most of the time, the body just needs a bit of time to heal the affected area, which is often helped by a few adaptations in the exercise regime.

- **T**ake away aggravators – initially, get rid of the things that make the injury feel worse during exercise, hours after and the next day (if you keep picking a scab, it will never heal)

- **A**dd in exercises that feel good – load the tissues, increase circulation, and promote healing / add in mobility work to reduce excessive tension

- **B**uild resilience to the aggravators – injury prevention 101 is build the strength to accommodate the stress. Once initial healing has taken place, we need to progressively build resilience in the tissues

Always consider what the athlete's current load tolerance is: It is common to see individuals load a movement and complain of discomfort and pain, and from this, they conclude that the movement is bad for them. However, if the individual can perform a Romanian Deadlift (RDL) with 20kg pain-free, but when they perform it with 100kg, it hurts, then it is not an issue with the movement, but instead, their tissues cannot currently tolerate the 100kgs of load – build load tolerance progressively (Progressive Overload).

The IIR Protocol

The IIR (Isometric, Isotonic, Reactive) Protocol is one I often use when returning an injured athlete back to sport. Often, athletes will get a great diagnosis and perform the early stages of rehab well. However, they skip the **Reactive Stage** and return to sport (RTS) unprepared.

In short, athletes often spend weeks performing controlled movements in a gym environment, and then once they are pain-free, they jump straight back onto the field, sprinting, changing direction, and jumping maximally. They then re-injure the same muscle and wonder why – because they haven't progressively worked back up to rapid eccentric and concentric contractions.

Stage 1: Isometric

Contractions with no change in muscle length – holding the position for 40+ seconds.

Stage 2: Isotonic

Eccentric (lengthening) and Concentric (shortening) contractions – progressively loaded.

Sub-Phases:

- **Tempo:** Specifically Slow Eccentrics and Pauses

- **RFD (Rate of Force Development):** Fast Concentrics

Stage 3: Reactive

Explosive/Elastic movements such as jumps and throws – plyometrics and ballistic training.

Contractions in response to a stretch: **Stretch shortening cycle (SSC)** (explained below)

- **Stored Elastic Energy:** Just like a rubber band, a stretched muscle wants to return to its original length due to the tough elastic properties of tendons (which attach muscle to bone). Imagine the recoil of a thick tendon such as the Achilles tendon – if genetics gift an athlete with a long Achilles tendon and subsequent training toughens the tendon, then this is going to greatly benefit their ability to jump

- **The Stretch Reflex:** There are receptors in the muscles and tendons (proprioceptors) that detect changes in muscle length (muscle spindles) and muscle tension (Golgi tendon organ). When there is a sudden change in muscle length, the muscle spindles send a signal to the spinal cord and a signal is sent back to contract the muscle. The Golgi tendon organ, on the other hand, can inhibit muscle contraction as a result of excessive tension that could result in injury. With progressive plyometric training, we can learn to capitalize on the stretch reflex (muscle spindles) and reduce the sensitivity of the Golgi tendon organ to maximize our ability to contract forcefully

Exercises are commonly described as Slow-SSC >250 milliseconds (0.25 seconds) or Fast-SSC <250 milliseconds. A vertical countermovement jump is considered slow-SSC as the duration of the SSC is approximately 500 milliseconds, whereas sprinting is classed as fast-SSC as the duration of the SSC is approximately 80-90 milliseconds.

Youth Deadly Dozen

I hope by this point it has become apparent that the Deadly Dozen Method is one of the most, if not the most accessible training systems in the world. However, you may have noticed that the Official Deadly Dozen Race is for 18+ year-olds, which is not very accessible for young folk.

This being said, I have created race variations for all ages, as I feel the Deadly Dozen Method is one of the best ways to get the youth not just physically active, but strong, fast, fit, and disciplined.

First things first, lifting weights does NOT stunt growth, and although lifting weights (as with all physical activities) carries some level of risk, studies show that the injury risks associated with lifting weights are far lower than the many sports young people play in school.

In actuality, young people should absolutely be lifting weights to help build the strength in their structures to accommodate the high forces that they are subjected to not only while playing sports but also during other daily activities, like playing with friends or helping their parents out around the house and garden – a stronger kid is going to be far more useful in the garden!

Now, we all know sport is brilliant for kids, but not everyone is into sports like football, hockey, and rugby. But I am yet to meet a kid who hasn't enjoyed some aspect of gym training when exposed to different styles of lifting weights. I have had young kids brought to my gym by their parents because all they do is play video games, are overweight and hate all forms of physical activity. Now if I told them to run on a treadmill for 10 minutes, they would probably hate me. But when I give them a pair of DBs and teach them how to perform an incline DB press, 99.9% of the time, they enjoy it, and the other 0.01% probably just find me annoying. In short, lifting weights is novel to kids, and most find it empowering.

Note: I wouldn't hammer their legs too much on the first session – there's a reason people skip leg day and that's because it is hard. You have to toughen people up slowly.

This all being said, I am happy to report that the amount of young people who are joining gyms these days is growing. The bottom line is young people will often drift away from the sports they play, especially as they become adults and take on adult responsibilities like work and family commitments. However, the gym is something that is more likely to be kept up throughout adult life, as it is usually a key part of an individual's physical and mental wellbeing. Therefore, the gym style of physical training should be pushed from a much younger age, and the accessibility of the Deadly Dozen Method makes it ideal for this.

Deadly Dozen will introduce kids to how they can progressively develop the fundamental movements such as hinge, squat, lunge, push and pull, while also providing a framework for developing other components of physical fitness, such as aerobic and anaerobic fitness. It is an ideal system to incorporate into schools because it doesn't require much equipment, the equipment it does require is easy to maintain and is unlikely to break, and it provides a clear progression through the different race variations and standards we have created for each.

The youth race variations are also great regressions for adults who are working up to the Official Deadly Dozen Race Weights.

All of the youth race variations have optional Journeys (usually runs, but can be row, ski, cycle) between each Labour. However, I would initially take these out: Remember, the ability to work hard is something that needs progressive development.

Note: My number 1 piece of advice when training kids is to guide them through the correct methodologies, but also give them the autonomy to select training styles and exercises that they like.

The Deadly Dozen has 4 categories, with the 1ˢᵗ category being the adult race (18+)

1. **>18:** 400m Runs – Full Reps and Distances on Labours.

2. **15-17:** 200m Runs – Half the Reps and Distances on Labours + weights reduced

3. **12-14:** 120m Runs – a Third of the Reps and Distances on Labours + weights reduced

4. **<12:** 40m Runs – a Third of the Reps and Distances on Labours + weights reduced

Here is the table for the main adult race, so we can compare it to the others over the following few pages.

18+ Adult Race: 1x Lap of 400m Track

Adult Event	Description: Male	Description: Female
400m Run		
KB Farmers Carry (240m)	2x 24kg KB	2x 16kg KB
400m Run		
KB Deadlift (60 Reps)	1x 32kg KB	1x 24kg KB
400m Run		
DB Lunge (60m)	2x 12.5kg DB	2x 7.5kg DB
400m Run		
DB Snatch (60 Reps: Alternate)	1x 15kg DB	1x 9kg DB
400m Run		
Burpee Broad Jump (60m)	Bodyweight	Bodyweight
400m Run		
KB Goblet Squat (60 Reps)	1x 20kg KB	1x 16kg KB
400m Run		
Plate Front Carry (240m)	1x 25kg Plate	1x 20kg Plate
400m Run		
DB Push Press (60 Reps)	2x 12.5kg DB	2x 6kg DB
400m Run		
Bear Crawl (120m)	Bodyweight	Bodyweight
400m Run		
Plate Clean & Press (60 Reps)	1x 15kg Plate	1x 10kg Plate
400m Run		
Plate Overhead Carry (180m)	1x 15kg Plate	1x 10kg Plate
400m Run		
DB Devil Press (20 Reps)	2x 10kg DB	2x 5kg DB

15–17-Year-Old Race: 200m Runs: 2x 100m Lengths (Track) or 20x 10m Lengths (Gym, etc).

15-17 Event	Description: Male	Description: Female
200m Run		
KB Farmers Carry (120m)	2x 16kg KB	2x 12kg KB
200m Run		
KB Deadlift (30 Reps)	1x 20kg KB	1x 16kg KB
200m Run		
DB Lunge (60m)	2x 5kg DB	2x 3kg DB
200m Run		
DB Snatch (30 Reps: Alternate)	1x 7.5kg DB	1x 5kg DB
200m Run		
Burpee Broad Jump (30m)	Bodyweight	Bodyweight
200m Run		
KB Goblet Squat (30 Reps)	1x 12kg KB	1x 8kg KB
200m Run		
Plate Front Carry (120m)	1x 15kg Plate	1x 10kg Plate
200m Run		
DB Push Press (30 Reps)	2x 6kg DB	2x 4kg DB
200m Run		
Bear Crawl (60m)	Bodyweight	Bodyweight
200m Run		
Plate Clean & Press (30 Reps)	1x 10kg Plate	1x 5kg Plate
200m Run		
Plate Overhead Carry (90m)	1x 10kg Plate	1x 5kg Plate
200m Run		
DB Devil Press (10 Reps)	2x 5kg DB	2x 3kg DB

"It is better to conquer grief than to deceive it." – **Seneca**

12–14-Year-Old Race: 120m Runs: 2x 60m Lengths (Track) or 12x 10m Lengths (Gym, etc).

12-14 Event	Description: Male	Description: Female
120m Run		
KB Farmers Carry (80m)	2x 12kg KB	2x 8kg KB
120m Run		
KB Deadlift (20 Reps)	1x 16kg KB	1x 12kg KB
120m Run		
DB Lunge (20m)	2x 3kg DB	2x 2kg DB
120m Run		
DB Snatch (20 Reps: Alternate)	1x 5kg DB	1x 3kg DB
120m Run		
Burpee Broad Jump (20m)	Bodyweight	Bodyweight
120m Run		
KB Goblet Squat (20 Reps)	1x 6kg KB	1x 4kg KB
120m Run		
Plate Front Carry (80m)	1x 10kg Plate	1x 5kg Plate
120m Run		
DB Push Press (20 Reps)	2x 4kg DB	2x 2kg DB
120m Run		
Bear Crawl (40m)	Bodyweight	Bodyweight
120m Run		
Plate Clean & Press (20 Reps)	1x 5kg Plate	1x 2.5kg Plate
120m Run		
Plate Overhead Carry (60m)	1x 5kg Plate	1x 2.5kg Plate
120m Run		
DB Devil Press (6 Reps)	2x 3kg DB	2x 2kg DB

"Don't explain your philosophy. Embody it." – **Epictetus**

<12's Fun Run: 40m Runs: 4x 10m Lengths

This race only uses: 1x 2kg KB / 2x 1kg DBs / 1x 2.5kg Plate

<12 Event	Description: Male	Description: Female
40m Run		
DB Farmers Carry (40m)	2x 1kg DB	2x 1kg DB
40m Run		
KB Deadlift (12 Reps)	1x 2kg KB	1x 2kg KB
40m Run		
BW Lunge (20m)	Bodyweight	Bodyweight
40m Run		
DB Snatch (12 Reps: Alternate)	1x 1kg DB	1x 1kg DB
40m Run		
Broad Jump (20m)	Bodyweight	Bodyweight
40m Run		
BW Squat (20 Reps)	Bodyweight	Bodyweight
40m Run		
Plate Front Carry (40m)	1x 2.5kg Plate	1x 2.5kg Plate
40m Run		
DB Push Press (12 Reps)	2x 1kg DB	2x 1kg DB
40m Run		
Bear Crawl (20m)	Bodyweight	Bodyweight
40m Run		
Plate Clean & Press (12 Reps)	1x 2.5kg Plate	1x 2.5kg Plate
40m Run		
Plate Overhead Carry (20m)	1x 2.5kg Plate	1x 2.5kg Plate
40m Run		
Burpee (6 Reps)	Bodyweight	Bodyweight

"While we wait for life, life passes." – **Seneca**

Ultra Deadly Dozens

Although the Official Deadly Dozen Race is incredibly hard to complete, I have created race progressions for those crazy individuals who want to go above and beyond.

Both Labours and Journeys can be increased by 25, 50, 75 and 100%. The 3 specific race variations listed below increase the Journeys by 100, 200 and 300%.

Double Deadly Dozen (DDD)

- 800m Journeys (Runs)

Triple Deadly Dozen (TDD)

- 1200m Journeys (Runs)

Quadruple Deadly Dozen (QDD): (12x 1 Mile = 12 Miles!) AKA The Dozen Miles

- 1600m Journeys (Runs)

Deadly Dozen +

The standard race and the above variations can involve Labour increases of 25, 50, 75 and 100%:

- DD+25 / DDD+25 / DDT+25 / DDQ+25
- DD+50 / DDD+50 / DDT+50 / DDQ+50
- DD+75 / DDD+75 / DDT+75 / DDQ+75
- DD+100 / DDD+100 / DDT+100 / DDQ+100

Labours	Standard	+25%	+50%	+75%	+100%
KB Farmers Carry	240m	300m	360m	420m	480m
KB Deadlift	60 Reps	75 Reps	90 Reps	105 Reps	120 Reps
DB Lunge	60m	75m	90m	105m	120m
DB Snatch	60 Reps	75 Reps	90 Reps	105 Reps	120 Reps
Burpee Broad Jump	60m	75m	90m	105m	120m
KB Goblet Squat	60 Reps	75 Reps	90 Reps	105 Reps	120 Reps
WP Front Carry	240m	300m	360m	420m	480m
DB Push Press	60 Reps	75 Reps	90 Reps	105 Reps	120 Reps
Bear Crawl	120m	150m	180m	210m	240m
WP Clean & Press	60 Reps	75 Reps	90 Reps	105 Reps	120 Reps
WP Overhead Carry	180m	225m	270m	315m	360m
DB Devil Press	20 Reps	25 Reps	30 Reps	35 Reps	40 Reps

The Ultra Race progression is the **Duodecuple Deadly Dozen, AKA The Duodecuple**: 12x 4800m (12x 400m), which is a total of 57.6km / 35.8m – will anyone ever complete a **Duodecuple+100**.

The Duodecuple can be done as a Row, Ski (same Journey distance – 100%: 57.6km), Cycle (double the Journey distance – 200%: 115.2km), or Swim (quarter the Journey Distance – 25%: 14.4km).

Conclusion

I have already talked in-depth about my inspiration for the Deadly Dozen Fitness Race and Training Methodology, and my journey toward writing this manual. Therefore, I am simply going to use this conclusion to say thank you for taking the time to read my work.

Thank You! **You are what makes all the hard work worthwhile.**

As I have mentioned previously, I am NOT an academic. I am just a husband and father of three who loves physical training and spends hours every evening writing in his office when his wife and kids go to sleep.

I am not a talented writer, but I love writing and putting my knowledge and ideas onto paper, and most of all, I love the idea that the hundreds of hours that I have put into writing this manual will be worth it because you, as a reader have gained something of value.

If you have found this manual useful, please let me know with a review. And feel free to drop me an email at any time if you have any questions: **info@deadlydozen.co.uk**

Coach Jason Curtis

P.S. I hope you have enjoyed the quotes I have sprinkled through the manual (in no particular order). Here's a few more for you to ponder on:

"You have power over your mind, not outside events. Realise this, and you will find strength." – **Marcus Aurelius**

"There are three things in your composition; body, breath and mind." – **Marcus Aurelius**

"We cannot choose our external circumstances, but we can always choose how we respond to them." – **Epictetus**

"Whenever there is a human being, there is an opportunity for kindness." – **Seneca**

"Well-being is realized by small steps, but is truly no small thing." – **Zeno**

"Never judge how you feel until you have got your heart rate up." – **Coach Jason Curtis**

G.Y.H.R.U: Get Your Heart Rate Up!!!

Deadly Dozen Affiliate

Maximize your reach by joining our inner circle and becoming a Deadly Dozen Affiliate / Master Coach (MC).

For just £12 per month, you can become an **Official Deadly Dozen Affiliate** and reap a whole host of benefits.

As a Deadly Dozen Affiliate, not only do you and your clients get BIG race discounts, but you also gain your own unique login to our **Online Hub**, which is packed full of resources and educational content and is ever-growing. Within the hub, you can download our branding and marketing materials and even gain 30% commission on all book and course sales you make, for example, the Deadly Dozen Training Manual - many of our affiliates earn more than £30-150pm on sales which is automatically paid directly into their PayPal account.

Note: If you want to run **Official Deadly Dozen Races**, get in touch via **info@deadlydozen.co.uk**

What you get:

- Ability to promote your gym / yourself as an Official Deadly Dozen Centre / Master Coach and use our logo and branding for promotion - run Official Deadly Dozen classes and workshops

- Discounted entry on Deadly Dozen Races: 20% Off (this stacks on top of any other discount)

- A 30% commission code on all our online courses + eBooks - you earn 30% of the course / book sale!

- Access to a HUGE portfolio of educational resources that cover all things health, fitness and performance

- New programs + workouts every month - master our methodology!

- Inside access to training tutorials and technique videos - master the race!

- Mentorship / email support from our race director Coach Jason Curtis and his team of Master Coaches

- Access to take the Deadly Dozen Master Coach (DDMC) Exam

- Get your gym / your business info listed on the Deadly Dozen website

Note: You can only promote yourself as a Master Coach once you complete the exam and gain your certificate – the DDMC exam can be found within the Online Hub.

Check out the link below to become an Official Deadly Dozen Affiliate Today!

https://courses.strengthandconditioningcourse.com/p/ddaffiliate

Free Content

Link and QR Code on the final pages.

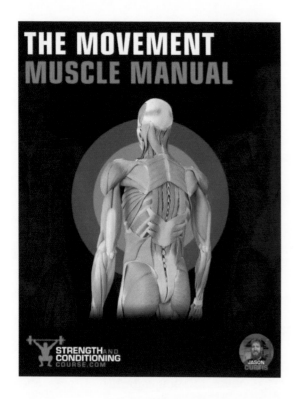

This unique muscle manual categorizes muscles by their movements, giving you a much better understanding of how muscles assist and oppose each other to perform actions.

You also get a FREE second version of the muscle manual, which lists:

- Origin.
- Insertion.
- Action.
- Antagonist.
- Innervation.
- Blood Supply.
- Daily Use.
- Gym Use.

This FREE Excel Tool Tests:

- **Lower Body Force Production/Power**

- **Reactive Strength**

- **Linear Speed**

- **Aerobic Fitness (MAS)**

The tool then generated 4-week targets and exercise recommendations.

This is a must-have tool for any coach, fitness professional or enthusiast who wants to test athletic capabilities!

My Courses

Link and QR Code on the final pages.

A good session starts with a great warm-up, and there are countless ways to maximize the effectiveness of this essential part of a session.

In this course, we delve deeper into how we can optimize the warm-up protocol to minimize our risk of injury and maximize performance on the subsequent session. We also look at how we create a warm-up that acts as an important part of the session where various physical attributes can be developed long-term.

- Running Drills.
- DROME's.
- Potentiation.

Become a Warming Up Specialist (WUS).

The development of strength is the foundation of physical performance because, before all else, you need the strength in your structures to support the fundamental movements that you carry out each day.

This HUGE course consists of 240+ narrated slides and 4+ hours of video tutorials for over 100 exercises – video tutorials for every exercise within this manual.

Become a Strength Training Specialist (STS).

My Courses

Link and QR Code on the final pages.

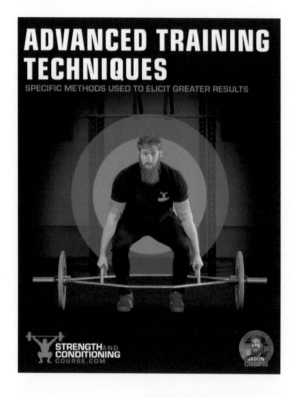

If you want to learn how to smash plateaus and take your training to the next level, this short course is perfect for you.

This course includes over 50 advanced training techniques, many with numerous variations.

A must for those that want greater results!

Become an Advanced Techniques Specialist (ATS).

This course is a step-by-step guide to the Snatch and the Clean & Jerk.

With over 230 narrated slides and countless hours of video tutorials, this course takes a systematic approach that will help you to master the Olympic lifts.

This is a must-have course for any coach or lifter who is looking to gain an in-depth understanding of the Olympic Snatch, Clean and Jerk, and progress both their own lifting ability and their ability to coach others.

Become an Olympic Weightlifting Specialist (OWS).

My Other Books

Link and QR Code on the final pages.

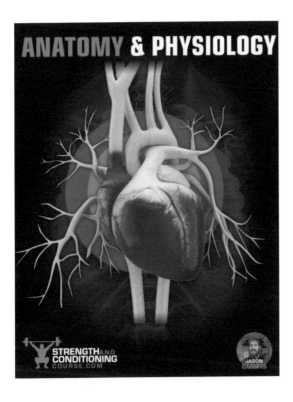

This manual is perfect for those looking to qualify as fitness professionals, experienced coaches looking for a refresh, and enthusiasts looking to learn more about the human body - we make anatomy accessible!

This manual takes a simplified, straight-to-the-point look at nine key sections, with dozens of large, full-colour diagrams and illustrations.

- The Cardiorespiratory System
- The Skeletal System
- The Muscular System
- The Nervous System
- The Endocrine System
- The Energy Systems
- The Digestive System
- The Components of Fitness
- Injuries

With 140+ mobility and 85+ strengthening exercises for over 50 specific muscles within the human body, this manual takes a comprehensive look at how movement occurs and the best ways to optimize it – it is a must-have for fitness professionals and enthusiasts!

Not only does the manual look at how to target specific muscles with mobility and strengthening exercises, but it also looks at fundamental movement patterns and how to perform primary lifts such as the back squat, bench press and deadlift.

Every exercise within the manual is accompanied by a full-colour picture and step-by-step instructions on how to perform the exercise with proper form.

My Other Books

Link and QR Code on the final pages.

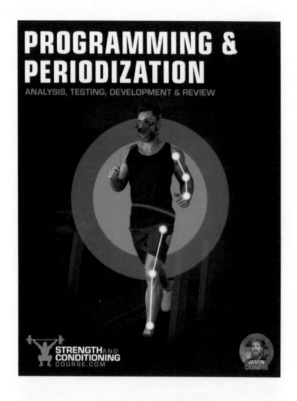

This manual is the first of our BIG 8 Pillars of Strength and Conditioning Series and shows you how to bring the key components of strength and conditioning together.

The BIG 8 Pillars of Strength and Conditioning:

- Programming & Periodization.
- Warming Up.
- Strength Training.
- Ballistic Training.
- Olympic Weightlifting.
- Plyometrics.
- Speed & Agility.
- Metabolic Conditioning.

Become the Expert!

The SCC Training Log has been designed by expert Strength and Conditioning coaches who have years of experience working with athletes and the general public.

What you get within the log:

- How to Quantify Training Loads.
- How to Test.
- Methods of Strength Development.
- How to Program.
- Goals, Strength and Weaknesses and Injury Trackers.
- 1RM Table.
- 100 Log Pages.

All within a convenient A5 logbook.

Check out all my content by using the link below or scanning the QR code:

www.courses.strengthandconditioningcourse.com/p/home

Or go to my LinkTree: www.linktr.ee/sccacademy

Purchase any of my other books here:

www.jasoncurtis.org

If you purchase any of my books (along with this one), it would be MASSIVELY APPRECIATED if you could leave me a review on Amazon – reviews help to promote my books to a much wider audience, so if you get a spare minute to leave one, thanks in advance, I really do appreciate it!

Bibliography

1. ACSM (2014a). Guidelines for Exercise Testing and Prescription. 9th edition. Philadelphia, PA: Wolters Kluwer/Lippincott Williams and Wilkins.

2. American Academy of Orthopaedic Surgeons. (1983). Joint Motion: Method of Measuring and Recording. Chicago: AAOS.

3. Baechle, T., and Earle, R. (2008). Essentials of Strength Training and Conditioning. 3rd edition. Champaign, IL: Human Kinetics.

4. Balady, G.J. et al. (2000). General Principles of Exercise Prescription. In ACSM's Guidelines for Exercise Testing and Prescription. (Franklin, B.A. et al, eds) pp.138. Lippincott Williams and Wilkins.

5. Barlett, R., Gratton, C. and Rolf, C.G. (2009). Encyclopaedia of International Sports Studies. London: Routledge.

6. Billat, V.L. et al. (1999). Interval Training at V02max: Effects on Aerobic Performance and Overtraining Markers. Medicine and Science in Sports and Exercise, vol. 31(1), pp.156-163.

7. Bompa, T. (2015). Periodization Training for Sports. 3rd edition. Champaign, IL: Human Kinetics.

8. Bompa, T.O. and Haff, G.G. (2009). Periodization: Theory and Methodology of Training. 5th Edition. Champaign, IL: Human Kinetics.

9. Cheung, K. et al. (2003). Delayed Onset Muscle Soreness: Treatment Strategies and Performance Factors. Sports Medicine, 33(2), pp.145-164.

10. Chu, D. (1996). Explosive Power and Strength: Complex Training for Maximal Results. Champagne, IL, Human Kinetics.

11. Cook, G. (2011). Movement: Functional Movement Systems: Screening, Assessment, Corrective Strategies. West Sussex: Lotus Pub.

12. Cooper, C.B. and Storer, T.W. (2001). Exercise Testing and Interpretation: Cambridge: Cambridge University Press.

13. Corrigan, B., and Maitland, G.D. (1994), Musculoskeletal and Sports Injuries. Philadelphia, PA: Elsevier Health Sciences.

14. Costanzo, L.S. (2010). Physiology. 4th edition. Philadelphia, PA: Saunders Elsevier.

15. Crossley, J. (2006). Personal Training: Theory and Practice. London: Routledge.

16. Chu, D. (1996). Explosive Power and Strength: Complex Training for Maximal Results. Champagne, IL: Human Kinetics.

17. Daniels, J. (2013). Daniels' Running Formula. 3rd Edition. Champaign, IL: Human Kinetics.

18. Dick, F.W. (2014). Sports Training Principles. 6th Edition. London: Bloomsbury.

19. Earle, R.W. and Baechle, T.R. (2004). NSCA's Essentials of Personal Training. Champaign, IL: Human Kinetics.

20. Enoka, R. (1988). Neuromuscular Basis of Kinesiology. Champaign, IL: Human Kinetics.

21. Fitts, P.M. and Posner, M.I. (1967). Human Performance. Belmont, CA: Brooks/Cole Pub. Co.

22. Fleck, S.J. and Kraemer, W.J. (2014). Designing Resistance Training Programs. 4th edition. Champaign, IL: Human Kinetics.

23. Gray, H. (1980). Gray's Anatomy. 36th Edition. Edinburgh: Churchill Livingstone.

24. Hall, M.M., Rajasekaran, S., Thomsen, T.W. and Peterson, A.R. (2016). Lactate Friend or Foe. American Academy of Physical Medicine and Rehabilitation, 8(3), pp.s8-15.

25. Heywood, V.H. and Gibson, A.L. (2014). Advanced Fitness Assessment and Exercise Prescription, 7th Edition. Champaign, IL: Human Kinetics.

26. Jeffreys, I. (2018). The Warm-Up. Champaign, IL: Human Kinetics.

27. Kenney, W.L. et al. (2012). Physiology of Sport and Exercise. 5th edition. Champaign, IL: Human Kinetics.

28. Leger, L.A. and Lambert, J. (1982). A Maximal Multistage 20-m Shuttle Run to Predict V02 Max. European Journal of Applied Physiology and Occupational Physiology.

29. Lorenz, D. and Morrison, S. (2015). Current Concepts in Periodization of Strength and Conditioning for Sports Physical Therapist. International Journal of Sport and Physical Therapy, vol. 10(6), pp.734-747.

30. Matveyev, L. (1981). Fundamentals of Sports Training. Moscow: Progress.

31. McGinnis, P.M, (2013). Biomechanics of Sport and Exercise. 3rd edition. Champaign, IL: Human Kinetics.

32. McKinley, M.P. et al. (2012). Human Anatomy. 4th edition. New York: McGraw Hill Education.

33. Muscolino, J.E. (2010). Kinesiology: The Skeletal System and Muscle Function. 2nd edition, Missouri: Mosby.

34. Noakes, T. (2002). The Lore of Running. Champaign, IL: Human Kinetics.

35. Richards, J. (2008). Biomechanics in Clinic and Research. Philadelphia: Churchill Livingstone, Elsevier.

36. Robergs, R.A., Ghiasvand, F. and Parke, D. (2004). Biochemistry of Exercise-Induced Metabolic Acidosis. American Journal of Physiology, 287(3), pp.R502-516.

37. Sadler, D. (2005). Sports Power. Champaign, IL: Human Kinetics.

38. Selye, H. (1984). The Stress of Life. New York: McGraw-Hill.

39. Solomon, E.P., Schmidt, R.R. and Adragna, P.J. (1990). Human Anatomy and Physiology. 2nd edition. Florida, USA: Saunders College Publishing.

40. Tabata, I. et al. (1996). Effects of Moderate-Intensity Endurance and High-Intensity Intermittent Training on Anaerobic Capacity and V02 Max. Medicine and Science in Sports and Exercise, vol, 28 (10), pp/1327-1330.

41. Tortora, G.J. and Derrickson, B.H. (2009). Principles of Anatomy & Physiology. 12th edition. New Jersey: John Wiley & Sons.

42. Verkhoshansky, Y.V. (1969). Perspectives in the Improvements in Speed-Strength Preparation of Jumpers. Yessis Review of Soviet Physical Education and Sports 4 (2): 28-29.

Music Theory
Practice Papers
2017
Model Answers

ABRSM Grade 2

Reflects new
question types
in use from
2018

Welcome to ABRSM's *Music Theory Practice Papers 2017 Model Answers*, Grade 2. These answers are a useful resource for students and teachers preparing for ABRSM theory exams and should be used alongside the relevant published theory practice papers.

For more information on how theory papers are marked and some general advice on taking theory exams, please refer to **www.abrsm.org/theory**.

Using these answers

- Answers are given in the same order and, where possible, in the same layout as in the exam papers, making it easy to match answer to question.

- Where it is necessary to show the answer on a stave, the original stave is printed in grey with the answer shown in black, for example:

- Alternative answers are separated by an oblique stroke (/) or by *or*, for example:

    getting slower / gradually getting slower

- The old-style crotchet rest is accepted as a valid alternative to the modern symbol .

- Answers that require the candidate to write out a scale or chord have been shown at one octave only. Reasonable alternatives at different octaves can also receive full marks.

- Sometimes the clef, key and time signature of the relevant bar(s) are included for added clarity, for example:

© 2018 by The Associated Board of the Royal Schools of Music
Published by ABRSM (Publishing) Ltd, a wholly owned subsidiary of ABRSM
Cover by Kate Benjamin & Andy Potts
Printed in England by Halstan & Co. Ltd, Amersham, Bucks, on materials from sustainable sources
Reprinted in 2018